DATE DUE

JUL 2 0 2015		

Gerald Hamilton

Tom Cullen

The Man Who Was Norris:
The Life of Gerald Hamilton

edited and with an introduction by

Phil Baker

Dedalus

Supported using public funding by
ARTS COUNCIL ENGLAND

Published in the UK by Dedalus Limited,
24-26, St Judith's Lane, Sawtry, Cambs, PE28 5XE
email: info@dedalusbooks.com
www.dedalusbooks.com

ISBN printed book 978 1 909232 43 3
ISBN ebook 978 1 910213 00 1

Dedalus is distributed in the USA by SCB Distributors,
15608 South New Century Drive, Gardena, CA 90248
email: info@scbdistributors.com   web: www.scbdistributors.com

Dedalus is distributed in Australia by Peribo Pty Ltd.
58, Beaumont Road, Mount Kuring-gai, N.S.W. 2080
email: info@peribo.com.au

Publishing History
First published by Dedalus in 2014
First ebook edition in 2014

Printed in Finland by Bookwell
Typeset by Marie Lane

The Author

Tom Cullen was born in Oklahoma in 1913 and went to France with the U.S. army during the Second World War. He remained there after the war before moving to Britain, having fallen foul of the American authorities for his communist beliefs.

He was the author of several respected biographies, including Maundy Gregory and Dr. Crippen, but his biography of Gerald Hamilton was blocked for legal reasons.

He died in 2001 in London.

The Editor

Phil Baker has written two books for Dedalus: *The Dedalus Book of Absinthe* and *The Devil is a Gentleman: The Life and Times of Dennis Wheatley.*

He is the author of books on Samuel Beckett, William S Burroughs and the London occult artist Austin Osman Spare, and reviews for a number of papers including *The Sunday Times* and *Times Literary Supplement.*

"It's marvellous… the way you've maintained standards of right and wrong and yet left Norris an endearing person. And you've made him both silly and witty, like a character in Congreve. He's awfully good."

E.M. Forster to Christopher Isherwood,
11 May 1935

Contents

Introduction:

The Importance of Being Gerald

"Uncle Gerald, your charm is a mystery" was W.H. Auden's 1939 toast to Gerald Hamilton, and Hamilton's undeniable charm was, indeed, mysterious. Despite his physical and perhaps moral ugliness, he had a strange charisma and he remains a fascinating character.

Hamilton's old-world charm carried him through a precarious life. One of the few people to be interned in both world wars as a threat to British national security, he became a communist agent between the wars before drifting to the right and recovering his faith in the "sacred cause" of absolute monarchy. Along the way he met everyone from the last Tsar to Aleister Crowley (who kept tabs on him for the British Special Branch when they shared a flat in Weimar Berlin) and he never lost his impeccable manners or his love of wine and food, whatever life threw at him in the way of personal and global crises. "We live in stirring times;" he liked to say, "tea-stirring times."

Hamilton is most famous, of course, as the inspiration for the seedy but beguiling Mr Norris in Christopher Isherwood's classic *Mr Norris Changes Trains*. The present book is emphatically not about the genesis of that novel, and it would be foolish to consider the novel to be simply about Hamilton. The "real" Mr Norris is the fictional one, who lives in the same realm as King Lear, Robinson Crusoe and Sherlock Holmes. Isherwood himself, one of the most nuanced and layered of autobiographical writers, has considered the relation between the man (or rather the mental image of a friend, a sort of "robot"; "Gerald-as-I-choose-to-see-him") and the character in his Prologue to Hamilton's autobiography (one of several, and none of them reliable) *Mr Norris and I...*

It might be more accurate not to say that Norris was Hamilton but, rather, that for the rest of his life Hamilton was Norris; an association he clearly relished, despite occasional protests to the contrary. This book is the story of his life outside the character, a life in which he went on to hobnob with fascist leader Sir Oswald Mosley and Establishment traitor Guy Burgess, and to scheme schemes undreamed of by Norris, from whitewashing apartheid South Africa to promoting Chiang Kai-shek's Nationalist China.

There is already a charming but partial picture of Hamilton in later life to be found in John Symonds's exceptional memoir *Conversations with Gerald*. This presents Gerald the reactionary bon viveur, pontificating about food and drink, fussing over soups and risottos, and staying in on Saturdays to avoid "football crowds, drinkers of bad beer, and fornicators in general." Never lost for the right thing to say, Gerald recalls being offered some perilously old 1874 Chateau Lafite which 'died' within seconds of the bottle being opened; there were long faces all around, before he brightened the party by observing "It is a privilege to have assisted at its obsequies." Whether he is condemning the British royal family as merely bourgeois or introducing Symonds to some of his favourite cheeses ("Chambourcy, Monsieur, Le Roy, Boursault, Fontainebleau," and particularly the goat's cheese Capricet) Symonds's Gerald comes over as provocatively opinionated but harmless and oddly endearing.

That was not how everyone saw him. The writer Julian Maclaren Ross described Hamilton as "the last of the dangerous men", comparing him in that respect to Crowley, and he had a bizarre, unsubstantiated story that a young friend of Gerald, intervening in a dispute on his behalf, had been stabbed to death: when the boy's parents complained, Hamilton's unsympathetic comment was allegedly "Goodness gracious me! Young men today seem to want to live forever!"

Hamilton's friend Robin Maugham received money for blackening Hamilton's name with a 1966 exposé in *The People* newspaper, in which Hamilton was described as "one of the most evil men alive today", but Stephen Spender and John Lehmann were more sincere in their judgment of Hamilton as a bad man, the latter firing a parting shot at him in his poem 'The Rules of Comedy', which ends "I'm sorry you died friendless, ugly, broke" (friendless being far from true, while being ugly and broke never cramped his style). There is a more unexpected reference in William Burroughs's novel *The Place of Dead Roads*: "An old-queen voice, querulous, petulant, cowardly, the evil old voice of Gerald Hamilton..."

Hamilton was also associated with perversity, in part via the masochistic Mr Norris, whose tastes were the subject of drollery by novelist Kyril Bonfiglioli ("I do have a few bits of equipment myself which other folk might think a bit frivolous. A bit Mr Norris – you know") and Barry Humphries ("I had written a macabre little song with a sexually perverse undertone. Somehow I had contrived to rhyme 'plastic rainwear' with 'Mr Norris changes train-wear'...")

More famous in his lifetime than he is now, Hamilton entertained his public with no fewer than three autobiographies (one of them illustrated with a drawing of him escaping from the British authorities disguised as a nun, by the cartoonist and illustrator Ronald Searle). The public were also treated to Robin Maugham's five-part *People* exposé of him as "the wickedest man in the world" ("*Gerald Hamilton*", ran the first headline: "*Traitor, Con-Man and Crook (Even his Name is a Fake)*") which was advertised on prime-time television. Writer and broadcaster Dan Farson had already interviewed Hamilton in Soho's Caves de France cellar bar for a television programme called *Bohemia*, and asked him "Is it true that you are the wickedest man in Europe?" "Oh, that's very kind of you," said Hamilton, "wittiest man in Europe, well, really…"

*

Tom Cullen's book was written while Hamilton and his curious celebrity were fresher in people's minds, less than a decade after his death. It was, however, blocked in Cullen's lifetime, in part because Robin Maugham seems to have made a bizarre claim that he had been libelled by an allegation that he knew Hamilton's death was faked, in order to escape his creditors, and that Hamilton had been seen being driven round Sloane Square in a taxi a week afterwards.

Maugham's real objection, I would suggest, was not to a cock-and-bull story about dead people riding taxis, but to a clear innuendo that Hamilton procured young men for him. He might further have objected to Cullen's entirely accurate depiction of the *People* series as a flagrantly insincere potboiler, quite cynically cooked up in cahoots with Hamilton himself.

I learned of this seemingly lost biography while researching Hamilton's entry for the *Dictionary of National Biography*, and tracked it to America. I already admired Cullen as a writer and researcher after reading his biography of Maundy Gregory, so I was excited to find that Cullen's friend Reed Searle had kept the Hamilton manuscript safely after rescuing it from the destruction of Cullen's more general papers in London.

Like many people who write, I find the idea of unpublished work emotive: a friend of mine was murdered on the night after he had finished his first book, and one of the last things he saw must have been the theft of his computer with the book in it, while my own last thought during a serious car crash was not that I was going to die but that I was never going to publish my book on Samuel Beckett. I felt for Cullen, and felt that his very fine book deserved to exist in the world. In addition to preserving memories of Hamilton himself, it sheds interesting light on various byways of social, sexual and political history, and it is a valuable corrective to some of the legends that have grown up around Hamilton – largely of his own embroidering. It seems that Hamilton did not, in fact, work with the notorious broker of unmerited honours and peerages, Maundy Gregory, despite his own shady endeavours in the same field, and in particular it seems that he was not a friend of the Irish Republican hero and martyr Sir Roger Casement: a cornerstone in Hamilton's personal myth.

Any biography is necessarily a partial picture. One of Cullen's angles is to bring out Hamilton's affinities with the characters of Restoration comedy, following from E.M. Forster's comparison of the fictional Norris to a character in Congreve – as cited in the epigraph to the book – and the perception of Isherwood, Auden and their circle that there was something "enchantingly 'period'" about Hamilton. I would suggest, however, that although the Restoration comparison works well, the period they were thinking of was primarily Edwardian and late Victorian, with Hamilton's exquisite manners and elegant walking sticks belonging to the age of wax fruit, antimacassars, and Oscar Wilde.

Forster's comment that Isherwood had maintained standards of right and wrong, while making Norris endearing, also bears on the perennial question of just how bad Hamilton was, and how we choose to frame and describe his behaviour. Seen from one angle, a man who can defraud the Save the Children Fund while running guns for the IRA and professing pacifism is something more than just a loveable rogue – and yet, to quote Norris, "There are some incidents in my career, as you doubtless know, which are very easily capable of misinterpretation."

Are there any mitigating circumstances? We could see a formative experience, not dwelt on by Tom Cullen, in the shock of Hamilton being sent away from home and bullied at his first school – he was a boarding-school 'survivor', as people might say today – which may have cauterized his character to some extent, and made him unpleasantly self-reliant. He might also have been capable of more loyalty, somewhere in his make-up, than he is usually given credit for. Along with his personal cult of Charles I, royal martyr, Hamilton maintained a more flesh-and-blood fidelity to the memory of his wife Suzy Renou – the second of two paid marriages of convenience – whom he never slept or lived with but remained fond of, and to that of his friend, danceband leader Ken 'Snakehips' Johnson, who was killed when the Café de Paris was blitzed. Their two photographs, in silver frames, sat on the mantelpieces of the various digs, bedsitters and furnished rooms that Hamilton occupied in his later years.

*

Christopher Isherwood not only had a genius for friendship but he was an ethical individual, and his own loyal affection for Hamilton must be a point in Hamilton's favour. Although he finally judged that Hamilton's persistent dishonesty was tiresome, "like a greedy animal which you can't leave alone in the kitchen", he was remarkably forgiving of Hamilton's depredations on himself. The most famous of these was Hamilton's ineffectual but profitably self-interested role in trying to help Isherwood's friend Heinz escape conscription into Hitler's army, which involved long-drawn-out and expensive attempts to obtain visas from Belgium and then Mexico: in the event, Heinz was to survive service on both the Western and Russian Fronts. Not long afterwards, with Isherwood and Auden having gone to America in 1939, Hamilton leaked a personal letter from Isherwood to the 'William Hickey' gossip column in the *Daily Express*, which helped to sour British public feeling against the emigrés.

Isherwood nevertheless sent Hamilton money to help him in his old age, even though he had few illusions about him. In *Mr Norris Changes Trains* he had deftly given Norris his moral come-uppance in the figure of his demonic manservant Schmidt – "quite literally a familiar", he said in a 1964 interview – and made their relationship an inspired, understated nod towards such doomed pairs as Dr Jekyll and Mr Hyde, and Dorian Gray and his picture. Seeing Hamilton on television in 1970 ("quite marvellously himself"), Isherwood noted his simultaneous aspects, "so polished and gross and charming and hideous", and the way he rolled his eyes like something in a horror film: "it's almost as terrific as the picture of Dorian Gray."

Isherwood was also generous enough to help Tom Cullen with the present book, answering queries and reading the manuscript in 1980, although he finally found it saddening (he records in his journal that he read it together with a biography of the musician and saloniste Misia Sert, "both of them ultimately downers"). It would have been his first inkling that even Hamilton's work for the Save the Children Fund was not as blameless as he had always believed, and it would also have put him through an account of his old friend's death, seemingly in a state of anguished repentance for his misdeeds.

Isherwood's underlying affection for Hamilton comes out in a dream he had in 1940, when Hamilton was already forgiven over the visa scheme and the leaked letter. As he recounted it to Hamilton a couple of years later:

> I had an almost clairvoyant dream in which I sat with you in that park in Amsterdam near the Emmastraat, watching the ducks on the lake. Nothing special happened, but it was unforgettably vivid, with the weeping willow and the sunlight on the water and the quacking of the ducks, and you, elegant as usual in grey, with a soft grey hat and your walking stick with the gold band; and there was a friendly relaxed atmosphere of mid-morning leisure.

It is a dream that brings together Hamilton's charm and the thoughts of another Gerald, the philosopher and mystical thinker Gerald Heard. In Isherwood's original account, recorded in his journal:

> This morning, lying in bed, half-awake, I had a very strange experience. I remembered – or rather, relived [...] – an instant of a certain morning, four years ago. I was sitting in a small park in Amsterdam, with Gerald Hamilton, and looking through the overhanging branches of a willow at a patch of brightly sunlit water, in which some ducks were swimming [...] for a couple of seconds, I actually was the Christopher of 1936 [...]

Now, for the first time, I feel I have some inkling of what Gerald [Heard] is really talking about.

The clairvoyant vividness is that of an almost mystical timeslip, pivoting not around a madeleine but a park and a friendship.

It is on that note of friendship that Isherwood deserves the last word. On first learning of Hamilton's death in 1970, he wrote that he no longer cared about Heinz's passport, and the still unclear details of just how far Hamilton might have swindled them, "But I do remember all the fun we had together. He had a very cozy personality and an animal innocence, you felt he was only acting according to his nature."

Phil Baker

Hamilton's birthday, 1968: Sibylla Jane Flower; Bevis Hillier; Lady Antonia Fraser; Hamilton; James Pope-Hennessy; James Reeve; Mark Amory.

Prologue: October 1954

Maskwell: "Ha! But is there no such Thing as Honesty? Yes, and whosoever has it about him, bears an Enemy in his Breast... Well, for Wisdom and Honesty, give me Cunning and Hypocrisie; oh, 'tis such a Pleasure, to angle for fair fac'd Fools!"

> – Congreve, *The Double-Dealer* (1694)

Le tout Londres was there at No 34 Tite Street on the morning of Saturday, October 16, 1954, according to the *Figaro* correspondent, meaning presumably that everyone who was anyone in the arts – poets, painters, writers, actors – was present for the unveiling of the blue plaque on the house where Oscar Wilde had lived. The occasion: the centenary of Wilde's birth. Certainly the organizers of the unveiling ceremony had tried to make it inclusive, inviting everyone from Allan Aynesworth, who was the original Algernon in *The Importance of Being Earnest*, to one of the bridesmaids at Wilde's wedding in 1884.

"The funny part is that I can't remember inviting Gerald Hamilton," Mrs Irena Barton, an attractive woman of French-Russian origin, tells me. "At that time I don't think I had even heard of Gerald Hamilton." Without Irena and her husband Eric, a bookseller in Richmond, there would have been no unveiling. It had all started with Irena writing a letter to *The Times* to suggest that "something should be done" to mark the Wilde centenary, a letter which had elicited some anonymous abuse, but also a 2/- book of stamps from a schoolgirl who wrote that this was all she could afford.

Now, sitting in the front parlour of her home on Richmond Hill, Mrs Barton searches her memory for how Gerald Hamilton first came into the picture. "I think he simply foisted himself on us," she says; "I think he gate-crashed." Invited or not, Gerald was to give Mrs Barton more headaches than the other one hundred and nineteen guests combined. "Starting about a fortnight before the unveiling Gerald telephoned almost daily to bombard me with questions." What was the prescribed dress for the occasion, Gerald wanted to know. Should he wear a lounge suit, or striped trousers and morning coat? If the latter, how could he be certain that he would not be the only male guest so attired? "These were some of the weighty matters on which Gerald sought enlightenment," Mrs Barton explains, laughing and shaking her head in wonderment. Then, too, Gerald wanted to know the exact order of the day – what was scheduled to take place and when. Did Mrs Barton anticipate that there would be trouble of any sort? A hostile reception by what Gerald referred to as "the rowdier element"?

"Gerald gave me to understand," Mrs Barton continues, "that, as a pacifist of long-standing, he could not be a party to any event that might end in violence." "One would have thought that it was Gerald's reputation that was being rehabilitated," Mrs Barton concludes. And in a sense this was the case. Gerald, who was in his sixty-fourth year, was coming in from the cold. His isolation was an enforced one: Gerald was not long out of Wandsworth Prison where he had served just one third of a nine-month sentence for a bankruptcy offence; he claimed that, taking advantage of coronation year, he had petitioned the Queen for a remission.

Gerald Hamilton was one of the very few Britons to be interned under the Defence of the Realm Act in both world wars, his presence at large being deemed to be inimical to national security. And now in October 1954 Gerald, whose prison pallor no amount of pancake make-up could hide, was down on his luck. He had left nearly everything he had that was pawnable with Auntie, *chez ma tante,* which was Gerald's term for the pawnbroker. He had sold to a rare book dealer the letters he had received from Max Beerbohm, Christopher Isherwood, and Lord Alfred Douglas, plus his copy of *Mr Norris Changes Trains* which Isherwood had inscribed "To the onlie begetter".

He had even been reduced to applying to Thomas Cook and Sons for a job as a London guide, but nothing had come of his application. So being an official guest at the Tite Street unveiling and at the Savoy luncheon afterwards, mixing on equal terms with *le tout Londres*, as it were, held a peculiar psychological significance for Gerald. He needed reassurance. He needed to know that having passed his three score years he had not lost his touch.

*

In appearance, Gerald had not changed much with the decades. He was still the world's ugliest man in the opinion of many, to whom this was a source of fascination. "I remember taking my two daughters – they were both in their teens – to meet him," recalls Mrs Gillian Mansel, who typed Gerald's letters for him, "and they were both appalled that I could work for anyone so ugly. But one forgot his looks when confronted with his charm, his old-world manners."

Gerald's wig, which had once held the young Christopher Isherwood spellbound, had long since been discarded. Isherwood describes his guilty reaction when Mr Norris catches him staring at it:

I must have been staring very rudely, for he looked up suddenly and saw the direction of my gaze. He startled me by asking simply:

"Is it crooked?"

I blushed scarlet. I felt terribly embarrassed.

"Just a tiny bit, perhaps."

Now Gerald's head was completely bald, though he liked to maintain that it had sprouted "a septuagenarian stubble". Otherwise his features were much the same as Isherwood had first catalogued them from the "sculpturally white" forehead to the chin "which seemed to have slipped sideways … like a broken concertina", and not forgetting the eyes, "light-blue jellies, like naked shell-fish in the crevices of a rock". Gerald's nose drooped over thick lips which were almost comic in their sensuality. "Really, Gerald should wear a fig-leaf over his mouth," one of his friends remarked.

What was there about Gerald that attracted Isherwood to him when the two met for the first time in Berlin in the winter of 1930–31? The disparity in their ages (Christopher was twenty-six, Gerald forty) suggests one possible answer; Christopher may have seen in Gerald a surrogate father. Isherwood has written how, as a boy, he revolted because he was never allowed to forget his real father, who had been killed in the First World War. "As an adolescent orphan he was subjected to reminders by schoolmasters and other busybodies of his Hero-Father." For this reason Isherwood perhaps chose as a father substitute Gerald, who was to play Falstaff to Christopher's Prince Hal.

Another tie which drew Isherwood and Hamilton together was their sexuality, as Isherwood writes in *Christopher and His Kind*. Back in Berlin in the winter of 1930–31 both cruised the gay boy-bars with which that capital abounded. "When it came to breaking the laws which had been made against the existence of their tribe," Isherwood writes, "Christopher was happy to be Gerald's fellow-criminal."

But it was not only as a surrogate father and a fellow homosexual that Gerald appealed to Isherwood. "From Christopher's point of view, Gerald was enchantingly 'period'," Isherwood writes. "He introduced Wystan [Auden], Stephen [Spender] and other friends to him, and soon they were all treating him like an absurd but nostalgic artwork which has been rediscovered by a later generation."[1]

Gerald was like a fugitive from the Restoration comedy of manners, which has been described as the most licentious in the history of the English stage. His was the amoral outlook captured by Wycherley and Congreve in their comic masterpieces. It was as though Gerald had been caught up in the cogs of some time warp, and had orbited for three centuries, before being deposited in the twentieth century to astound and delight Isherwood and his friends with his queerly-cut toupées, his courtly manners, and his police record. His young friends may not have been aware of the source of their delight but in Gerald they were watching a character out of Congreve, not as a stage reincarnation, but as "the word made flesh".

Gerald had affinities of his own with the seventeenth century. Even as a schoolboy at Rugby he had made a cult of the Stuarts. "At a very early age I insisted upon wearing mourning on January 30th, the day on which Charles the First was beheaded," he writes, "and, later, I ate no food but dry bread on that day – not a light undertaking for a very greedy

---

1 As I have suggested in the introduction, Tom Cullen's sense of Hamilton as a some-what Restoration figure works well with E.M. Forster's sense of Norris as a character out of Congreve, but it is likely that when Isherwood and his friends saw Hamilton as "enchantingly 'period'", the period was primarily pre-First World War. [Ed.]

schoolboy." Then came the day of rejoicing. On May 29th, the day the monarchy was restored, Gerald would invite his school cronies to "an orgy of ice-cream" at Hobley's, the Rugby pastry shop. And throughout his life, in various Hamilton diaries, January 30th is ringed as the "anniversary of the martyrdom of St Charles".

*

Saturday October 16 dawned dull, with the sky threatening rain. Gerald was among the first to arrive in Tite Street, which had been roped off, and where chairs had been set up for the official guests. No 34 (which had been No 16 when Wilde lived there) had lost whatever charm it may once have possessed. A sombre, red-brick terraced house of four storeys, it had been requisitioned by the Borough of Chelsea and now housed council tenants.

Sleek limousines (that of Chelsea's mayor had a pennant flying over its bonnet) drew up and disgorged their equally sleek occupants. As might be expected, the theatre was most heavily represented, among those who had come from the green room to pay homage being Dame Edith Evans (the Lady Bracknell of her generation), Peggy Ashcroft, Esmé Percy, Michael Redgrave, and Micheal MacLiammoir. They were joined by representatives of the other arts such as T.S. Eliot, Sacheverell Sitwell and Augustus John.

To at least one observer the gathering suggested a religious revival meeting, the spirit of reconciliation being as heavy as the clouds which threatened rain. Old friends embraced; old enemies likewise. Vyvyan Holland, Wilde's eldest son, could be seen hobnobbing with Lord Cecil, descendant of Wilde's ancient adversary, the Eighth Marquis of Queensberry.

The only discordant voice was that of Gerald Hamilton, loudly complaining because the Union Jack, and not the Irish tricolour, was used to cover the blue plaque. "Well, no, but really my dear fellow, an abominable piece of impertinence," Gerald muttered to Claud Cockburn. But then Gerald could be more Irish than the Irish when it suited him. Just as he fooled most of his friends into thinking that his name was really Hamilton, so did Gerald gull them into believing that he was a true son of Erin, when in reality his name was Souter and his forebears Scottish. His protests were cut short when Sir Compton Mackenzie pulled a cord, and the Union Jack fell away to reveal "Oscar Wilde, 1854–1900, Wit and Dramatist, lived here". That night the plaque would be defaced by vandals throwing a pot of paint.

*

In the River Room of the Savoy, where the invited guests were enjoying champagne cocktails before the celebratory luncheon, Gerald could be heard denying for the umpteenth time that he had served as model for the Mr Norris who changed trains. "Really not my style at all, old chap - some of Mr Norris's mannerisms are mine I admit, some of his *obiter dicta* likewise – but all that sex and insinuendo, really!" – and at this point Gerald rolled his eyes upwards as though calling on heaven to be his witness. "Do I look like the type who goes in for whips and strumpets in scarlet boots?" Then, as though fearing an answer, he hurriedly remarked that "it was really very naughty of Christopher, the dear boy".

In the River Room, where chairs had been pushed back, brandy snifters filled, and cigars lit, the guests could congratulate themselves not only on a good meal, but on the fact that so far there had been no mention of the infamy which they had ostensibly been called together to redress. True, there had been one awkward moment earlier when Sir Compton Mackenzie, holding aloft a priced catalogue of the sheriff's auction that had taken place at No. 34, had told how Lot 237, tin soldiers and other toys belonging to Wilde's two sons, had been knocked down for thirty shillings. But the awkwardness had been smoothed over with Sir Compton remarking, "We are nicer people today."

Sir Max Beerbohm, in a message read at the luncheon, chose a safe course by confining himself to Wilde's table talk, "the most spontaneous and yet the most polished" it had been his privilege to hear. It was a verdict with which Gerald Hamilton, who had pilfered most of Wilde's epigrams at one time or another and passed them off as his own, might have concurred.

Laurence Housman, whose tribute likewise was read, came closer to treading on dangerous ground when he declared that Wilde, by his unhappy fate, had served the whole of humanity. He had "defeated the blind obscurantists; he had made people think," according to Housman. Wilde had made people think, yes, but in 1954 the "blind obscurantists" still had things pretty much their own way. The years following the Second World War had seen a fourfold increase in the numbers of persons proceeded against for homosexual offences (but had not Wilde himself warned that the road to sexual law reform was "long and red with monstrous martyrdoms"?). The French cultural attaché, in his tribute, made matters worse by linking Wilde's name with that of André Gide. It was with relief that the guests rose to drink the toast to Wilde's memory proposed by Sir Compton Mackenzie and seconded by the Irish ambassador.

They then made their way to the cloakroom, where along with their wraps they had "parked their guilt-complexes", in the phrase of Claud Cockburn, upon whom none of the irony of the occasion appears to have been lost. Bidden to witness a drama entitled "Oscar Aveng'd", they had been entertained by a farce entitled "The Tite Street Follies".

*

At least the Restoration poets were less hypocritical, more honest in their avowals as to what their plays were about, which was sex. Sex in all of its aspects – the coterie audience of aristocrats for whom these poets wrote was obsessed with sex as a reaction against the puritanism of Cromwell's Commonwealth. Not waiting for Freud, they were busy finding out about man's suppressed desires, the disparity between his inner and his outer nature.

Maskwell is the character in Restoration comedy whom Gerald Hamilton most resembles, and whom Gerald could have played on the stage to perfection – Maskwell, described as a "sedate, a thinking Villain, whose black Blood runs temperately bad", but whom a modern critic has likened to "a bad dream from the subconscious of the aristocracy".

Maskwell is the archetypal confidence trickster. "Tis such a pleasure to angle for fair-fac'd Fools," he cries, and one can almost see Gerald Hamilton nodding approval. Like Maskwell, Gerald had the "fair-fac'd Fools" at his mercy, for Isherwood and his friends had been brought up to believe in personal relationships as representing "something solid in a world full of violence and cruelty", in the words of E.M. Forster, who went on to say: "One must be fond of people and trust them if one is not to make a mess of life, and it is therefore essential that they should not let one down." The trouble with Gerald was that he was always letting one down.

Gerald played by a different set of rules. In vain his friends sought to make excuses for "good old, bad old Gerald", as they called him. He simply could not be all that bad, they reasoned. After all, he was such a bungler, so inefficient as a crook – everything he put his hand to came unstuck, they argued, forgetting the successful deals he pulled off. "Crime, as he practised it," writes Isherwood, "…is as demanding and unrewarding as witchcraft."

Not all who met Gerald were taken in by his Edwardian manners, his air of bonhomie. Some found him to be positively evil. Aleister Crowley, who met Gerald in Berlin in the early 1930s, was terrified of him, believing him to be in the pay of the NKVD, the Soviet secret police (Crowley discovered Gerald's duplicity by casting the I Ching). Lord Berners refused to dine with Sir Oswald and Lady Diana Mosley when he learned that Gerald was to be one of the company. "Lord Berners was the most broad-minded of men," Lady Mosley tells me. "He could not have cared less about Gerald's sexual morals, but he would not sit at table with a man whom he knew to be a crook." When Maurice Leonard sought permission to bring Gerald to a piano recital given by his friend Marc Anthony he met with a horrified reaction. "Have nothing to do with that man, I beg of you," Anthony warned him. "He is evil, and everyone who has had anything to do with him has come to grief. One of his friends committed suicide, another Gerald shopped to the police." The writer Julian Maclaren Ross told Gerald's friend John Symonds that a young man had been stabbed to death while fighting one of Gerald's battles for him. Accused by the boy's distraught parents of being responsible for their son's death, Gerald allegedly replied, "Good gracious me! Young men seem to want to live forever."

Gerald certainly had no conception of loyalty. Betrayal

was almost a conditioned reflex. It was not just a question of spying on Willi Muenzenberg, the Comintern boss he worked with in Berlin. Gerald's friends might have been surprised if they had known that starting in 1942, when he was released from Brixton prison as an 18B internee, Gerald was in regular contact with the Special Branch, Scotland Yard. His diaries, in particular, establish the fact that Gerald regularly saw Detective Inspector (later Chief Superintendent) G.G. Smith of Special Branch, the spy catcher credited with cracking the Portland Spy Ring. In addition, the Hamilton papers include letters from Smith, which indicate that the detective's visits to Gerald's flat in Glebe Place, Chelsea, were not social calls – the letters make use of some sort of code. Gerald's employment as an informer by Special Branch is discussed in a later chapter. Suffice it to say here that when Guy Burgess went missing in 1956, one of the first persons sought out by Smith was Gerald.

*

The unveiling of the Wilde plaque marked a stage in Gerald's climb to position of comfortable notoriety, if not celebrity. His confidence restored by the friendly reception he was given at the Savoy luncheon, Gerald was well on his way to becoming a Public Character. Soon no Foyle's literary luncheon would be complete without him. When John Gordon of the *Sunday Express* condemned *Lolita* as "the filthiest book I have ever read", Gerald was one of those invited to Graham Greene's flat in Albany to inaugurate the John Gordon Society, dedicated to "the defence of purity in public life".

As the years slipped past, Gerald appeared to be living proof that if the British love a Grand Old Man, they love a Grand Old Scallywag more. For in the fifties, long after

Isherwood and Auden had settled in America, it was the turn of a new generation – novelists Robin Maugham and Michael Davidson, painter Francis Bacon, journalists Tom Driberg and Maurice Richardson – to "discover" Gerald and to be thrilled by his awfulness. Only it was no longer "good old bad old Gerald", but simply "PFG": initials which stood not for "Please Forward Gold", as his friend Mike Steen would have it, but "Poor Fucking Gerald".[2]

In the sixties Gerald was taken up by still another generation, writers James Pope-Hennessy, Lady Antonia Fraser, and Bevis Hillier, and painter James Reeve being intrigued by this "darling dodo" in their midst. As late as 1969 novelist Colin Spencer was telling a friend, "You really must meet Gerald. He's the ugliest man in the world."

With Isherwood no longer on the scene to defend Gerald, each succeeding generation took on the task of excusing his worst excesses. For Gerald by now had become the epitome not only of bad taste, but of unfortunate timing. Gerald waits until the Sharpeville massacre in South Africa, in which sixty-seven rioting Africans were shot by police, to publish his travel-book apologia for apartheid, *Jacaranda* (which the South African government subsidized). As if that were not enough, he waits until the bronze statue of Sir Winston Churchill is unveiled at London's Guildhall to reveal to the world that he – not Churchill – was the model for the statue ("Only the head is Churchill's, the rest – four-fifths of the statue – is me.")

What was the secret of Gerald's hold on his friends? Was it his sheer awfulness? Was his attraction such as makes some people prefer kitsch to good art? Or did his friends simply look upon him as a test of loyalty? Whatever else, they looked upon

---

2 Hungry and in need of a first-class dinner, Hamilton was wont to look plaintive and say "Poor Fucking Gerald wants his beans!" – see for example Robin Maugham, *Escape from the Shadows* (Hodder and Stoughton, 1972) p.208. [Ed.]

him as a Life Force. Isherwood, in paying tribute to Gerald's survival value, writes "Gerald inhabited a world into which Christopher had barely peeped; one might call it 'real' for it was without hypocrisy, its ends and means were frankly criminal... Christopher was sometimes shocked and repelled by the glimpses he got of this world. Nevertheless, Gerald's example encouraged him to live his own life more boldly."

Awed by his "limpet-like tenacity" and "preternatural vitality", Maurice Richardson says much the same thing. "When on Judgement Day, at the special session which will have been allotted for the singular case of Hamilton, Gerald, the Recording Angel, hoarse after his long recitation, closes his recital, I shall advise Gerald to make the following plea in mitigation: 'My zestful hedonism was often an encouragement to others'."

One

November 1890: Premature and Perfect

"If indeed to be premature is to be perfect – as Oscar Wilde assured the egregious Nineties," Gerald writes, "then I must have come into the world in a very unusual state of perfection." Gerald Frank Hamilton Souter, to give him his full name, was born on November 1 1890 at Shanghai, where his father was agent for the China merchant firm of Holliday, Wise and Company of Manchester. Unfortunately Gerald's premature entrance cost his mother her life, Edith Minnie Holliday Souter dying within a fortnight. Gerald later claimed to believe she died from "postnatal depression that the boy she had brought into the world was not a girl".

When he was four months old Gerald was bundled off to England in the care of two Chinese amahs, thus permitting him to observe in later life that anything Oriental in his behaviour was due to the fact that he had been suckled by Chinese breasts. Once arrived at Tilbury, the orphan was deposited in the arms of a maiden aunt, Mary Anne Holliday, familiarly known as Aunty May, and whisked off to the country to be reared. Gerald was eight years old when he saw his father again; when Frank Thomas Edward Souter suddenly materialised from nowhere to reclaim his son, like the wicked enchanter in a fairy tale, Gerald was instantly antagonistic. "I nursed a feeling of the most profound dislike towards him," he writes; "I could hardly bear to be in the same room with him, and I would invariably burst out crying when I was told 'Father is here'." On one occasion when his father came to fetch him for a drive in Hyde

Park, young Gerald locked himself in the water closet, nor would he come out until assured by his Aunty May that Souter *père* had quit the premises.

How does an eight-year-old boy set about to destroy the intruder in paradise garden? Does he shoot the father with a poison arrow dipped in curare, or atomize him with the ray-gun he has seen advertised in *The Beano*? Small boys in their imaginations have availed themselves of these and other means to eliminate the hated rival. One hardly needs Gerald's favourite author Oscar Wilde as a reminder that "All the great crimes of the world are committed in the brain". However, Gerald was more subtle. He destroyed his father by substituting a stereotype for the real man.

But first, it was necessary to invent an entirely spurious background for Souter *père*. "My paternal ancestry was, may I say, faintly ducal," Gerald writes in his usual arch manner, the duke in question being James Hamilton (1811–1885), first Duke of Abercorn, Privy Councillor, and Knight of the Garter (Gerald maintained that His Grace was so enamoured of his blue Garter sash that he wore it to bed). Gerald's father, "Francis Ernest Hamilton", was supposed to be the nephew of this eccentric duke, whose arms and motto (*Sola nobilitas virtus* – Virtue alone is nobility) Gerald appropriated as his own.

The deception fooled none of Gerald's friends, who made a guessing game of the father's true identity. Because Gerald was so anti-Semitic a number of his friends, Maurice Richardson among them, concluded that his father must be a Jew – a South African Jew, according to some. Richardson had a bizarre explanantion for his conviction that Gerald's origin was Jewish. He referred to the latter's appearance at a London magistrate's court. "Poor Gerald was being given a bad time by the prosecution," Richardson recalled, "and in his desperation he turned to the bench, crying 'I swear on my mother's head that I am telling the truth'. Now I maintain that such a strange oath could only have been learned from Jewish parents." Others thought that the father was central European, while James Pope-Hennessy was certain that he had been a greengrocer in London's East End.

*

Frank Thomas Edward Souter was born in Bombay in 1864 of a distinguished Indian civil service family with Scottish connections that could trace its ancestry back to Robert the Bruce. Gerald's paternal grandfather was Sir Frank Henry Andrew Souter, Police Commissioner of Bombay Province, and one of the heroes of the Indian Mutiny (his capture of the rebel chief of Nurgoond earned him his knighthood). Gerald's uncles were all either civil servants or carved out careers for themselves in the Indian Army, Gerald's father being the only Souter to opt for a commercial career. One of the uncles, Major Maurice Souter, whose braggadocio earned him the family nickname of "Marbot", after Napoleon's boastful general of that name, was to cover himself with glory in the 1914–18 war at Agagia, in Egypt, when he led the Dorsetshire Yeomanry in a charge against the Senussi, and captured their Turkish leader Gaafar Pasha. The exploit earned Major Souter a colonelcy and the DSO, which he maintained should have been the VC. Thereafter he went about, an embittered man, muttering, "Iron has entered into my soul."

The male Souters were a hard-riding, pig-sticking, polo-playing lot; excitable, talkative, almost incoherent. Drawing upon these male relatives, Gerald painted for the benefit of friends a picture of his father as a hard-drinking, Jorrocks-type country squire, whose culture was limited to a knowledge of claret and of horse flesh. In reality Gerald's father was abstemious, cantankerous, opinionated. "Frank Souter had a large store of knowledge, which he doled out grudgingly," observes the Hon Terence Prittie. "He would brook no contradiction, but had the happy faculty of being always right" – right, that is, except when it came to his operations as an investment broker on the stock exchange: his relatives were burned more than once by the dud shares in which he advised them to invest. That Frank Souter also had his human side is evident from his love of ballroom dancing, at which he excelled (Gerald too, despite his corpulence, was surprisingly nimble on his feet.) Souter in fact was a patron of the annual East London Costermongers' Ball, mingling with perfect ease with the pearly kings and queens of Cockneydom.

At that first encounter between father and son, Mr Souter was dismayed to see that, in his absence, Gerald had been turned into a mollycoddle. For whether or not Gerald's mother had expired regretting that the son she had borne was not a daughter, Aunty May seemed determined to rectify this. She did so by dressing Gerald as much like a girl as she dared, giving him dolls to play with, and spoiling him outrageously. Gerald was, by his own admission, a sickly-looking, decidedly effeminate youth, and he attracted bullies. "My long hair, my delicate complexion, and my general appearance of being a second little Lord Fauntleroy must have worked a distinct provocation," he writes.

Horrified by life at Aunty May's, the father quickly removed Gerald from her care and sent him first to a prep school in Berkshire, where "the organized bullying… was conducted with a refinement and persistence worthy of a greater cause", and then to Rugby, where Dr Arnold had perfected a system for turning out Christian gentlemen. Mr Souter entered Gerald's name for School Field House, where Rupert Brooke's father was Housemaster. The fact that Rugby barred Roman Catholics may also have influenced Frank Souter, who was strongly anti-Papist. But an upright, Protestant English gentleman was exactly what Gerald, with his genius for defying his father, had no intention of becoming. To this Arnoldian ideal Gerald opposed the *carpe diem* philosophy of Congreve's Bellmour: "Come, come, leave business to Idlers, and wisdom to Fools. ...Wit be my faculty; and Pleasure my occupation."

*

The only mention of Gerald's name that occurs in *The Meteor*, the school's monthly publication, is in connection with his debut before the Rugby Debating Society on March 7, 1908, when he defended the motion "That, in the opinion of this House, Cromwell injured rather than benefited England". "Mr G.F.H. Souter made, by way of a maiden speech, a spirited onslaught on certain absurdities levelled against King Charles", the school magazine reports. "Cromwell", the write-up continues, giving the gist of Gerald's argument, "had been called the father of modern Socialism, since he was the first to take the law into his own incapable hands. He was, in fact, an ambitious hypocrite, cloaking his designs under the cover of religious piety."

The appeal that Stuartism, that most romantic of lost causes, holds for adolescent public schoolboys is an evergreen one. One thinks of Esmond Romilly, Winston Churchill's nephew, who at the age of thirteen journeyed from his prep school at Seaford to London to lay white roses at the foot of Charles I's statue in Whitehall on the anniversary of the king's execution – this same Esmond Romilly who later was to become a communist and fight on the side of the Republicans in Spain.

Very likely Restoration permissiveness also attracted Gerald, for he was more sexually precocious than his School Field contemporaries, from all one can gather, having been initiated into homosexual practices at his Berkshire prep school, where "acts of indecency" were of common occurrence, as he notes. Then too Gerald, while still a lower form boy, got hold of Burnet's life of John Wilmot, the second Earl of Rochester, poet, wit, libertine and practical joker who, as one of his pranks, enticed Charles II disguised to a brothel, then arranged to have all his money stolen. Rochester was a notorious womanizer, but not averse to the charms of page boys, as his verse makes clear:

> Then give me Health, Wealth, Mirth and Wine,
> And if busy Love entrenches,
> There's a sweet, soft Page of mine
> Does the trick worth Forty Wenches.

These traits served to endear the mad earl to Gerald.

As noted earlier, when the May 29 anniversary of the Restoration rolled around Gerald would treat his cronies to an orgy of ice cream. The youthful Gerald became such a fanatical Stuartist that he worked out elaborate genealogical tables purporting to show how Edward VII was a usurper, and Prince Rupprecht of Bavaria was the legitimate King of England. From these schooldays dates Gerald's antipathy to the British Royal family, the exception being Edward VIII, with whom he sided at the time of the abdication. According to Gerald, they were all usurpers.

*

Gerald no longer spent his school holidays with his Aunty May, but with his father and his Souter relatives. He got to know these Indian Army uncles of his quite well, for one or another of them was always home on leave. As time went by they made a considerable fuss over their nephew, and for a strange reason: Gerald was destined to be the last of the Souters. The hereditary line ran out after him. A curse of barrenness appears to have descended upon this excitable, talkative breed. One Souter uncle died before reaching maturity, four uncles and one aunt never married, another uncle and an aunt each married, but produced no children. This was to leave Gerald in a unique position to avenge himself on his father.

Of the Souters Gerald liked best his Aunt Helena (known to the family as Dolly) who, with her younger sister Marguerite, had been educated at the court of Grand Duke Louis IV of Hesse-Darmstadt. It is something of a mystery how these girls, daughters of a Bombay police commissioner knighted by Queen Victoria, yet with no claim to being either of the landed gentry or the *noblesse de robe*, gained *entrée* to the grand ducal court. Yet Aunt Dolly became a close friend of Princess Alix of Hesse-Darmstadt, whose marriage to Nicholas II was to make her the last Tsarina of Russia. I have seen photographs of the Tsarina which she autographed for Aunty Dolly, including one of the Imperial family inscribed: "From your loving Alix, 1901–1902." Gerald was to trade on this connection when in 1912, armed with his aunt's letter of introduction, he visited Nicholas and Alexandra at their summer palace at Tsarkoe Selo, and made the acquaintance of their haemophiliac heir and his sinister shadow, Rasputin.

But to return to Rugby, Gerald had already gained the reputation among schoolmates of being a "royalist snob" by October 1907, when Princess Henry of Battenberg, Edward VII's sister, visited the school, and Gerald was chosen as one of three boys to address her. After saying his few words Gerald bowed so low that he almost toppled over, according to his account. Later a bully, who was doubtless republican in outlook, administered a swift kick to Gerald's backside with the words, "That's for sucking up to Ma Batters."

"When people suggest that I left Rugby under a cloud, I reply that it must have been under a cloud of incense" – this was Gerald's usual explanation for his abrupt departure from Rugby in 1908, while still in the fifth form. Gerald is alluding to his visits to the local Catholic church – or "Tolly" church as it was known, a tolly being schoolboy slang for a candle – which was strictly out of bounds to Rugbeians. On one of these occasions, Gerald, after assisting at mass, was presented with a rosary by "an astonished priest [who] recognized me as a Rugby boy", and he bore this treasure in triumph back to School Field House. The visits, of course, were one more gesture of defiance, aimed more at his father than at the schoolmasters standing in *loco parentis*.

Popery, however, was not the reason Gerald gave to Maurice Richardson for his expulsion from Rugby. Gerald told Richardson that he had been caught in bed with another boy. Homosexuality was no new phenomenon at Rugby, which in this respect was no different than other public schools. Waves of overt homosexual behaviour swept the school with the periodicity of chickenpox or the mumps. To prevent such outbreaks games had been instituted, as had compulsory cold baths. Various rules had been framed with the object of removing temptation. A boy must not walk out with a boy from another House, nor in the first instance make friends with older (later it would be younger) boys. But the rules were honoured more in the breach, according to Gerald, who writes that "fervent and romantic friendships between elder and younger boys flourished at Rugby". "Probably no schoolboy could pass through a public school completely unscathed", he adds. Gerald in fact enters an impassioned plea for such ephebian relationships. "Both masters and parents," he writes, "are far too apt hysterically to condemn as 'unnatural vice' what is in fact a very natural occurrence…"

For those boys whose minds dwelt too often and too lovingly on sins of the flesh Dr Arnold had recommended "personal correction", perhaps unconsciously adopting a euphemism commonly employed by prostitutes. Dr Arnold removed the birch from the hands of the housemasters and placed it in the itching fingers of Sixth Form prefects. JK Stanford, who was at School Field House with Gerald, recalls that for their sins lower formers were "beaten… with a birch or a cane or a long-handled hair-brush". As Gerald entered Rugby late, he was excused the ardours of fagging, but most likely he experienced "correction" and in later life he developed a taste for chastisement, as did his fictional counterpart Mr Norris. Gerald showed his friend Peter Burton a pornographic essay on Rugby caning, seemingly written by himself, in the form of an October 1914 letter from a Rugby schoolboy to a friend at another school. It will be recalled that Norris was the author of such works as *Miss Smith's Torture-Chamber* and *The Girl With the Golden Whip*.

Having broken the Eleventh Commandment by being caught, Gerald was called into W.P. Brooke's study one morning in July, 1908. It was all very civilized and, at the end of the interview, Gerald shook hands with Brooke after being told by the kindly if absent-minded housemaster that he must leave; it was for the good of the school.

*

At Rugby Gerald identified himself with the "aesthetes" as opposed to the "hearties" (at Rugby these latter were known as "bucks"). He abstained from taking part in athletics of any sort, which automatically made him a "remnant". "I believe that I alone can claim to have spent four solid years at Rugby without ever having been promoted out of the remnants," he was to boast in later life.

Bertrand Russell criticized the Arnold system as "sacrificing intellect to virtue". Certainly the emphasis in Gerald's day was all on character building, to the exclusion of originality of thought. "What we look for here," Dr Arnold told his pupils, "is first religious and moral principles; secondly, gentlemanly conduct; thirdly, intellectual ability." Gerald imbibed few Arnoldian principles of morality and conduct. As for his intellectual formation, Gerald was to remain an unabashed philistine with no ear for music, no eye for painting, and no mind for literature. "I only read books written by friends," he said, "or in which I am mentioned."

On the other hand Rugby gave him a cachet which was to prove invaluable to his operations as a confidence trickster – the cachet of being "an English public school gentleman". The old Rugby school tie was to get Gerald out of more than one tight corner. Like the egregious Captain Grimes in Waugh's *Decline and Fall*, Gerald could boast "There's a blessed equity in the English social system that ensures the public school man against starvation." "One goes through four or five years of perfect hell at an age when life is bound to be hell anyway,"

Waugh's character explains, "and after that the social system never lets one down". Once sent down, Gerald never again visited Rugby. He gave as his excuse for shunning the school that it held too many sad memories, referring to his school mates – Rupert Brooke's brother Alfred, who was Gerald's special friend, among them – killed in the 1914–18 war.

*

Frank Souter was enraged when he learned that his son had been expelled from Rugby, and in particular when he learned the reason. Gerald had let the Souters down – not only his father, but all those Indian Army officers who were counting on their nephew to carry on the line.

Gerald's disgrace was complete. "My father assured me that it was a waste of time to send so useless a son to Oxford at all, and that, if I refused to go into the Army, I must take up some career. He suggested putting me into an office." But Gerald had no intention of being shelved in some musty counting-house, for which, in any case, he would have been totally unfit. In any event Gerald would reach his majority in three years, at which time he was due to come into an inheritance from his mother. Meanwhile he would become a remittance man. The arrangement was that his father made Gerald an annual allowance of £500, which his Aunty May agreed to match. He chose as his destination China, perhaps because Shanghai was as remote from the playing fields of Rugby as it was possible to get.

*

What eighteen-year-old, accustomed to start each school day with a plunge into a cold bath, could resist the *luxe* of the East, and the blandishments of servants who addressed him as Glory of the East, Protector of the Poor, and Shelter of the World, while they prostrated themselves at his feet? Gerald was not made of such stern stuff. One of his first acts, in setting up a bachelor establishment, was to engage two such worshipful servants: Ah Sung, or "Gazelle Eyes", a catamite, who spent most of his waking hours in posing in fine silk gowns in front of a mirror; and Kwei Ching, a native of Soochow, who was as ugly as Gazelle Eyes was exquisite, but who was twice as faithful.

Gerald then decided to give the social life of the International Settlements a twirl. His mother's relatives in Shanghai included Uncle Cecil Holliday, senior partner of the Holliday, Wise firm, and Aunt Alexandra, who was married to a younger son of the millionaire philanthropist, Sir Thomas Hanbury. Thanks to their introductions, Gerald became a member of the Race Club, where the gambling stakes were vertiginously high, and of the Shanghai Club, which he claimed had notices posted "No dogs or Chinamen allowed".

By the end of six months the social life had begun to pall ("I had not crossed two continents in order to enjoy an imitation, however splendid, of London life," Gerald writes). Besides, the moral standards of the pillars who propped up the Shanghai Club were "considerably lower than in Europe", he observes. "Even the husbands of Shanghai accompanied the bachelors on their frequent excursions 'down the line' – the row of large houses at the corner of Kiangse Road and the canal, inhabited by American ladies who sold their favours for the established price of fifteen Mexican dollars..." It was not the laxness of morals but the hypocrisy that bothered Gerald.

So, six months after his arrival in Shanghai Gerald took the step which would irrevocably cut him off from the British colony, including his Holliday relatives: he decided to wear Chinese dress, which in their eyes was tantamount to 'going native'. Gerald's decision was taken "partly out of compliment to the country I was living in," he writes, "but, chiefly because I considered Chinese dress to be more comfortable, more healthy and more beautiful."

Gerald was not the only Englishman to hold to this belief. Sir Harold Acton wore native costume during the years he was in China, as did Sir Edmund Backhouse, master forger, pornographer, and fantasist, who claimed to have been the lover of a British prime minister (Lord Rosebery) and of the Dowager Empress of China. ("I doubt whether Backhouse and Hamilton had common friends," Hugh Trevor-Roper wrote in response to my query after I had noted they were both in China at the same time: "I suspect that their very similarities would have kept them apart.")

Gerald's sojourn in China was simply an interregnum, a marking time until he came into his mother's money, and could then tell his father to go to hell. As though to hasten the showdown with his father, Gerald gambled feverishly on the Shanghai Stock Exchange in rubber shares, made £3,000 in a deal involving Langkat Sumatra Rubber, then lost all this and more when the bubble burst. Thereupon he became ill from anxiety and was nursed by Catholic nuns at the Shanghai General Hospital ("I spent many long weeks there in a large room, with Kwei Ching squatting on a verandah outside"). Once recovered he underwent a conversion to the Church of Rome, one of the nuns having made him promise that if his life were spared, which at one point seemed problematical, he would become a Catholic. Gerald writes of his baptism on the eve of the Feast of the Immaculate Conception, "I fully realised that this step would irrevocably sever the ties that bound me to my father…" In later life Gerald admitted it was this, and not the keeping of a promise, that was his prime consideration in joining the Church of Rome.

Before leaving Shanghai, Gerald, in his newly-found zeal, made an attempt to convert Kwei Ching, giving the latter a graphic account in Chinese, pieced out with pidgin-English, of the events leading to Calvary. "Possibly my enthusiasm was infectious, possibly it was simply the love that every Chinese has for a story – at any rate, Kwei Ching was visibly moved.

After a long time he asked, "And when did that happen, Master?" "A long, long time ago," I replied, "many centuries ago"… "And where did it happen, Master?" "Very many thousand miles from here," I answered. The ghost of a smile then began to brighten Kwei Ching's features, so long saddened by my recital. "Oh, Protector of the Poor, if it happened so long ago and so very far from here, let us hope that there is no truth at all in this terrible story of a god crucified."

*

Gerald's showdown with his father took place not at the father's house in Egerton Crescent, South Kensington, but at the father's club, the St James's on Piccadilly, and it was brief almost to the point of being anti-climactic. The father had received lurid accounts from old business associates in Shanghai of Gerald going native. The atmosphere, therefore, was one of permafrost when the two met in the leather recesses of the club. First of all, Frank Souter read the riot act to his son for having become a Catholic. "You can become a Parsee or a Buddhist, or a damned Fire-Worshipper, for all I care, but I will have no son of mine a Catholic," Souter *père* is quoted as saying. Of his conversion Gerald was to write later "It was never a positive act of belief in one Church or creed, but rather a negative gesture of disbelief in the tenets of the Church of which my father was so militant a supporter."

Next, the father had certain testamentary duties to perform. On November 1, 1911, Gerald's twenty-first birthday, he would come into £38,000 left in trust for him by his mother: a considerable sum, the father pointed out, for any youth who had just attained his majority to manage. Frank Souter, who in his son's absence had prospered as a stockbroker in the City, was possibly hoping that Gerald would entrust part of the money to him to invest. If so, disappointment once more was to be his due, for Gerald's reply upon being asked what he proposed to do with the money was, "Why, to squander it of course."

The two men came down the steps of the St James's Club, and parted without so much as a handshake or a word of farewell, the elder Souter turning east towards Piccadilly Circus, the younger west towards Knightsbridge. Gerald was on his own. His father did not cut off his allowance immediately, but henceforth Gerald was the master of his own destiny.

Two

November 1915: Raided

At midnight, November 11 1915, Gerald's beautiful flat at Dacre House, Westminster, showed signs of disarray, testifying to the imminent and indeed hasty departure of its occupant. Already Gerald's library had been removed to a warehouse for storage, and there were dust covers on the Chinese Chippendale in the dining room, whose walls Gerald had had decorated in a silver-grey. Elsewhere a wardrobe gaped empty and dresser drawers were pulled out, as Savage, his manservant, transferred to the open valises the things Gerald would need on his journey. Gerald could not shake off the dust of London quickly enough, assailed as he was whenever he ventured into its streets by posters urging him to 'Enlist To-Day and Bring Victory Nearer.'

Earlier he had made enemies by "boldly deploring that it was no longer possible for me to communicate with my many German friends". "I even went so far as to claim that an Irishman had the right to regard the war through neutral eyes," he writes, revealing that for wartime purposes at least he had assumed another nationality. Now, no longer able to bear the stern, accusing gaze of Lord Kitchener, "I resolved to leave London at once for Spain." Actually he was bound for Rome, this confusion in destination being but one of a number of distortions and outright lies in Gerald's version of the events which were about to unfold.

Gerald claims that he had dined alone, and that while Savage finished packing he had retired to his Rose Dubarry

51

bedroom, and was reading "when I heard a violent banging on the street door, and my bell was rung with great vehemence". "I slipped on a dressing-gown while Savage… opened the door of the flat," he continues. "A quantity of staff officers in uniform, headed by Lord Athlumney, the Provost Marshal, and followed by two plainclothes detectives, came bursting in… each with a revolver in his hand."

The detectives were Inspectors Tappenden and Leach of Scotland Yard's Special Branch, who had been tailing Gerald for days. The presence of the 6th Baron Athlumney, whose rank as Provost Marshal was that of colonel, and of the other staff officers in uniform remained unexplained in Gerald's version of the raid. The drawn revolvers were pure invention, as were several other details. True, at some time during the course of the evening Gerald had slipped into a dressing-gown – a yellow silk affair, which he claimed had belonged to a Chinese emperor.

But far from being alone and tucked up in bed with a book when the raiding party came bounding in, Gerald was entertaining three servicemen – an Army officer, and two members of His Majesty's Brigade of Guards. According to the *Daily Telegraph*, Inspector Tappenden asked Gerald, "What are you doing with these young soldiers here?" To which Gerald, who at twenty-five was probably the same age as his guests, replied, "They are friends of mine". *The Times*, in its account of the raid, added that Gerald "acknowledged handing a £1 Treasury note to a soldier", a transaction which, in its implication to readers, was tantamount to taking the King's Shilling for enlistment in the legion of the damned.

The interrogation having ended, the officers proceeded to search the flat. In Gerald's study, the so-called Chinese Room, whose yellow ceiling contrasted with walls of black, they confiscated Gerald's passport, his chequebook, and a quantity of letters which were found in the drawer of a Foochow lacquer writing-table.

The officer and two guardsmen were marched off under military escort to face courts-martial charges of 'conduct unbecoming' (there was to be a spate of such arrests in weeks to come, thanks to the correspondence seized in Gerald's flat). Curiously, Gerald himself was not arrested until the following day when he was picked up as he boarded a train for London at Oxford (he had hurried to Oxford to see his Aunt May and to reassure her, should she have chanced to read about the raid in the press). On Saturday, November 13, Gerald, who gave his profession as 'art dealer', was arraigned at the Westminster Police Court on a charge of gross indecency, pleaded not guilty, and was remanded in custody. Inspector Tappenden, in opposing bail, hinted that the Special Branch was pursuing inquiries with a view to charges of a more serious nature, having to do with national security.

*

When Gerald came down the steps of his father's club at the end of the last chapter he seemed set to conquer the social world to which he aspired. After all, he was a personable young man, not handsome, but endowed with a certain charm. More important, he had independent means. In the four years that had since elapsed, what had gone wrong? How had he been blown off course ?

Gerald had celebrated his independence suitably enough by hearing mass in the crypt of St Peter's, Rome, on his twenty-first birthday, November 1 1911. Afterwards he was received in private audience by Pope Pius X, to whom he presented an expensive clock with a musical chime to mark the Angelus, a typical Geraldian gesture. "The Pope, I heard afterwards, was very nervous because he spoke no language except Italian and that with a very strong Venetian accent," Gerald relates. The tension was relieved when His Holiness discovered that Gerald spoke Italian. "As I knelt and kissed the ring of St Peter, I felt I was a very great hypocrite as I had learned Italian in anything but respectable company."

That winter in Rome marked Gerald's introduction to so-called Black Society, the Catholic aristocracy that clustered round the Vatican and assisted at its various ceremonies. He made particular friends with Cardinal Merry del Val, the Papal Secretary of State, and was a guest of the Papal Chamberlain at the latter's residence in the Via Pompeo Magno. In time Gerald would be on a friendly footing with three Popes,[3] his greatest influence being with Pope Paul VI, whom he first knew as Cardinal Montini.

But Gerald was not in Europe as a pious pilgrim. It was in a continuous round of pleasure that he managed to run through his mother's inheritance in four years, squandering it at the rate of £10,000 a year. Nor was he repentant. "I suppose I should regret today that I wasn't wiser with the money I came into," he mused in the course of a radio interview years later. "But honestly I don't regret it. Money spent and gone, well there it is. You can't get it back, and you certainly had enjoyment from it." His father cut off his allowance in the Spring of 1913 "since I refused to settle down, or to adopt a commercial

3 Possibly four: he certainly met Pius X (in office 1903-14), and his presenting him with the elaborate clock was reported in the *Observer*, April 12 1914; he certainly petitioned Benedict XV (in office 1914-22) for the SCF; he claims – in *Conversations with Gerald*, p.88 – to have made the acquaintance of Pius XII (in office 1939-58) on SCF business when he was still Monsignor Pacelli; and he seems to have known Paul VI (in office 1963-1978) relatively well from before the War, when he was still Cardinal Montini. [Ed.]

career," as Gerald explains. Gerald retaliated that autumn by changing his name by deed poll from "Souter" to "Hamilton".

It was his solicitor, Reggie Newton,[4] who initiated Gerald into the mysteries of reversionary interest. "I could always raise such money as I required upon my parents' marriage settlement, by the terms of which my father had the usufruct of my mother's not inconsiderable fortune... until his death, when it went to me... " Inevitably Gerald's demand for quick cash landed him in the arms of the money-lenders, but, as he explains, "I have never had a head for figures, and as long as I had ample money for the moment I neither knew nor cared what might happen afterwards."

With the money he was thus able to raise Gerald had furnished the flat at Dacre House, Westminster, with Chinoiserie, and it had become quite a showpiece ("strangers often telephoned to ask me if they might come and look at it"). But Gerald was seldom there to enjoy it himself, spending most of his time on the Continent. "I must admit that the wanderlust from which I then suffered," he writes, "was as unreasonable as it was imperative." Hardly had Gerald set foot on English soil than he was off again, to Berlin, Constantinople, Paris, Madrid "in search of new emotions and experiences". Sometimes in London he did not even bother to unpack his bags, knowing that he would be off again, driven by his unreasonable daemon.

As mentioned earlier, one of the first journeys undertaken by Gerald after he had come of age was to Russia where armed with a letter of introduction from his Aunt Dolly – "playing the Dolly card", as he called it – he sought and obtained an

---

4 Reginald Newton was the son a of a famous but crooked solicitor, Arthur Newton, who acted for Oscar Wilde's co-defendant in the Wilde trials of 1895, later briefed counsel on behalf of Dr. Crippen, and was eventually struck off. Concerning Reginald, Maurice Richardson remarks "I could never make up my mind whether he was acting in the interests of Gerald or of the prosecution." [Tom Cullen]

audience with Nicholas II at the Tsar's summer residence at Tsarkoe Selo. Gerald recorded his impressions of that audience in *As Young as Sophocles*. "A small door in the wall opened, and the Emperor, dressed in a very simple Russian costume, with tall boots, came into the room and greeted me with a grave, frank courtesy," Gerald writes. Gerald, who was pleased that the Tsar spoke English fluently, was struck by "the extraordinary melancholy of his eyes, which every now and then drooped as he spoke. The impression he conveyed was rather that of a country gentleman than of a monarch."

Characteristically, Gerald, who had lost none of his schoolboy devotion to the Stuarts, compares the Tsar with Charles I, noting that their "edifying private lives stand out in strange relief amidst surroundings of incredible corruption and profligacy". If noble in thought, both monarchs were "weak in action", Gerald reflects, "under the fatal, if well-intentioned influence of [their] wives". As if on cue, the Tsarina had appeared at the conclusion of Gerald's interview with her husband, and she was followed shortly thereafter by their son, the Tsarevitch ("a most nervous, timid lad"), in a sailor suit and attended by a Cossack giant. The Tsarevitch being much taken with a gold pencil-case which Gerald carried, the latter made the little boy a present of it.

Undoubtedly it was Gerald's passionate advocacy of the Stuart cause which drew him to the castle of Leustetten where he was received by the Princess Ludwig of Bavaria, afterwards Bavaria's last queen, and the mother of Crown Prince Rupprecht. In so-called legitimist circles this princess was known as Queen Mary IV of England, for with the extinction of the male Stuart line the legitimists had been forced to fall back on to the descendants of the female children of Charles I to find a suitable pretender. Gerald found the princess severe

and formal ("I noticed that never for a moment did she seem
to relax") in contrast to the *gemutlichkeit* he had encountered
at Tsarkoe Selo.

Despite their apparent aimlessness, Gerald's travels had
a certain logic. As though sensing that the social life he
observed was doomed – did he, one wonders, fancy himself as
a Stendhal or a Proust, storing up material for a masterpiece? –
Gerald was determined to see as many of the European courts
as possible; and in the next few years there was scarcely a
prince or princeling, a *margrave* or a *graf*, that he overlooked.
He became adept at parleying a letter of introduction to an
ambassador into an invitation to a court ball embossed with
the pompous *Zum allerhöchsten Befehl*. It was a strange
obsession. To most young men of his age the dreary round of
courts which Gerald followed would have been a *via dolorosa*
such as penitents undertake during Holy Week, scourging
themselves as they go along. But not so Gerald, who took
great pains with each of his genuflexions.

Typical was the Saxon Court at Dresden, where "upon
a raised dais, each member of the royal family had his own
particular whist-table... playing whist with those whom he
wished to honour". "Every arrival," Gerald adds, "had to
pass by each whist-table, waiting till royalty deigned to look
up, when, with a low curtsy or profound bow... the courtier
passed on to the next table... until the last was reached." The
tedium of this absurd ritual was, for Gerald, relieved by the
presence of royal pages, "good-looking boys in their teens,
the flower of the Saxon aristocracy... in their brilliant and
uncomfortable cornflower-blue uniforms". (Those page-boys
in the cornflower blue provide another kind of logic behind
Gerald's strange peregrinations, for his travels were governed
as much by his quest for homosexual adventures as they were

by his adulation for royalty.)

In London, by contrast, the society which Gerald frequented was anything but top drawer. He was inclined to blame Souter *père* for the fact that he had never attended a Levee at St James's Palace, though how his stockbroker father could have secured the entrée for him is beyond understanding. "I had, however, an opportunity of meeting those who lived and breathed in the rarefied atmosphere of Court circles, thanks to Arthur Ponsonby," Gerald claims. He is referring to the son of Sir Henry Ponsonby, Queen Victoria's private secretary, but Arthur Ponsonby was a rising Labour politician when Gerald knew him and unlikely to breathe that rarefied atmosphere of which Gerald writes.

The people Gerald mostly frequented in London could loosely be described as bohemians, and they included the remnants of the old Oscar Wilde set who continued to gather at the Café Royal. Foremost among these was Lord Alfred Douglas. "Bosie's quarrelsome disposition involved him in innumerable law cases and endless squabbles," Gerald writes, "but I flatter myself that I avoided any serious dispute through the forty years we were friends... He loathed Socialism and despised particularly the Bloomsbury intelligentsia." Gerald managed the seemingly impossible task of remaining friends with both Bosie and Robert Ross, the art critic, whom Bosie accused of poisoning Oscar Wilde's mind against him. In pursuit of his vendetta against Ross, Bosie, whose homophobia dated from his conversion to Catholicism, wrote to the prime minister, two high court judges, and the public prosecutor denouncing Ross as "a filthy bugger", thus forcing Ross in 1914 to sue him for criminal libel. Bosie also sent a postcard to Queen Alexandra, who retained Ross as her adviser on the purchase of paintings, asking Her Majesty, "Do you know that your friend Robert Ross is a notorious sodomite?"

Gerald told John Symonds that the only time he discussed Wilde with Bosie was in Paris in the twenties, when they visited Wilde's tomb at the Père Lachaise Cemetery. "As we stood looking at it Douglas said to me that he had had a love affair with Wilde, but that Wilde had never used him 'in the manner of the sinners of Sodom'." Years later, when Gerald was in Germany, Bosie allegedly wrote him a long letter "in which he gave me all the details of his sexual life with Wilde". John Symonds asked him where the letter was now, and Gerald launched into a melancholy diatribe. "Everything always gets seized in my life," he complained; "somebody low like a bailiff must have chucked it into a wastepaper basket." "What couldn't I get for it today?" Gerald sighed. "A thousand pounds."

Among Gerald's bohemian friends was the colourful Florence Abdy, the widow of Sir William Abdy and a generous hostess to leading dancers, actresses, and variety artists of her day. Flo was a prostitute walking a beat in the Haymarket when she encountered Sir William, who, paralyzed from the waist down, was being wheeled in a bath chair from the Carlton Hotel to a taxi. "I do not myself believe in the magical attributes of the 'glad eye'," Gerald writes, "but on this occasion 'a glance of infinite meaning' must have been exchanged, for Sir William... without more ado, invited the lady to lunch with him at the Café Royal."

Sir William did more: he married the lady, and installed her at Melton Hall, his country seat in Surrey, where she became known as "Over-Flo Abdy", owing to her tendency to invite more guests than the hall could properly accommodate. A bell was rung at 8 o'clock in the morning, Gerald claims, so that when the maid brought the morning tea the visitors were found in their right beds.

Gerald could be an amusing dinner companion, and he was sought after by minor Mayfair hostesses, including a Mrs Ross-Cochran, who paid the price for being a slave to an antique fashion. In Restoration times faded beauties used to enamel their faces "filling up the Chinks in rivell'd Skin, as House-painters do the Cracks in Wainscot", as Shadwell remarks of Lady Fantast. On Mrs Ross-Cochran the effect of such calcining was to make her appear like a Japanese doll, according to Gerald. One day Gerald received a note from Mrs Ross-Cochran's secretary asking him to call round, which he did. The secretary came straight to the point. "Mrs Ross-Cochran is devoted to you," she began. "There's nobody who entertains her more, who makes her laugh as much." Gerald said that he was pleased to hear this. "Yes," the secretary replied, "but there are certain disadvantages." The secretary then recalled a recent dinner party at which a minor disaster had occurred: "Mrs Ross-Cochran laughed so much that a crack appeared across her cheek." "I quite understand," said the penitent Gerald. "I shall try not to be so funny again."

*

"It is not to be wondered at that many crooks clustered round me like bees attracted by the smell of honey," Gerald writes, "since I had more money in my pocket than was necessary, and I was spending it most royally." Many of the petty crooks who were drawn to the honeypot were continentals who had come to London in the summer of 1911 for the coronation of George V, attracted by the easy pickings to be had from the wealthy visitors who thronged the capital.

Among them was Rudolf Stallman, alias the Baron von

Koenig, alias the Baron von Rossbach, alias Rudolphe Lemoine, who had arrived from Germany a year earlier as a fugitive from justice – he was wanted by Berlin police in connection with £4,000 he had won at cards. It was to be Stallman's private boast that in a lifetime of crime, during which he amassed a fortune, this instance of cheating at cards was to be his sole conviction in a court of law. As it was, he fought like a tiger against extradition in proceedings which involved Sir Edward Grey and Count Metternich, the British and German foreign secretaries respectively, before he was finally deported to Germany in August 1912.

All of this was behind Stallman, who had served a nominal prison sentence by the time Gerald met him as Baron von Rossbach in London in 1913. The two men took to each other at once, though Gerald pretends that he did not twig Stallman's true identity until much later, writing: "Mr Berry Wall, an extravagant and foolish old gentleman with a harmless taste for very large buttonholes, and very small manicure girls, asked me if I knew who the Baron von Rossbach really was. I said I had known him in London and in Paris, and believed him to be an Austrian nobleman. Mr Berry Wall, bubbling over with the importance of his information, told me that he was really the Baron von Koenig, the notorious millionaire crook." When Gerald met Stallman, who was to play a major role in his life, he frequented those London gaming clubs from which he was not barred, but in 1913 he had more important business.

Stallman's connection with German intelligence would make a fascinating study in itself. One gets only tantalizing glimpses of it in his various court appearances at the extradition proceedings. Thus *The Times* of August 9 1911 reports, "Count Stallmann [sic]... says that he is really wanted [i.e. for extradition] because of his knowledge of certain espionage proceedings connected with the case of Lieutenant Helm, the German officer who was arrested a year ago in England on a charge of spying." Again, when he went into the witness box at the Bow Street magistrates court Stallman was asked whether he knew a certain Lieutenant Backhouse. "You mean the German spy? Yes," Stallman replied, going on to deny that he had won £700 from Backhouse at cards.

That German intelligence should employ a known crook such as Stallman is not as far-fetched as it might seem. Nor was the German government alone in following such a practice. In wartime most governments recruit spies from among the underworld elements who in peacetime constitute one of the chief sources of information for their police.

Gerald was in Paris with Stallman, and the two of them preparing to set out on a motoring holiday through Bavaria in the latter's Mercedes, when the mobilization order was signed heralding France's entry into the Great War. ("One evening as I was dressing for dinner," Gerald writes, "von Rossbach burst into my room and said, 'Tell Savage to pack your trunks to-night and leave to-morrow... The mobilization order will be posted up everywhere during the night'.") Stallman/von Rossbach's next move was a curious one. Instead of returning to Berlin immediately and placing himself at the disposal of his emperor, Stallman, with his wife and two children, made a bee-line for Madrid, as though by prior arrangement. Here, over the next four years, he was to head an intelligence network which included the whole of the Iberian peninsula, extending as far north as the Pyrenees, Stallman having rented a villa conveniently near the French border at Fuentarrabia. It was to Madrid in the summer of 1915 that Gerald was irresistibly drawn, as though by a magnet.

Earlier, following Stallman's advice, Gerald had caught

the first cross-channel ferry from Dieppe to Folkestone, arriving in London on the August Bank Holiday Monday to find the Cowes yachting regatta cancelled, and the government reassuring the populace that the wheat harvest would last at least four months. The next day, Tuesday, the 4th August, England declared war on Germany.

From the outset Gerald had found himself out of sympathy with Britain's declared war aims. "For King and Country" meant little to one who, since reaching his majority, had roamed restlessly from one European capital to the next. Nor could he get worked up over the fate of the Belgians whose country had been overrun. On the other hand, Gerald had many good friends in Germany, including his current lover, Fritz von Retzow, who was stationed with his regiment at Goldap when the war broke out.

Von Retzow was killed on the Polish front in May 1915, six months before the raid on Gerald's flat. "My friend" Gerald writes, "had begged leave from his superior officers not to fight on the Flanders front, for fear of having to fight against me." Was he now to look upon these friends as "the enemy", or as the jingo press would have it, "grey invading hordes" and "barbaric Huns"? "My heart instinctively revolted against the clamour and folly," he writes.[5]

It is difficult to assess how deeply Gerald's pacifist views were held. He claimed that they stemmed from an interest in Buddhism acquired during the years he had spent in Shanghai, and that he was impressed by the Buddhists' respect for life in all forms. Whether from pacifist objections, or from distaste for this particular war, Gerald gave an excellent impersonation of a draft dodger on the run when he arrived in Madrid to be

---

5 Hamilton published a short story with a pacifist theme, 'The Enemy: An Unpleasant Story', in the magazine *Colour*, May 1915 ("… this cursed war, brought about by England's rapaciousness and interference…"). [Ed.]

Stallman's guest.

For one thing, he had suddenly switched nationality to become an Irishman, this would-be aristocrat who had prided himself on his "faintly ducal" ancestry that had linked him to the Abercorns. For another, Gerald, claiming the privilege of Irish neutrality, rashly accepted the invitations which Stallman procured for him to parties and receptions at the German embassy. His attendance at these functions was duly reported to the British ambassador, who in turn transmitted the information to Whitehall. This explains why the moment Gerald landed back in England in October 1915, ostensibly to arrange with his bankers to remit money to him abroad, he was tailed by Special Branch detectives. Not only that, but Gerald's telephone was tapped, and his mail opened on orders of Basil Thomson, head of Scotland Yard's combined CID-Special Branch operations. As he read the reports of the detectives assigned to Gerald, Thomson was clearly puzzled, not knowing for certain whether in Gerald he was dealing with an enemy agent or simply a "moral degenerate".

Three

April 1916: Good Friday

Nor was Basil Thomson the only one puzzled. Apart from the Special Branch, Gerald, prior to his arrest, had managed to excite suspicion in a quite different quarter. For no sooner had he unpacked his bags at his flat in Dacre House than he had presented himself at the Foreign Office with a letter of introduction from Arthur Ponsonby. His reception in Whitehall is recorded in a minute from Charles (later Sir Charles) Wingfield to a subordinate named Aladon:

> Wingfield to Aladon, 4.xi.15: "Mr Gerald Hamilton, who has been appointed Siamese Consul in Rome, called today to see someone who would give him advice as to how he could best use his influence to benefit Great Britain as well as Siam. As nobody else wished to see him... I saw him. I thanked him for his zeal and suggested he should get in touch, not with Sir R. Rodd, as he suggested, but with Mr. Consul Morgan. He seemed 'rather an ass' if I may so express myself."

In reply, Aladon suggested that "it might be as well to warn Sir R. Rodd and Mr Morgan of this gentleman's 'good intentions' which may end in being meddlesome".

Gerald maintained that he had been offered the Siamese Consul-Generalship by the Siamese Minister in Rome, who was charming, rich, and who shared Gerald's sexual predilections (when Gerald was in Rome the diplomat had placed one of his cars at Gerald's disposal). Whether or not this official had actually offered Gerald the post (and he may only have suggested it in passing without intending that his offer be taken seriously) Gerald had certainly set about things in a curious fashion, in trying to make himself *persona grata* at the Foreign Office.

His friend Arthur Ponsonby was anything but forthcoming when the Foreign Office queried him about Gerald. "Hamilton," he wrote, "is the son of a scotch [sic] laird who it is said has not been very kind to Hamilton… He is neurotic and a few years ago became a Roman Catholic upon which occasion his father cut him off without a shilling." Ponsonby was inclined to blame the Church of Rome for Gerald's neurotic behaviour, concluding, "I think now he regrets his change of faith but in many ways is a good chap but somewhat a prig, using the term in its best sense."

It was not until a fortnight after Gerald's arrest that Basil Thomson was able to inform Wingfield, who had continued to keep a watching brief on the exotic bird that had briefly flown into his ken, that there was "no question of espionage regarding Gerald Hamilton, and the only reason the Military authorities are making further inquiries… is that so many letters from officers were found in his flat." "He is a thorough degenerate," Thomson adds, "and should not be allowed inside any public office." (This is a little puritanical, coming from one who in the not too distant future was to be arrested in Hyde Park in the act of having sexual congress with a prostitute who bore the intriguing name of Thelma de Lava.)

Meanwhile, Gerald had been allowed to languish at Brixton prison, bail having been refused on three occasions when he came up on remand before the magistrate, Mr Horace Smith, whom he describes as "having one foot in the grave and the other in the lavatory". "He had the habit of getting up and leaving the court and returning five minutes later with the request that the case should begin all over again," Gerald explains.

Finally, on December 6, through the expedient of applying for bail to a judge in chambers, Gerald was released on two sureties of £1,000 each furnished by his Aunt May and by Captain Wise, an old friend of the Holliday family. He would have rotted in jail, Gerald reflected bitterly, had he waited for his father to come to his rescue.

Gerald spent the interval before his trial at Stonyhurst, a Jesuit seminary in Lancashire, as the guest of Father C.C. Martindale, a worldly priest who enjoyed shocking his superiors by drawing parallels between Christianity and Mithraism. Earlier, when Gerald had undergone a crisis of faith, he had sought Father Martindale's advice, and had been given absolution for his sins in what must rank as one of the most bizarre confessions on record; bizarre because it took place in full view of the audience during a performance at the Palace Music Hall. With Basil Hallam onstage singing 'Gilbert the Filbert', the Jesuit urged Gerald to hold his theatre programme in front of his lips so that he could not be overheard by his neighbour, and to bare his soul. "Father Martindale indicated the moment of Absolution by opening his watch", Gerald later recalled. Just at that moment Hallam was leading a rousing chorus of

> O Hades, the ladies,
> They leave their wooden huts,
> For Gilbert, the Filbert,
> The Colonel of the Knuts!

*

On Thursday, February 10 1916 Gerald was found guilty of gross indecency after a jury trial at the Old Bailey, and sentenced to two years imprisonment with hard labour, which was the maximum penalty allowable by law.

The report of the case, which appeared in identical form in *The Times*, the *Daily Telegraph*, and the *News of the World*, emanated from an agency man who either was overworked, inebriated, or both, it being so garbled as to be unintelligible. Under the heading 'WESTMINSTER FLAT CASE: THE CONDUCT OF CERTAIN PUBLIC HOUSES', the *Times* report began as follows:

At the Central Criminal Court, before the Recorder, the trial was concluded of Gerald Hamilton, 25, on bail, upon an indictment charging him with misdemeanour. The defendant pleaded "Not Guilty". The accusation was made in respect to alleged behaviour at a flat occupied by the defendant in Westminster, the rent of which was £150 per annum. It was stated that among the things found at the flat was a passport issued to the defendant which showed that he had travelled to Rome, Paris and Madrid. The jury found the defendant Guilty.

Special Branch had searched the warehouse where Gerald had stored his books, and there detectives had found a bundle of photographs that were "the most absolutely loathsome things that a disordered mind could conceive", according to the prosecutor, who was glad to say that "the things were foreign".

The balance of the *Times* report was taken up by remarks concerning two public houses mentioned in the case, with the Recorder asking whether police had taken steps to revoke their licences. One of them was the Covent Garden Hotel in the

Strand, said to be a rendezvous for "sodomites" where soldiers and sailors went when they were hard up for beer money. The correspondence the police had seized in Gerald's flat led directly to its being raided.

In passing sentence, the Recorder said it was clear that the defendant "had been carrying on this kind of business for a long time", although exactly what the business was is not clear from the report. In perusing this account a *Times* reader might be excused for inferring that Gerald Hamilton, aged 25, was either (a) the proprietor of a public house whose licence had been or was about to be revoked, or (b) a pornographer who specialised in filthy pictures which, thank God, were of foreign import.

Nowhere does the report make mention of the "misdemeanour" of which a jury had found Gerald guilty, nor is there any indication of the evidence adduced against him (did the officer and the two guardsmen testify?), nor of his defence, if any. Whatever the nature of his business, Hamilton obviously was a man of substance who spent his time in travel between Rome, Paris, Madrid, and London, where he had a *pied-à-terre* at Westminster for which he paid £150 per annum; this apparently was what mattered most to our reporter.

Basil Thomson, however, still was not satisfied that Gerald had not been trafficking with the enemy, so he arranged for a stool pigeon named Ansell to be planted on Gerald as his cellmate. The unsuspecting Gerald, in turn, gave full throat to his pro-German sympathies with the result that no sooner was he freed in November 1917, after serving twenty-one months of his sentence for gross indecency, than he was re-arrested and interned for the duration of the war without trial under Clause 14B of the Defence of the Realm Act.

Before this could happen, however, Gerald experienced

one of those lightning conversions that change the course of a man's life. He became a follower of Roger Casement.

*

On Good Friday 1916, Casement had been put ashore from a German U-boat in Tralee Bay in what was to prove the sorriest invasion since Louis Napoleon landed at Boulogne with a moulting eagle. Casement's mission: to stop the insurrection against the British due to take place in Ireland on Easter Sunday, which was doomed in advance for lack of arms. In the event, Casement had been promptly arrested, the Easter Rising had aborted, and in the words of WB Yeats "a terrible beauty" had been born.

While waiting to stand trial for treason at the Old Bailey, Casement was transferred from the Tower of London to Brixton, where Gerald was serving his sentence for gross indecency. Gerald's frissons on learning that Casement was a fellow prisoner were those of a Jean Genet submitting to the unseen presence of Harcamone, the murderer, in death row. "Harcamone was taken to a special cell... It was from the cell, where I see him as a kind of Dalai Lama, invisible, potent and present, that he emitted throughout the prison those waves of mingled joy and sadness," writes Genet, who might almost be describing Casement's effect upon the prison population of Brixton, at that moment swollen by Irish Volunteers rounded up as the aftermath of the Easter Rising.

From this propinquity sprang the myth of Gerald's friendship with Casement; his fantasy of having met the handsome, bearded Irishman in 1912 at the home of Mrs Alice Stopford Green, widow of the historian J.R. Green, and of Casement's immediate and profound effect upon him. "My character, plastic at all times, received perhaps a deeper impression from this great Irishman than from any other single individual I have ever met," he was to write, going on to describe Casement's "beautifully modulated voice, the humourous sparkle in his eyes, his habit of stroking his short beard".

From claiming friendship with Casement to claiming that Casement was responsible for him languishing in prison was a further embroidery of Gerald's unblushing myth. Casement was to be the cover-up used by Gerald to blot out that conviction for gross indecency. What Gerald did was to telescope events to make it appear that his two periods of confinement at Brixton were in reality one; and that the one – his internment under Clause 14B – was due solely to "my close connection with Casement and my desire for Germany to win the war, which I believed would mean complete freedom for my country Ireland".

Forgetful Gerald contradicted this in an article he wrote in August 1966, in which, referring to the fact that he was shadowed by detectives when he arrived in London in the autumn of 1915, he writes "I was the object of suspicion not because I was at the time associated in any way with Casement, but because of my assocaition in Madrid with leading Germans."

As a re-writer of history Gerald reminds one of those "invisible menders" employed by valet services; a little old lady whom one sees sitting in the window of such establishments intent upon teasing bits of coloured wool to cover a cigarette burn in someone's favourite tweed jacket. Similarly, by teasing bits of fact with bits of highly-coloured fancy Gerald sought to make it appear that when arrested in London he was on the verge of joining Casement in Berlin in order "to dissuade him [Casement]… from any undertaking likely to cause loss of life in Ireland". "I knew positively that a rising in Ireland had been planned but postponed until the aid promised by Germany was forthcoming," he adds.

With Casement's arrest after being put ashore from a German U-boat, Gerald found himself seriously compromised, according to his story, though he does not explain how or why this was so. Suddenly one morning London's hoardings blossomed with the exhortation "Hang Hamilton!" according to Gerald, this being the work of Horatio Bottomley who, in the columns of *John Bull*, was demanding that Gerald should mount the scaffold with Casement. However, when the 'Gerald Hamilton Confesses' series ran in *The People* in January 1966 its sub-editors made a diligent search of *John Bull* for any mention of Gerald. There were plenty of stories about "Germ-Hun" atrocities, but no reference to Hamilton, nor to Casement for that matter. Gerald was insistent that he had the relevant cuttings in an old trunk, but they never materialized.

Worse still, according to Gerald, Basil Thomson summoned him, and in an effort to extract information from him threatened him with "You are sitting in the chair your friend Casement recently sat in. You know what is going to happen to him, don't you? Well I expect the same fate now awaits you."

(In Paris, years later, Gerald encountered his ancient adversary in the lift of the St Lazare Hotel, they being the sole occupants. "The lift was one of those old-fashioned cage-like French lifts that move very slowly," Gerald recalls. "I immediately turned on Sir Basil and never in my life have I been so abusive to any human being as I was on this occasion. He kept trying to stop the lift, but, in the end, the lift went to the top floor." "I thoroughly enjoyed myself that morning," says Gerald.)

There appears to be no more truth in this story than there is in Gerald's extraordinary claim that while Casement was being held in Brixton he, Gerald Hamilton, was able to exchange messages with him "thanks to the frequent visits of my solicitor". While in prison Casement was under observation twenty-four hours a day for fear that he might commit suicide and thus cheat the gallows. Two guards stayed with him in his cell at all times while overhead a light burned night and day. Despite these precautions Gerald maintains that Casement, presumably through the good offices of Reggie Newton, Gerald's solicitor, was able to slip him a copy of a biography of Lord Carson with Casement's annotations in the margin, a book which "I have preserved as my most precious relic".

"It is a cruel thing to die with all men misunderstanding – and to be silent forever," Casement wrote on the eve of his execution. Little better perhaps is to die a martyr with all manner of men attempting to clamber aboard the bandwagon, and to capitalize upon one's martyrdom.

*

Casement was a passive homosexual whose partners were for the most part "rough trade" he picked up in bars or public gardens in London or Paris, Lisbon or Lima, wherever his travels took him. His so-called *Black Diaries*, which cover the period 1901–1914, are studded with such expressions as "huge", "enormous", "long and thick about 7" and "wobbling down right thigh".[6] "Casement looked at men exactly as most men look at women," in the words of his latest biographer. The only wonder is that he felt impelled to write it all down.

Gerald Hamilton shared with Casement the life-long habit

6 These diaries did Casement's reputation great damage and it was claimed in some circles that they had been fabricated by the British government. They are now accepted to be authentic. [Ed.]

of keeping a diary. Unfortunately his pre-1940 diaries went up in flames during the blitz, together with other papers stored in a Thames-side warehouse. The surviving diaries cover the period 1940–1970 with the exception of the year 1941, a large part of which Gerald spent in prison. The diaries for the most part are of a type obtainable from Boots the Chemists called "Home Diary and Ladies' Note Book", and containing among other useful information First Aid, Gardening, and Mothercraft hints.

Gerald uses these diaries mostly to record appointments he has kept during the day, but they contain certain peculiarities. For one thing, starting in March 1942, they are written in French, whether for purposes of concealment, or simply to give Gerald practice in writing the language, is not clear. For another, they contain a simple code by means of which Gerald notes such sexual encounters as he may have had during the day – at the beginning of the entry he writes the name of his sexual partner followed by an X or an XX, as the case might be. These symbols reveal Gerald to have enjoyed a prodigious sex life, which lasted right up to his death in 1970 at the age of eighty; a sex life which one feels would have interested Johnson and Masters and the Kinsey Institute. The 1940 diary, for example, which is the earliest surviving, reveals that Gerald, in his fiftieth year, had 172 sexual encounters with fourteen different men, who sometimes performed solo, sometimes in combination.

Unlike Casement, Gerald, as a diarist, is not concerned with the grosser aspects of sex. He is inclined to gush, however, about the "gorgeous boy" he has picked up the night before in Ward's Irish Bar in Piccadilly. Samples with the French argot translated roughly into English slang equivalent; "February 28 1942: Supper Chez Auguste with Peter Watson. Met David

R[oss] and went crazy;" February 28 1943: "I saw 'Heaven' at Ward's last night, which prevented me from sleeping;" "October 4 1958: Went to the William IV pub where I saw a real beauty."

In the last years of his life Gerald kept the diaries in a locked suitcase underneath his bed. Peter Burton is under the impression that he was only half joking when he referred to the "State secrets" that were thus locked away.

Gerald shared Casement's penchant for "rough trade", meaning dockers, lorry-drivers, and other working-class types, especially those in uniform. The guardsman's red tunic magically transformed any man in Gerald's eyes, as indeed it does to this day in the eyes of many inverts. The history of homosexual prostitution among guardees is as old as the Brigade of Guards itself. Referring to the period just prior to the Great War an American visitor to England writes of the gay scene. "The skeptic has only to walk around London, around any English garrison centre… to find the soldier prostitute in almost open self-marketing." The American goes on to picture "the fine flower of British soldier prostitute, dressed in his best uniform, clean shaven, well groomed and handsome with his Anglo-Saxon pulchritude and vigour, smilingly expectant. He is sure to be approached by some admiring stranger or regular 'friend', and asked to take a drink or offered a cigar; and so is brought delicately to a bargain, at a tariff from the modest five shillings or three-and-six to a sovereign".

By the 1940s, when the surviving volumes of Gerald's diaries begin, the tariff had risen considerably. Guardsmen expected at least a pound to be left for them on the mantelpiece, £3 if the guardsman had allowed his gentleman friend "to take a liberty", by which phrase sodomy is meant. Gerald was always generous with his guests who were in the military service, paying their train fare if they were stationed at Aldershot or Pirbright, as well as slipping a *pourboire* into their hand as he said goodbye at the door.

Such at any rate is the testimony of an ex-Royal Air Force man whom I shall call André, who met him in 1943 when Gerald was living in a studio flat at 56 Glebe Place, Chelsea. André himself was billeted in a house in Regent's Park which the RAF had requisitioned, so he was able to see Gerald two or three times a week. As André's French was fluent (born of a Russian mother and a German father, he was educated in France) the two conversed mostly in that language, giving Gerald the opportunity to polish his usage of it. More important, André was an excellent cook, and enjoyed catering for the small dinner parties Gerald gave at Glebe Place. Mostly they were for Gerald's gay friends, among whom was his landlord Sir Frederick O'Connor, the Tibetan explorer. But some of the parties were mixed – André recalls meeting Lady Furness at one such gathering. André, for his part, saw to it that Gerald never suffered from wartime rationing. "In Regent's Park we kept pigs and chickens, so Gerald always had fresh eggs, and, whenever we slaughtered a pig, a leg of pork."

When I met André, who is now in his late fifties, at his flat in Hammersmith, he told me how Gerald ensured that a never-ending stream of guardees passed through his bedroom. "Gerald had an arrangement with a sergeant in the Foot Guards named Bob whereby Bob procured other guardees for him – for a consideration, naturally. Gerald always recompensed Bob for his trouble. The drill was that if you were in London on a pass you telephoned Gerald to see what his plans were. If he wanted a *partouze*, or just to see you alone, you went around to his place." Apparently Gerald made no wartime concessions to what Isherwood calls his "almost surgical standards of cleanliness", but would usually insist upon his guests having a bath after their arrival, or better still, bathing them himself, taking obvious pleasure in playing the nanny. The service types themselves did not object – it was "better than the Turkish", they pronounced. The purification rites over, the fun and games would begin, with Gerald acting as master of the revels.

André was able to clear up a mystery which had puzzled me in going through Gerald's diaries. In decoding the shorthand method whereby Gerald recorded his sexual encounters I was staggered at how prolific they were. To take a not untypical example, the entry for Saturday, January 31 1948 indicates that Gerald had sex first with Bill, then with Bill and David, then with Bill and Syd. The following day it was Jimmy, then Syd and Bobbie as a twosome, with Gerald, who was pushing sixty, noting he was *"tres fatigué"* at the end of the entry. As the diaries progressed the name of Syd, who was apparently a recruiting sergeant for the Territorials, and a married man with children, occurs more and more frequently, usually in tandem with Jack, an ex-boxer who now owns a working men's café south of the Thames. These two appeared to be a double act of long-standing.

"Gerald was primarily a voyeur," André explained to me. "He got his kicks from watching others perform, rather than from performing himself. At least, this was the case when I knew him during the war – what he did before then I wouldn't know, though I imagine that his behaviour wasn't any different." "Gerald didn't like to be interfered with," André continued. "I tried it once or twice, but he didn't encourage me."

Had he ever known Gerald to indulge in sado-masochism, chains, bondage, whips? André, who was thinking back thirty years, could not remember Gerald ever having asked to be whipped, nor of ever having seen Gerald whip anyone. "Of course, people do different things with different people," he conceded. On the other hand, Maurice Leonard, a friend of Gerald's of later date, remembers calling on Gerald one morning to find him in low spirits and covered with welts and contusions. "Obviously Gerald had allowed his little games to be carried too far," Leonard comments, adding "he was a masochist and entertained some weirdo customers."

Another friend of Gerald's recalls dropping in on him unexpectedly to find Jack, the ex-boxer, cowering on the floor while Gerald stood over him with a cane. For what it is worth, John Symonds, Gerald's literary executor, discovered just such a cane, carefully wrapped and enclosed in a laundry box, while going through Gerald's effects: it was about 18" long, as big in diameter as a man's little finger, and of the flexible type favoured by schoolmasters.

On a lighter note, the late Sir Francis Rose told me of the farce that resulted when Gerald evidently got his dates mixed up. Rose had been inveigled to the studio flat in Glebe Place by the promise of meeting a Catholic priest who was 'dying' to meet him, according to Gerald. "The door was opened by a white-faced sailor who showed signs of incipient hysteria," Rose recalled. "God knows what had been going on before I arrived, but I feared the worst." Next to arrive on the scene was a guardsman in uniform. "Gerald, the guardsman, and I had no sooner settled down to tea, which was served by the *matelot*, who kept dropping things, than the doorbell rang again. Gerald shooed the two servicemen into his bedroom and answered the door himself.

"In swept a magnificent creature dressed as a bishop, with purple neckcloth, gaiters, and purple stockings, as I recall. This was Montague Summers, who styled himself a priest of the Roman profession, though there is no record of his ordination as such, and who certainly was an authority on demons, witchcraft, and magic. Evidently it was Summers that I had been summoned to meet. But before we could converse, the doorbell rang yet again. This time it was none other than the Mage himself, Aleister Crowley."

Crowley was once asked what he thought of Summers by Lance Sieveking, author of *The Eye of the Beholder*, who quotes his reply.

"I haven't seen Monty Summers for years," answered Crowley, knocking the end off his cigar with the air of an executioner. "He takes care of that. He knows what would happen."

"What would happen?"

"I should change him into a toad."

Poor Gerald, in vain did he try to make small talk – the Magi sat very straight in their chairs and glared at one another in silence. Finally, Summers could contain himself no longer. "Don't you think," he said, addressing Crowley, "it is rather presumptuous to style yourself as the Great Beast 666 as foretold in the Book of Revelations?" At that point Gerald dropped and broke one of his best bone china teacups.

Four

December 1919: Holy Innocents' Day

Whenever two or more of Gerald's friends meet today it is customary for at least one of them to play the devil's advocate. "Yes, yes, all that you say of Gerald is true. He was an unprincipled scoundrel, a wicked old rogue. He would gladly have stolen the pennies from his dead father's eyes, or sold his grandmother for cat's meat. But there is one achievement you can't take away from him, and that is his work for the Save the Children Fund. Gerald *did* see the Pope in Rome, and he *did* persuade His Holiness to take up a collection for the fund in all Catholic churches throughout the world. In this respect, you can say that Gerald saved the lives of thousands of German and Austrian children who otherwise would have perished through starvation, or succumbed to the diseases of malnutrition." So runs the Gospel according to St Gerald.

Occasionally a dissenting voice is raised. "I have the deepest suspicion that very little of the money Gerald collected ever found its way into the coffers of the Save the Children Fund," Alan Neame, who collaborated with Gerald in writing *Blood Royal*, told me. "The only reason Gerald was employed by the fund was that he was supposed to be close to Queen Ena of Spain, and the Save the Children people were anxious for the Spanish to set up a branch of their organization."

Such dissent is rare, however, the majority opinion, as voiced by Christopher Isherwood, being "It is difficult to find anything sinister in the hard work he [Gerald] did for the Fight the Famine Council and the Save the Children Fund, after

World War One".

The astonishing thing is that within six months of exchanging his grey prison uniform for a civilian suit Gerald was on his way to Rome with all expenses paid as the SCF plenipotentiary to the Vatican. How had he accomplished this feat? All his life Gerald operated on the theory, proven correct in his case, that the public's memory is mercifully short. Nothing fades so quickly as the ink of yesterday's headlines. By the time he emerged from Brixton prison into the sunlight once more, that headline WESTMINSTER FLAT CASE and the garbled account which followed it in *The Times* had long since been forgotten.

When he walked into the offices of the Save the Children Fund one morning in May 1919, for his appointment with Lord Parmoor, Gerald could be certain that his claim to be a Catholic and a pacifist who took a passionate interest in the welfare of children ("I have always regarded children as a peculiarly sacred trust," he was to write, "In their hands and not in ours lies the future...") would be accepted at face value with no questions asked. Besides, whether he knew it or not, Gerald's timing was impeccable. He had walked in on the SCF at that moment which occurs in the life of every newly founded organization which determines that either it gathers momentum and spurts ahead, or it stands still, eventually to wither and die. The SCF was in a state of crisis.

*

The SCF, and the shorter-lived Fight the Famine Council which preceded it, were products of the British sense of fair play. They were born of widespread disgust with Lloyd George's policy of "Squeezing Germany until the pips squeak" which meant in practice squeezing old people, women and children (an estimated 700,000 died in Germany alone within six months of the Allied blockade being imposed against the defeated Central Powers). Among the first to realize that "something must be done" was Miss Eglantyne Jebb, whose relief work among Macedonian peasants in the Balkan wars had taught her that children were war's first civilian casualties. Miss Jebb's initial target was a modest one: to raise £1,000 to buy milk for Vienna's starving children. The response to her appeal was overwhelming. Robert Smillie of the Mine Workers, for example, pledged his union to raise £10,000 for Miss Jebb's milk fund, an amount which the men at the coalface trebled in coming weeks.

Miss Jebb quickly realized that if the SCF was to operate effectively in alleviating want it must be international in scope. She set her heart on founding an SCF International Union with headquarters in Geneva. This meant securing the blessing of Pope Benedict XV, for many of the countries in which the SCF would be operating – notably Austria – were predominantly Catholic. It was at this point that Gerald walked through the door.

Miss Jebb's co-founder, Lord Parmoor, whom Gerald saw, is perhaps best remembered as the father of Sir Stafford Cripps, though Lord Parmoor himself was to have a brilliant career in law and politics, which included being Britain's chief delegate to the League of Nations. But in 1919 his chief interest was famine relief – i.e. persuading the British government to lift the blockade against the Central Powers and to float a loan that would help get them on their feet again. It was probably Gerald's pacifist views that most impressed Lord Parmoor, who had been active in championing the cause of conscientious objectors. There and then, Gerald was engaged to go to Rome for the Vatican mission.

No one at SCF headquarters bothered to check Gerald's credentials; indeed no one was in a position to do so. As with other organizations that mushroom overnight, the SCF's internal structure made it easy prey for charlatans. For a time the otherwise level-headed Miss Jebb herself was bamboozled into endorsing a product known as Vita-Bread, which was a veritable "bread of heaven", according to the patentee, a Mr Graham, who claimed that the recipe had been handed down to him from on high, and that it was guaranteed to cure babies of rickets.

Gerald left London for Rome on June 12 1919, six days before his public examination in bankruptcy was due to begin. While Gerald was still His Majesty's guest at Brixton a petition in bankruptcy had been filed against him by a Llandudno jeweller[7] for debts amounting to £313, to which five other creditors had attached claims. Now from the safety of Paris, where he stopped off en route to Rome, Gerald wrote to the Registrar in Bankruptcy (on stationery bearing the Duke of Abercorn's crest) regretting his inability to attend the hearing "owing to my presence here upon a really important business". Moreover, "If a receiving order is made against me while I am here," he warned, "it will effectively prevent me ever earning anything with which to repay my debt." He was nevertheless adjudged bankrupt in his absence on September 3 1919.

While in Paris Gerald looked up George Gavan Duffy, Roger Casement's solicitor, to whom he had been given a letter of introduction by Art O'Brien, the Sinn Fein representative in London. Duffy came from a distinguished family, his father,

---

7 And not just any old Llandudno jeweller but almost certainly Wartski's, the Faberge specialist, whose Imperial Russian aspect would have appealed to Gerald. Harry Wartski was so fond of Llandudno that when his firm opened a branch on London's Regent Street in 1911, it was given the name of Wartski of Llandudno. [Ed.]

Sir Charles Gavan Duffy, having been one of the founders of the Young Ireland movement and a friend of Carlyle's. When Casement was arrested Duffy had accepted his defence, even though this meant giving up his partnership in a firm of solicitors in Gray's Inn. His reward was to be his appointment as the Irish Free State's first Minister of Foreign Affairs. In June 1919, however, when Gerald first met him, Duffy was busy in Paris preparing the Irish case for self-determination to go before the Versailles Peace Treaty commission. At his headquarters at the Grand Hotel on the Boulevard des Capucines, Duffy already styled himself "Ambassador of the Irish Republic". Here, the fact that Gerald was a jailbird for once worked in his favour, for he was able to retail news of the Sinn Feiners whom he had met at Brixton. From the outset the two men hit it off well. Gerald was to be retained to do many an errand for the Sinn Fein movement, including gun-running when the Irish struggle entered its "Black and Tan" phase.

However, when Gerald was released from prison in January 1919 it was almost certainly as a result of a deal whereby he would act as a spy for the British government inside the Sinn Fein movement. The Government may even have facilitated his entry as a Save the Children Fund envoy to use this as a cover for his spying activities.[8]

Gerald, who had not seen Pope Benedict XV in five years, records that he found him "much changed and aged by the terrible trials of the war". Always pale and matchstick thin, the Pope's shoulders were more stooped, his limp more pronounced than ever. His Holiness had been treated shabbily by both belligerents in the late war, his seven-point peace proposals which called for the substitution of "moral force" for material might having been brushed aside (the Germans

---

8 See p.95 for Gavan Duffy's ostracizing Gerald. [Ed.]

referred to him as "*der franzosische Papst*" while the French stigmatized him as "*le pape boche*".) In view of the frail state of the Pope's health, Gerald had been warned by Vatican officials not to show His Holiness the photographs of starving children with which he had come armed, for fear that they might upset the Pontiff. Gerald refrained from doing so at his first audience with Benedict, who "listened with keen attention" to all that Gerald had to say about the work of the SCF and asked him to submit a memorandum for his perusal.

During his second audience with the Pope, which took place in September, Gerald disregarded the warning and produced the photographs, which showed seven and eight-year-olds with their bodies so emaciated they looked more like kindergarteners. They had large, dull eyes, overshadowed by rickety foreheads. Their bellies, swollen by hunger oedema, were supported on legs whose joints were dislocated. The Pope was horrified. So moved was he that he issued an encyclical ordering a special collection to be taken up on Holy Innocents' Day, December 28 1919, in every Catholic church, and the proceeds to be sent to the SCF in Geneva for distribution on a non-sectarian basis. Gerald's mission to Rome thus ended in triumph.

Before leaving Rome, Gerald carried out his first assignment for Sinn Fein, which was to plant a forged document with the Rome daily *Il Tempo*, with the object of sowing dissension among the delegates gathering for the Versailles peace talks. The forgery took the form of a secret defence treaty, allegedly signed by Germany and Japan in The Hague in October 1918, and its reproduction in the columns of *Il Tempo* had the desired effect of stirring up an international hornet's nest. "The Japanese Embassy immediately issued a *démenti*," according to Gerald, "but this was believed by no one." Whitehall thought it smelt a Muscovite rat, but its man in Rome was better informed, cabling that *Il Tempo* had bought the supposed treaty "for a small sum from a Sinn Fein agent, and… its publication was intended to embarrass the Presidential campaign for ratification of the Peace Treaty". This apparently refers to President Wilson's efforts to get the U.S. Senate to ratify the Versailles Treaty. Gerald was paid 50,000 lira by the newspaper, and what financial arrangement Sinn Fein had with him is not known.

*

Gerald made three blunders in travelling to Berlin on SCF business. To begin with, he travelled on a "yellow passport" issued by the German embassy at Berne, his own British passport being stamped "Not Valid for Germany". Secondly, on his arrival he failed to notify the British Military Mission, which was still very much a presence in occupied Berlin. Lastly, Gerald, although he was on legitimate SCF business, neglected to provide himself with proper credentials from the SCF International Union at Geneva. Instead Gerald was high-handed in his dealings with German charity officials, bandying the names of Lord Parmoor and Lord Robert Cecil, and relying upon bluster to carry the day. Result: universal suspicion, which Gerald's manner did nothing to dispel.

On November 9 Sir Charles Marling telegraphed the Foreign Office in cypher as follows: "Mr Abrahamson of the British Red Cross has learnt… that a Mr Hamilton, an Irishman, 35 years of age and a recent convert to the Roman Catholic Church, has arrived lately in Berlin from Berne. Hamilton called on Dr Elizabeth Rotten as representative of the Save the Children Fund and stated that he had been instructed by Lord R Cecil and Lord Parmoor to inform her that an International Conference would take place at Geneva at the end of November... He further stated that he had requested, in the name of the Pope, the Archbishop of Paderborn to be the President of the German Committee... Can you give me any information as to the genuine character of Hamilton's mission?"

In the ensuing correspondence, in which everyone concerned but Gerald was asked to give an opinion, what is striking is the readiness of one and all to throw Gerald to the wolves. First, Lord Robert Cecil replies that he has no recollection of ever having spoken to Hamilton "or indeed heard of him, and I feel sure that I never sent him or anybody else on such a mission as you describe to Dr Rotten, whom I only know by name". Next, W.A. Elkin, of the SCF office in London, in a letter marked "Strictly Confidential", acknowledges that Gerald's mission to Berlin is an authorized one, but reveals that the international conference then envisaged has been postponed. Elkin then proceeds to do a hatchet job on Gerald's reputation, writing that "since he first approached us we obtained certain unsatisfactory information as to his reputation in Catholic circles and as to his character... our Hon. Sec. who could give you the facts is at present in Geneva. I know, however, that she consulted a leading Roman authority in this matter, that he was able to give her information which confirmed suspicions she already felt, and as a result of this it was felt that Mr Hamilton was an unsuitable person to work through".

The "Hon.Sec." was of course Miss Eglantyne Jebb, but what were those "suspicions she already felt" concerning Gerald that were confirmed by "a leading Roman authority"? Had she learned about Gerald's prison record, and about the charge of gross indecency of which he had been convicted?

Whatever Miss Jebb had learned, she failed to communicate it to the SCF International Union in Geneva, with the result that Gerald, far from being regarded by the latter as "an unsuitable person to work through", was next entrusted with a delicate mission to Spain. Altogether he was carried on the International Union's payroll for another year. A simple breakdown in communications? A question of the right hand not knowing what the left was doing? Unfortunately Miss Jebb left no papers which might throw light on the matter. What is known is that she was determined to avoid any public scandal which might harm the SCF in its infancy.

As it was, nemesis was preparing to overtake Gerald in the person of W.T. Mackenzie, a Scot, who owed his sudden accession to the post of SCF treasurer to the fluke that his was the only name Miss Jebb could think of on the spur of the moment when pressed to add a suitable Catholic to the SCF Executive (Mackenzie was a convert). It was an inspired choice. As treasurer, he not only brought order out of the fund's financial chaos, but pruned its administrative expenses so that more than nine-tenths of the monies collected went for direct famine relief. In Geneva, as if to set an example of frugality, Mackenzie chose to live in an attic, located appropriately enough in the rue Calvin. "It really might have been a monk's cell, with the missals and books of devotion, the crucifix and the religious pictures," Miss Jebb wrote to her mother.

Undisturbed in his monastic digs, Mackenzie began to pore over the SCF ledgers, and noted that a disproportionate amount of the £359,695 collected in 1919 for famine relief[9] had been dissipated as "personal expenses", the worst offender in this respect being Gerald Hamilton. It was perhaps understandable

---

9 At today's values equivalent to around thirteen million by retail prices or fifty million by earnings. [Ed.]

that Gerald, as the SCF's representative, should travel first-class, and put up at the best hotels, but all of those expensive luncheons, those bottles of vintage port, those after-dinner brandies – were they essential to the task at hand? Mackenzie would have been less than human had he not contrasted his own hairshirt existence with Gerald's, his anchorite cell in the rue Calvin with Berlin's Eden Hotel and Madrid's Ritz, where Gerald stayed regularly. Undoubtedly Mackenzie's thinking ran along these lines as he began to investigate Gerald's expense accounts.

*

Gerald's mission to Spain, whose object was to persuade the Spanish to set up a branch of the SCF, was a failure, due partly to Machiavellian intrigue on the part of the Spanish clergy, and partly to the fact that an Austrian delegation had got in ahead of him. The latter, who were representatives of the Archbishop of Vienna, in effect persuaded the Spanish hierarchy to bypass the SCF by sending their contributions directly to Austrian Catholic agencies for distribution to the needy. There was nothing Gerald could do but bow to defeat. The International Union had already advanced Gerald 5,000 Swiss francs to defray his expenses. When he asked for another 2,000 Mackenzie wired him to return to Geneva.

In May 1920 Gerald was summoned by the International Union's executive to give an accounting of his fund-raising activities in Spain. He had precious little to show for the months he had spent there, mostly in Madrid. By March 6 he had collected only 50,000 pesetas, which included 10,000 pesetas donated by a State lottery winner, plus a subscription opened by the newspaper *El Hoy*. He told the executive that, after that, the monies he had collected had been sent directly to "needy areas in France" – an odd choice given the desperate need not only in Germany and Austria, but in Russia, Hungary, and Poland. Apparently Mackenzie thought so too, for as late as August 1920 he was still pressing Gerald for a detailed accounting of his expenditures. Gerald replied that all the relevant information had been forwarded to Monsignor Maglione, the Papal Nuncio at Berne, behind whose soutane Gerald now took refuge (the monsignor was sympathetic to the cause of Sinn Fein). Gerald then tendered his resignation to the SCF. Had he not done so he faced prosecution for misappropriation of funds.

The final word belongs to Miss Eglantyne Jebb. As pointed out earlier, Miss Jebb left no papers, but she often spoke of Gerald to her niece, Miss Buxton. In response to my query concerning Gerald, Miss Buxton writes: "I have a very vivid recollection of Aunt Eglantyne telling us hair-raising stories about Mr Hamilton. She was quite clear about it… that he was a rogue, and must be got rid of from the SCF. But it was a baffling problem as to how this could be achieved without a public row, which she was determined to avoid." The niece has a vague recollection of a scheme Gerald promoted whereby the SCF would acquire a fleet of lorries to transport food and other supplies across Europe to the needy. Gerald himself, of course, would act as middle man, getting his cut from the haulage deal. Her aunt's worries concerning Gerald lodged in Miss Buxton's mind. "I was young at the time," she writes, "but all this made such an impression on me that for the rest of my life I have had a joke about the name. Whenever there was any mention of the name Hamilton, I would say to my friends, 'Beware of anyone called Hamilton – he is probably a fraud and a rogue'."

*

From raising funds for starving babies to putting guns into the hands of Sinn Fein volunteers – the disparity between these two assignments is so great that Gerald, in his memoirs, feels called upon to justify the latter activity. "That I accepted such a charge as this may surprise the reader, already tired of my pacifist outbursts," he writes. "At the time the outrages of the Black and Tans in Ireland... had stung me temporarily out of my phlegmatic pacifism into a desire to take a more active part in assisting my martyred country." As Gerald indicates, with the Black and Tans terror in the autumn of 1920 the struggle for independence had entered a new, and as it happened, final phase. Meanwhile, Michael Collins's "flying columns", which were the republican response to the Black and Tans, were in desperate need of guns and ammunition in order to pursue their particular form of guerilla warfare.

The smuggling of rifles and Tommy guns to Ireland was the responsibility of Liam Mellowes, "Director of Purchases". The drill was that the arms were deposited in German warehouses where sailors from British ships collected them in small parcels and delivered them into the hands of IRA agents in British ports. Sometimes the guns were dismantled and the pieces packed with other hardware, such as rollers for mangles, for conveyance direct to merchants in Ireland as ordinary goods. Because they were shipped in small caches the guns eluded the British authorities, who were on the lookout for large arms consignments. Although Gerald is understandably coy as to the exact nature of his role, his job was largely one of squaring German port authorities and customs officials with judicious bribes.

Gerald's work for Sinn Fein in Berlin brought him into contact with the Irish colony there, a weird collection of individuals who for the most part had known Roger Casement during his tragic days in Berlin, and who now lingered onstage like actors who had fluffed their exit cues. At the Romanische Café opposite the Kaiserkirche, where it had its own table, the colony met daily to constitute a tiny island around which the dirty tide of revolution and civil war swirled. These revenants from a dead past had sat in the café sipping their acorn coffee when the Kaiser had abdicated and a mob led by a Workers' and Soldiers' Council had stormed the imperial palace. They were still sitting there munching little iced cakes made from mouldy potato flour when Rosa Luxemburg's body was thrown into the Landwehr Kanal. Their talk then as now when Gerald first met them was not of riots, bloodshed, or revolt, but of how shamefully the unspeakable Bethmann-Hollweg had treated "poor Roger", and how that saintly martyr had been let down even by his own people, the Clan-na-Gael in New York.

Bellwether of the flock was Dr George Chatterton-Hill, a British subject married to a German, who in 1915 had formed the Deutsche-Irische Gesellschaft to enlist German support for Irish independence. He was ably abetted by Barry Gifford, one-time correspondent for *The Times* in Cairo, who was likewise married to a German. Then there were the American-born Frau Dr Grabisch, née Agatha Bullitt, sister of the William Bullitt who one day would become America's first ambassador to the Soviet Union; and lantern-jawed St John Gaffney, who had been sacked as American consul at Munich because of his friendship with Casement. These four, at least, could claim to have a legitimate interest in Irish affairs.

The same could not be said for some of the other hangers-on, whose Anglophobia was all they had in common. They included General Maritz, of Boer War fame; Baron von Horst, a German importer; and 'Colonel' Emerson, who had made a fortune with a headache powder known as "Emerson's

Bromides". Circulating on the fringe of the colony were two Indians – a firebrand named Chempakaramanam Pillai, and Vivendranath Chattopadhya, who was said to have been involved in a wartime plot to assassinate both Kitchener and Sir Edward Grey.

Gerald's Sinn Fein activities were bound sooner or later to attract the attention of the German government. Questioned by Dr Brinckmann, of the German Foreign Office, Gerald denied that he represented the Irish Republicans in any official capacity, but Brinckmann was not convinced. "Dr Brinckmann laughed," Gerald recalls, "and replied that various Irishmen, or pseudo-Irishmen... each had assured him that he alone represented Ireland in Berlin. I, on the other hand, came to tell him that I did not represent Ireland. For this very reason he must regretfully believe that I was the real Representative."

*

Gerald pokes sly fun at the Irish colony in Berlin, claiming that their "Irish politics were at that time limited to successive tea-fights". Bun-fighting on the terrace of the Romanische Café may have been their chief pastime, but the colony were united on one thing: their profound distrust of Gerald Hamilton. Baron von Horst, in particular, viewed Gerald with deep suspicion, but then the baron was "always of the opinion that everybody except himself was an English spy", according to Gerald. When Gerald became friendly with Brigadier-General Sir Edward Bellingham, CMG, DSO, and head of the British Military Mission in Berlin, the colony's worst suspicions appeared to be confirmed. "This friendship," Gerald admits, "was viewed with horror by the... so-called Irish clique in Berlin, who wrote long reports to Dublin about my frequenting members of the military mission."

Were the clique's suspicions well-founded? Was Gerald in fact playing the double agent? British informers were not thin on the ground in Berlin, judging from the anonymous reports in the Foreign Office files at Kew. Some of these reports emanate directly from the Director of Military Intelligence, others from nameless MI5 agents.

Many of them contain the sort of chit-chat plus wild rumours that Gerald was to show himself proficient in producing when later he worked for French Intelligence. Thus, in July 1920 a secret agent reports that Dr Chatterton-Hill's flat at Prinzregentstrasse 94, near the Pragerplatz, is a rendezvous for "a very large number of shady visitors, including ex-German agents, shipping men, and commercial people of the lower classes". "His flat is plentifully hung with photographs of Roger Casement, who was his closest friend." Many of the reports seek to establish a link between the Irish colony and the Bolsheviks. Thus Frau Dr Grabisch is reported as being about to accompany Vivendranath Chattopadhya to Moscow "to obtain financial support for a new Sinn Fein magazine". Colonel Emerson, "the notorious Irish-American Sinn Fein agitator", has offered to edit the magazine, the report adds. The colonel has suggested that Moscow be asked "to supply funds to raise a regiment of Northern Frontier tribesmen with some such name as 'Liberators of India' ".

But if Gerald had been paid to supply chit-chat about the Irish colony in Berlin and its associates one would expect him, in true double-agent fashion, to supply accurate details about the arms shipments which he arranged. These details too are not lacking in the Foreign Office and Home Office files, and as late as October 1921, with Irish Home Rule only two months away, British police and customs officials, acting on insider tips, were still seizing arms destined for Ireland from fishing vessels.

The evidence as to whether Gerald acted as a double agent in spying on Sinn Fein is inconclusive. One can only point to certain indicators, such as his connection with the British Military Mission in Berlin, and the universal distrust in which he was held by the Irish colony, plus the reports in the Foreign Office files which read as though they might have emanated from Gerald's pen. Perhaps the most telling indicator is the snub administered by George Gavan Duffy, who had made use of Gerald's services for the greater part of three years. With the signing of the Anglo-Irish peace treaty in December 1921 Duffy became the republic's first Minister of Foreign Affairs. Thereafter he had nothing further to do with Gerald, whose letters to him went unanswered. It was a little like Falstaff being cold-shouldered by his beloved Prince Hal.

*

Gerald would have argued that in operating as a middleman or "Mr Fixit" he was serving a useful purpose, even though such operations involved using the Save the Children Fund as a cover for gun-smuggling. The guns had furthered the goal of Irish independence, and the starving children did get fed, he would have pointed out. Was it not Adam Smith who said that in pursuing private gain the individual is led by an "invisible hand" to promote the public good? Unfortunately, in Gerald's case, the hand that guided was all too visible. It was his own, forever outstretched to take.

In seeking to justify the sale of honours by Maundy Gregory when Lloyd George was prime minister, Gerald writes, "With regard to the moral side of Maundy Gregory's activities I honestly do not see why people should hold up their hands in horror." "A rich man," he goes on to point out, "can always buy a valuable picture; why should he not buy a title?" Why not, indeed. Gerald claims that he was employed by Maundy Gregory in the 1920s in procuring foreign decorations for Gregory clients who coveted these "unconsidered trifles". Moreover, he claims that Gregory was extremely generous when it came to travelling expenses. "Maundy," he told Ian Dunlop, "would unlock a drawer in his desk containing stacks of five pound notes, toss a couple of stacks across the desk to me, saying 'Let me know if you need more'." In researching a book on Maundy Gregory I could find no evidence linking Gerald to the honours broker; therefore his claim to have known Gregory "intimately", and to have worked for him, must be treated with caution.[10]

Gerald also claimed that he did a brisk business in selling the Order of Saint Simeon Stylites for Tsar Ferdinand of Bulgaria, who was always hard-up for cash; but as "Foxy Ferdy" was forced to abdicate in 1918, or before Gerald had tried his wings as a go-between on a large scale, this claim must again be treated with caution. Gerald is said to have assured those who purchased from him the Portuguese Order of Christ, at £2,500 a time, that at a distance of ten paces one

---

10 Tom Cullen's Gregory book is *Maundy Gregory: Purveyor of Honours* (Bodley Head, 1974). It is possible Hamilton had at least a slight acquaintance with Gregory via André Simon and the Wine and Food Society, of which they were both members. However, it is also significant that Hamilton does not claim any connection with Gregory in his first two autobiographies, only says that their paths "did once or twice cross" in a letter to the *Spectator* (November 23 1963), and then suddenly remembers, or perhaps embroiders, four pages about him in *The Way It Was With Me* (1969). He claims there that a reviewer has taken him to task for not mentioning his connection with Gregory, as if this was already known to the reviewer, but the review in question – the stimulus for the *Spectator* letter – says no such thing: it complains of too much teasing discretion all round, and too little detail about Frank Harris and Roger Casement in particular. [Ed.]

could not tell it from the French Legion d'Honneur, both being worn suspended from broad red ribbons.

There is a further apocryphal story that Gerald, horrified at the wastefulness when he discovered that the Cross of the Stylites contained real gold and real jewels, persuaded Foxy Ferdy to call in the decorations on the pretext of conferring a higher honour on their recipient. The decorations were then melted down for their gold, and their gems extracted, while the new ones which replaced them were gold-plated, with jewels of glass.

Whereas Gerald's claims to have acted as an honours broker with Gregory are dubious, there can be no doubt as to his success in obtaining various favours from the Vatican. As pointed out earlier, before the war Gerald had been assiduous in cultivating the so-called Black Society of Rome. Word of his influence in Vatican circles must have got round, for Gerald's correspondence includes requests from Catholics to obtain everything from a Papal knighthood to a decree of nullity from the Rota dissolving the marriage of a Canadian whose wife had run off with another man.

Curiously, Gerald's greatest influence was with Cardinal Montini of Milan, who was to be elevated to the Holy See as Pope Paul VI. In soliciting the title of Papal Count for a wealthy American in the late 1950s Gerald writes to remind Cardinal Montini, "Your Grace may remember how helpful you were when I was instrumental, through the good offices of Mgr Barton-Brown as well as your kind self, in soliciting the title of Princess for Mrs S——, just before the war, which the Holy Father saw fit to grant this estimable and pious lady. There were other occasions when Your Grace deigned to help me with similar requests." The Holy Father referred to of course was Benedict XV, whom Gerald had persuaded to endorse the

Save the Children Fund. Again, Gerald would have argued that he was performing a public service in bringing these pious persons to the Vatican's attention. And if he received a 'cut' from the donations that these same pious persons made to a designated Catholic charity – it was no more than he deserved.

The moral question aside, it could be argued that the "Mr Fixits" of this world are often grossly over-paid. Frequently, for example, the services which Gerald performed involved nothing more than making a telephone call for the purpose of bringing two people together, having first convinced them that they had interests in common. A painter friend of Gerald's is temporarily hard-up and in need of a patron? Gerald knows a newly-made alderman who is dying to have his portrait painted in his robe. A publisher is looking for a title to add to his autumn list – Gerald brings him together with a "deb's delight" who has been in the headlines for eloping with an heiress. A shady firm is looking for a peer to embellish its board of directors? Gerald knows a baronet who needs the director's fee.

Under the heading of effecting introductions comes Gerald's acting as pimp for various friends, in particular for one wealthy homosexual novelist who kept Gerald in cakes and ale over the years.[11] Gerald would insert an advert in *The Times* to the effect "writer seeks secretary-companion for travel abroad", then interview the applicants, passing on to the novelist the ones he had short-listed. Unfortunately, Gerald appears to have gone more on looks than on character or ability, with the result that the novelist was lumbered with a succession of petty crooks and would-be blackmailers.

In the grey area bordering the criminal belong Gerald's

---

11 "Cakes and Ale", a sly Maugham allusion – to Robin Maugham in this case – via the title of a book by his more famous uncle, Somerset Maugham. [Ed.]

efforts on behalf of a race-track betting scheme run by a man with the felicitous name of McLuckie in which Gerald tried to induce Peter Watson to invest; also his dealing with a Canadian crook named Eugene Fields who was marketing a "hot-dog" machine in which leading London brewers were said to be interested, but who absconded after fleecing several of Gerald's friends.

The trouble with acquiring a reputation for being dishonest is that all kinds of people then ask one to do all sorts of things with which they would not themselves soil their hands. The most audacious request of all to Gerald came from X, an Old Etonian and the holder of a royal sinecure.[12]

This man was James Frere, sometime royal herald, who had a flat in Dolphin Square in which Gerald sometimes stayed. A bachelor with a keen interest in costume, Frere had worked in Intelligence during the War before being appointed Bluemantle Pursuivant of Arms. In this role he took part in both the funeral of King George VI and the Coronation of Queen Elizabeth II. He was initially responsible for dealing with the press, but unfortunately his arrogance and open contempt for journalists made him unsuitable for the job.

"Wisely" (in the words of his *Times* obituary) "he was soon relieved of this post" and instead confined to matters of dress and uniform, where he was much happier: he designed the staves (or "wands") which the heralds carried at the Coronation and indeed still use, instead of the less aesthetically appealing batons which they had previously had to carry.

After the Coronation he was promoted to Chester Herald (and in this period he also embraced the Roman Catholic Church, becoming a Knight of Malta). In 1960, however, he resigned, leaving his career at a low ebb. He then worked for

---

12 I have taken the liberty of inserting the following four paragraphs. [Ed.]

a while at the Law Courts and wrote a couple of books on monarchy and aristocracy, before retiring to the country where he tenanted "various grand, albeit usually dilapidated, castles and country houses from which his main source of gratification often appeared to come from the flying of his own flag." Frere's determination to live in the past (he had been regarded as anachronistic even at the College of Heralds) grew stronger as he declined into "virtually a fantasist's existence", and finally "became involved in the twilit Corvo world of dubious titles and bogus orders of chivalry. He acquired three Spanish marquisates and styled himself *inter alia* Mountjoy King of Arms, King of Arms and Chronicler of Pepinan, and Clairvaux King of Arms of the Order of the Temple of Jerusalem".

Frere's obituarist comments "it was deeply poignant that he should have felt the need to embrace such titles and offices the whole genre of which at one time he would have been the first to ridicule". Neverthless he was charming, amusing, well-informed, and always a generous host. It is clear that he and Gerald would have had plenty of things to talk about, one of which turned out to be insurance fraud.

*

In 1960 X asked Gerald to arrange to have his flat in SWI burgled during his absence in Malta, so that he could collect the insurance on the flat's contents. The request was perfectly serious, X being in desperate straits and having fled to Malta to escape his creditors. From Malta he sent detailed instructions to Gerald as to how the flat was to be burgled. First Gerald was to get hold of a property valuer, and to make sure that the evaluations on the furnishings, which included a painting by van de Velde, totalled £1,300 ("Naturally ask him to place as high a price on everything as possible", the friend cautions). Gerald was then to arrange with a lorry driver in Lambeth, whose name X thoughtfully provided, to go with his van and a helper to the flat in SW1, show the head porter a letter purporting to be signed by X and authorizing the removal of the furnishings.

There was only one snag: X had let the flat during his absence, so Gerald would have to make sure that the tenant was well out of the way when the burglary took place. "Can you please find out the tenant's pattern of life? What times he is out each day and so on?" X writes from Malta, adding, "If possible get to know him". Ironically, this temporary tenancy put paid to the scheme, because X discovered that his insurance policy did not cover theft if the flat were sublet.

Would Gerald have gone through with the plan if this flaw had not been discovered? I doubt it strongly. Crime as practised by Gerald may have been no more rewarding than witchcraft, as Isherwood suggested, but Gerald would certainly have needed a large financial inducement to have become mixed up in anything as crackpot as X's scheme, although Gerald's theft of a pearl necklace, in the next chapter, was very nearly as hare-brained.

Five

May 1924: Jewel Thief

During the next four years Gerald gave a passable impersonation of that most ridiculous of comedy characters, the jealous husband, who either is, or thinks he is, a cuckold. These were the four years Gerald spent in pursuit of a petty criminal of Polish extraction named Georg Skrzydlewski. The fascination which Skrzydlewski exercised for Gerald when the two met in a Berlin night club in 1921 was almost hypnotic.

Gerald does not identify the night club but doubtless it was one of the 132 *Nachtlokal* registered with the police as catering to homosexuals, possibly the Mikado where transvestites gazed at their reflections in bar mirrors, or the Verone-Diele on Kleiststrasse where lesbians steered their girl friends round the dance floor. But then all of Berlin danced in those days, partly to keep warm. As one observer has it, "War cripples and profiteers, filmstars and prostitutes… all twist and turn in gruesome euphoria."

The Pole's beauty was such that couples passing his table would stop and stare at him, according to Gerald, who has left a fairly detailed account of that first encounter. "I had noticed this young man already," he writes in *Sophocles*, "both on account of the vivacity with which he spoke, keeping his companions in fits of laughter, and on account of his extraordinary good looks." When the friend Gerald was with rose and bowed stiffly in Skrzydlewski's direction, "I naturally asked who on earth this young man might be – imagining that he was a prominent personality of some sort." But Gerald's friend informed him that the young Pole was one of the newly-disbanded Baltic troops who had marched on Berlin in the abortive Kapp Putsch the previous spring.

Gerald then suggested that his friend invite the Pole to their table for a drink. "Let him come to my table if he wants to meet me," was Skrzydlewski's reply; and so Gerald, "impelled by I know not what strange force", joined the young man who was to become his tormentor, and in five minutes they had become fast friends. "I had never before met anyone of such magnetic charm, at once so witty, so cheerful and yet so boyish," Gerald writes. Georg in fact was nineteen, twelve years younger than Gerald, who automatically adopted an avuncular attitude. Unhappily the former's boyish charm belied criminal tendencies; Skrzydlewski had been attracted to the Kapp Putsch by the prospect of loot, and had been living by petty theft ever since the coup had failed.

Gerald's affair with the Pole coincided with the most active period of his life as a Sinn Fein agent, shuttling back and forth between Berlin, Brussels and Rome. Had he dared, Gerald would gladly have locked Skrzydlewski up during his absence from Berlin, or have resorted to any other desperate expedient in order to keep the Pole away from "bad company", meaning potential rivals. It is difficult to recognize in the love-sick Gerald the ice-cold cynic who took the concupiscence of others for granted. Yet Gerald in love demanded absolute fidelity and chastity, and flew into a rage if he thought the loved one was cheating. Once Gerald returned to Berlin to find Skrzydlewski missing from his usual haunts and, enquiring, learned that the Pole had been arrested for burglary. Freeing Georg from prison involved "payment of a sum of money, coupled with, I must truthfully add, a little judicious bribery and the use of such influence as I then possessed". Gerald met Georg at the gates of the Alexanderplatz prison, but it was not until the Pole had stepped into the taxi, and they were speeding towards Gerald's apartment in the Schöenbergerufer that "I realized for the first time the full responsibility I had so lightly and rashly accepted… It was a sort of incubus which I had wilfully accepted, and under which I was completely powerless to express my own character."

Georg led Gerald a dog's life. "Sometimes he would absent himself for days, or even weeks, and then turn up again without warning of any kind," Gerald complains. Worse still, Georg was a drug addict, given to experimenting with most forms of auto-intoxication. When he wasn't inhaling ether he was shooting heroin. When in residence, he filled Gerald's apartment with the noxious fumes of his opium pipe, a cardinal sin in the eyes of his host, who abominated smoking in any form. "Needless to say, in a very short time the night life I was leading began to tell upon me very severely," Gerald grumbles, adding, "but Georg seemed to flourish all the more, and looked, as ever, the picture of robust health. I began seriously to believe in the possible truth of Wilde's *Picture of Dorian Gray*."

But Gerald was hooked. There was no escaping the hypnotic spell the Pole had cast upon him. "I noticed that most people became weak and pliable in his presence, even if it was the first time they met him," Gerald writes. "His powers of persuasion were never put to the test. He had but to express a wish and people ran to obey him." Gerald could never bear to be away from Skrzydlewski long, but hastened his return to Berlin from his trips on Sinn Fein business. "Sometimes he was punctually on the platform to meet me," he recalls; "sometimes nothing had been seen or heard of him for several days."

That there was an element of sado-masochistic bondage

in Gerald's relationship with the Pole – indeed, in all of his lasting emotional relationships – is evident. He might grumble, but secretly he appears to have enjoyed being cuffed around. The Pole understood this. So in later life did Tinker Dare, the gypsy whom Gerald tried to turn into an unpaid servant. So too did the lance sergeant in the Irish Guards who was known to Gerald's friends as "the Gentleman Guardsman". The latter was brutally candid in his letters to Gerald from Dusseldorf, where he was stationed with the Rhine Army of Occupation after World War II ("I must tell you how you appear to me... a grumpy, stupid old bugger"), but then this was expected of him. "If at times I have been domineering and demanding that was in the nature of our friendship," he reminds Gerald.

Gerald's fits of jealousy on the other hand disgusted Tinker, who writes "Your idea that I should come straight home from work, sit, cook and sew for you and be in bed by nine... passes all understanding," announcing that he is off to spend a few days with "poor decent Romany folk where I can live once again and be happy."

"If ever you do find someone young and foolish enough to come and live and work for you don't ever be bossy and sarcastic," Tinker advises, "and give him some freedom. Don't put him in a rusty cage (for gilded in your case does not apply) and then he may stay with you."

On another occasion the gypsy's patience wore so thin that he found himself on the edge of violence. "Had I stayed, old and all as you are, I'd have poked you very hard," he informs Gerald.

*

Skrzydlewski introduced Gerald to a Berlin which Gerald,

in his wildest flights of fantasy, had never dreamt existed. This was the Berlin of the *Ringvereine* societies, gangsters who were the Weimar Republic's equivalent of today's mafia. Originally sponsored by the government as a means of rehabilitating criminals, the *Ringvereine* (there were over fifty of them in Berlin alone) became a form of mutual insurance for the underworld. Just as bourgeois youth had its *Wandervogel* whose members swore undying friendship while huddled around campfires, so the ex-convicts of Berlin's *Ringvereine* came together in solidarity, giving themselves such splendid names as "German Strength" and "Forever Faithful". When a member was arrested the *Ringvereine* not only provided him with a lawyer, but an alibi if necessary, and would offer to put the frighteners on witnesses who were scheduled to testify against him. If he were so unlucky as to be sent to prison, his pals would club together and support his family while he was inside.

The *Ringvereine* were not only providential societies but they operated protection rackets as well, Gerald discovered. Waiters, for example, had to be hired through the *Ringvereine*, which in turn offered the café owner police protection as part of its services. It was the kind of situation which Brecht exploited in *The Threepenny Opera*, where criminals and police consort in interchangeable roles.

Gerald was fascinated by this world which Skrzydlewski opened up to him, acting as his cicerone. In the louche nightclubs frequented by the *Ringvereine* he met such characters as Paul Magofski, an amiable pickpocket who went by the name of "Mifa", which were the initials of his cycling club. Georg also introduced him to Fassaden-Emil, the cat burglar; Pappel-Heine, the Chatterer, and Klette Klaus, whose speciality was doing apartment houses. Klette would start at the top and ring every doorbell on his way down until he found an apartment whose occupant was not at home, then he would burgle it. Most of this light-fingered mob were in their late teens or early twenties. As a sideline they pimped for the prostitutes in the Hallesches Thor, but they were not adverse to going with gentlemen who bought them gifts and otherwise treated them well. "After a few visits, they treated me as an equal, almost as one of them," Gerald told John Symonds, "and they never in my presence put a curb on their tongues no matter what they were discussing, crime or love."

In the comedy of manners, when a jealous husband wants to keep his wife to himself, and thus avoid the risk of being cuckolded, he sends her to the country, which is dreaded as "the last ill-usage of a Husband to a Wife", as Alithea remarks in *The Country Wife*. Acting from motives no more high-minded, Gerald installed his lover in a furnished flat away in Frankfurt, "but Georg behaved in exactly the same way as in Berlin", he laments. In desperation he tried to lure Skrzydlewski to Paris, where Gerald himself had taken an apartment in the avenue du Colonel Bonnet. Not unreasonably, in view of his criminal record, Skrzydlewski's application for a French visa was turned down. "Georg flew into a frightful rage and disappeared," Gerald recalls. "I waited in vain for a few days, and then returned to Paris resolutely determined never to forgive him this last mad freak of his." In the end the longing proved too great, and Gerald returned to Berlin just before Christmas 1921, when the two reconciled their differences. His affair with Georg did not end for another three years, three years of riding a roller coaster, so far as Gerald was concerned.

*

In Paris Gerald renewed his friendship with Rudolf Stallman, whose career had undergone several metamorphoses since the wartime days in Madrid when he had headed a German spy ring. Following the war Stallman had surfaced in Barcelona as head of a para-military police force formed to crush the anarcho-syndicalist movement in that city. A two week general strike in March 1919 had been followed by a lock-out, and a wave of bombings and political murders carried out by both left- and right-wing extremists. The fact that "Baron von Koenig", which was the name he went by in Spain, should be chosen to put down the unrest was a tribute to Prussian efficiency, Gerald suggests, adding that "the Baron won universal credit from his capitalist employers for the thoroughness of his work of extermination". "The baron's extermination policy included the rounding up and torture in Montjuich prison of union leaders, some of whom were shot dead 'while attempting to escape'." On one weekend alone police surgeons carried out twenty-one post-mortems on "persons who had met violent deaths".

The emergency over, Stallman had returned to Paris, and as "Rudolphe Lemoine" (Lemoine was his wife's maiden name) had launched an enterprise known as "La Franco-Coloniale Financière", an umbrella for multifarious investment activities such as bill-discounting, patents, mining stocks and shares. By the time Gerald renewed their friendship Stallman was already associating with such big-time crooks as Ivar Kreuger, the Swedish match king. When he introduced Gerald to Kreuger he warned him not to be witty as Kreuger did not like jokes of any kind. To which Gerald replied "I have waited in the anterooms of Crowned Heads without being drilled as to what I am to say or do – anybody would think I am about to meet

God." "Well," replied Stallman, "in a sense you are."[13]

In Paris Gerald met Frank Harris and became involved in the latter's ill-fated scheme to revive a defunct daily known as the *Paris Evening Telegram*. As usual, Gerald assumed the role of middle-man in introducing Harris to the good-natured but stupid Prince Aziz Hassan, an Egyptian potentate who was ripe for the plucking. There was also the matter of Gerald issuing a promissory note in the amount of 100,000 francs as a down payment for the purchase of the newspaper, but whether or not he forged Aziz's name to the note is not clear. All that saved Gerald's skin, and that of the redoubtable Frank Harris, was that the putative owner of the newspaper, a man named Cohn, turned out to be a bigger crook than they were.

Hamilton and Harris, it has been remarked, were the last of the gentleman adventurers – a gentleman adventurer being defined as one who, if forced to use a lead pipe, is careful to wrap it in a silk scarf. Harris, who was then living in the Villa Edouard VII at Nice, was sixty-eight when Gerald first met him, but trying desperately to appear twenty years younger. "Up to the end he successfully dyed his hair and moustache a deep jet black[14] and affected a light springy gait," Gerald writes. "He was a very short man, and he succeeded, to a certain extent, in counteracting this defect of nature by the use

13 Ivar Kreuger (1880–1932) became fabulously wealthy through multiple business and financial interests – most famously match production, in which he was heading for a world monopoly – but his empire was fraudulently grounded and under-capitalised, akin to a Ponzi scheme. Its collapse led to a further world crash after the Wall Street Crash, the Kreuger Crash, and Kreuger's suicide. In his day, his reputation was such that Dennis Wheatley includes him in a list of evil individuals in his Satanic thriller *The Devil Rides Out*: "Herod, Caesar Borgia, Rasputin, Landru, Ivan Kreuger and the rest" – *The Devil Rides Out* (Hutchinson, 1934) p.34. [Ed.]

14 Bernard Shaw was of the opinion that Harris would get more women if he dyed his hair white. "Think of the advantages of my senile appearance," he allegedly told Harris. "No woman could be afraid of me. They come and sit on my knee, Frank." [Tom Cullen]

of cork lifts inside the heels of his shoes."

Usually when Gerald called at the Villa Edouard VII it would be shortly before noon and Harris would be lying in bed dictating his memoirs to his devoted Russian secretary, Mlle Krim. Gerald, after noting the black stains on the pillowcase from Harris's hair dye, and how the paintings of nude women on the wall were so arranged that the bed's occupant could gaze upon them without turning his head, would exchange gossip with Harris, who was always glad to interrupt his dictation. Eventually Harris would dress, choosing a stiff collar, bow tie, straw boater, and spats, and the two buccaneers would set sail for an aperitif along the Promenade des Anglais. From their jaunty appearance one would never have suspected that they had hardly a franc between them.

*

Gerald, in his memoirs, skims lightly over the years that led from gun smuggling for Sinn Fein in Berlin to his arrest in Marseilles in October 1924. His reticence is perhaps understandable, for during this period he was involved in several shady deals, including the swindling of Abbas Hilmi II, the deposed Khedive of Egypt. It was in his 'Mr Fixit' capacity that Gerald came to the notice of the Khedive, who was Prince Aziz's cousin. Gerald was introduced to His Majesty as the man who could get him a *permit de séjour* for France, where Hilmi had been declared *persona non grata*, but where nevertheless he had a mistress, one Mme Solange,[15] stashed

---

15 Gerald told Timothy d'Arch Smith of an encounter with Mme Solange over breakfast in the dining car of the Blue Train, in which she was travelling from Nice with the Khedive. Noticing that she rubbed her neck as though in pain, Gerald commiserated with her. *"Ah, monsieur,"* she replied, *"si vous devriez faire ce qui je dois faire avec Sa Majesté, vous auriez mal au cou aussi!"* [Ah, monsieur, if you had to do what I have to do with His Majesty, you'd have a bad neck too.] [Tom Cullen]

away. Using the pretext that he was bringing pressure to bear on Quai d'Orsay officials on Hilmi's behalf, Gerald was able to extract a considerable sum of money – £100,000 he told Robin Maugham – from His Majesty. "He would toss over £10,000 to me as anyone else might hand out 10 shillings," Gerald claimed, but this, like all other sums mentioned by Gerald, must be treated with reserve. Gerald fell out with Hilmi after spreading rumours that the German crew of the Khedive's yacht had mutinied at Piraeus because they had not been paid.

By now Gerald had become increasingly reckless in his dealings. He appears to have jettisoned the maxim learned in Brixton prison "that the real criminal never sees the inside of a jail; it is only the insignificant and the careless, the tools and the fools, who come to be arrested at all". He seems to have aligned himself squarely with these latter, though whether he was more tool than fool is difficult to ascertain.

What he does not reveal in his memoirs is the reason for his recklessness, which was Georg Skrzydlewski. By now Georg, whom Gerald continued to see whenever he could get away to Berlin, was nursing a drug habit of enormous proportions. Keeping Georg supplied with heroin took all the money Gerald could lay his hands on, and Gerald had begun to despair of ever being able to satisfy the Pole's insatiable demand. This pressure goes far to explain the rashness of Gerald's next move, which involved the theft of a valuable pearl necklace, and which brought on to the scene, as Gerald's accomplice, a crook who styled himself Baron Alphonse Raymond Amendal Moral le Bailly de Tilleghem. It was in Brixton prison that Gerald first met the baron, who claimed to be a wealthy Belgian landowner, but who was being held by the British under Clause 14B as pro-German. Following the war Gerald had lost track of de Tilleghem until the spring of 1924 when he encountered him unexpectedly at the Sporting Club at Monte Carlo, where he had run up huge debts.

Gerald maintained it was the baron's gambling debts, not Skrzydlewski's drug habit, that led to his downfall. For in order to help his old pal Gerald introduced the baron to a San Remo jeweller named Perelli, who agreed to open a credit in de Tilleghem's name. Shortly afterwards Perelli informed Gerald that the baron (Gerald refers to him in his memoirs as "the Count") had run up a credit of 150,000 francs for which he had given a postdated cheque. "I was horrified," Gerald writes, but in view of subsequent events his horror may be discounted.

The scene now shifts to Milan where it was Gerald's turn to open a credit account with a jeweller in the via Manzoni named Gatti, who had formerly supplied gems to de Tilleghem's wife. Gerald, introduced as "Lord Hamilton", a well-known English nobleman desirous of selecting a really fine piece of jewellery for his fiancée, chose a necklace of matched pearls priced at £1,500, "the famous pearl necklace which brought so many tears into my hitherto not unhappy life", as he so poignantly describes it.

Putting as innocent a construction upon it as possible, Gerald was to claim that the transaction was a desperate bid to buy time: by selling the necklace the baron hoped to repay Perelli "and in due course, when his [de Tilleghem's] affairs were arranged, he would hand me a cheque to settle my account with Gatti". The robbing Gatti to pay Perelli explanation will not wash, however, in view of the aftermath. Once the necklace was in their possession the pair scarpered to Switzerland, converted the pearls into cash, divided the proceeds, and went their separate ways. On May 16 1924 Gatti swore out a warrant for milord Hamilton's arrest, and Gerald was now officially a jewel thief.

Nor does Gerald's version of being let down through his desire to help a pal hold water. Many years later de Tilleghem, who in the meantime had emigrated to the United States and become a naturalized American citizen, wrote to Gerald from San Francisco. "I have not read anything from your distinguished 'nom de plume' since '38, when you produced that kind of silly autobiography that put me in quite a false light," de Tilleghem begins, referring to *As Young as Sophocles* in which there is a full account of the theft of the pearl necklace. "But as it [the theft] all happened about twelve years before the publication of your book," the erstwhile baron continues, "I cannot blame you for it except that you have been the 'Deus ex Machina' in the whole bloody business."

To return to 1924, for the next five months it was *sauve qui peut*, with Gerald running scared. Thanks to the publicity given to the theft (it was splashed in the *Corriere della Sera* and picked up by other continental newspapers) he was forced to avoid the de luxe hotels which were his usual haunts. First Gerald rushed to Paris to see his lawyer, who assured him that there was no danger of him being extradited to Italy; then he roamed restlessly to Cologne, Munich, Bad Gastein, Vienna, and finally to Kiel, where he was reunited with Skrzydlewski. The pair spent an idyllic summer month at this northern seaport, where Gerald had rented the Villa Asgard.

Finally, tired of running, Gerald decided that the only solution to his troubles was to throw himself upon the mercy of the long-suffering Prince Aziz, who had meanwhile returned to Cairo. Gerald was confident that the prince, once the facts were presented to him in the right light, would bail him out. Accordingly, he booked a passage on the S/S Naldera, and on

October 18 took a train from Geneva for Marseilles where the ship was docked. Earlier that same day a court in Milan had sentenced "Lord Hamilton" *in contumacia* to three years imprisonment and a 10,000 lira fine.

*

Gerald looked more like a war profiteer or even a film producer than a fugitive from justice when he stepped down from a first-class carriage at Marseilles the following evening, with the astrakhan collar of his greatcoat turned up against the cold and a poodle named Kiki in his arms. He was followed by his German manservant, Wilhelm Madler, who was weighed down by expensive luggage. Whether or not he was hoping that his grand entry would create a sensation, the only witnesses on hand to savour it were a couple of detectives from the prefecture, who took Gerald into custody on a warrant for his arrest.

"The abrupt change, from the luxury in which I had been travelling to the indescribable squalor of the Marseilles *violon*, made me feel that I was taking part in some horrible nightmare," Gerald relates. All of his valuables and some 20,000 francs in currency were taken from him, and he was locked in a communal cell "full of the rowdiest and most unclean of the Marseilles *bas fonds*". The stir of surprise withheld from Gerald on his arrival at the railway station was now accorded to him in full measure by these same *bas fonds*, intrigued by the astrakhan collar, the queer thatch of hair which served Gerald as a wig (prematurely bald at thirty-four, Gerald had now begun to wear the hairpiece which so fascinated Isherwood in Berlin some years later). When it became apparent that Gerald's money had been confiscated,

114

and that hence he would be unable to bribe the guard to send out for wine, his cell-mates lost interest in him. That night Gerald fought for *lebensraum* on the trestle table which served as a bed for himself and five or six other inmates. "When one had attempted to deal with the army of lice, bed-bugs, and fleas, which had made all rest impossible, it was necessary to attend to the host of mosquitoes and gnats that buzzed in the foetid air."

That night too Gerald, for perhaps the first and almost certainly the last time in his life, toyed with the idea of suicide (under his wig in a tiny chamois bag Gerald had secreted two cyanide of potassium pills which he had purchased from a chemist in Kiel, he claims). But toyed is the operative word, for Gerald's love of life was too strong. He might have cheered up somewhat had he read the account of his arrest which appeared in the *Daily Express* in London under the headline:

£1500 Pearl Swindle:
Englishman Arrested
In Marseilles

The *Express* reporter, evidently confusing Gerald with his father, described him as one who had "relatives of high social position in England and is known to many people in London where he had been a prominent figure in dancing clubs".

The 1925 Index of Foreign Office papers contains the following entry: "Hamilton, G.B. Arrest in France and Expulsion to Italy", but the file to which this entry refers is missing, presumably destroyed as being "of no historical interest". When I asked the Foreign Office Records Department about the contents of the missing file I was told "Apparently, Mr Hamilton complained about the treatment he received during his expulsion from France to Italy in 1925. It seems that he was not the only one to complain, but in the opinion of H.M. Consul-General in Marseilles no purpose would be served in taking up the matters with the authorities."

Gerald would appear to have had good grounds for complaint, for, although he liked to pose as an Irish subject when it suited his purpose, he was, after all, a British subject travelling on a valid British passport, and as such, entitled to the protection of H.M. consular staff abroad. Although sentenced *in contumacia*, technically he was innocent under British law, for his defence against the crimes with which he was charged had yet to be heard in a court of law. One would have expected a protracted correspondence, with legal precedents cited, between Whitehall and the Quai d'Orsay before Gerald was handed over to the Italians. As matters stood, H.M. Consul-General at Marseilles appears to have acted in a high-handed manner, and Gerald to have been the victim of an extremely raw deal.

*

In addition to the contumacial sentence passed on him in Milan in the Gatti case, Gerald was made to stand trial at San Remo for having swindled the jeweller Perelli, was found guilty and sentenced to four years imprisonment, the sentence to run concurrently with that of the Milan court. Eventually both sentences were quashed by Courts of Appeal on technical grounds, but not until Gerald had remained behind prison walls for more than a year. Two months were spent in San Remo's fortress prison, erected in the fifteenth century to protect the town from Barbary pirates. "It would not be untrue to say that with the solitary exception of electric light, no improvement, sanitary or spiritual, had been brought to this loathsome prison since the day of its construction," writes Gerald, who adds that "homosexual practices of the most unspeakable nature were publicly resorted to, and rape employed if the weaker partner showed reluctance." In contrast, Milan's modern San Vittore prison was paradise. Here for fifty lire a month Gerald was able to get himself into a payment cell (*camerone di pagamento*), which was double the size of the ordinary cell, and to send out for his meals. Gerald must also have had access to a good prison library, for he filled a commonplace book with quotations from French, Italian, and German, as well as English classics.

Gerald wrote to Skrzydlewski several times, but received no reply. When Gerald returned to Berlin in the late twenties he left no stone unturned in his effort to locate the Pole, but could find no trace of him. Thinking that perhaps he was serving a long prison term, Gerald made inquiry of the dope peddlers and pickpockets with whom Georg had formerly consorted, but they too had lost track of him. Either Georg had died of a drug overdose, he concluded, or like Eurydice he had been swallowed up by the underworld. But more than three years after the idyllic summer they had spent together at Kiel, Skrzydlewski was still very much in Gerald's thoughts, judging by a poem among Gerald's papers dedicated "To G.S. in Berlin", and dated "Tunisia, Feb. 23" – the year is not given, but the poem is written on the back of a business letter dated 1928. Entitled "Idolatry", the poem reads in part:

> The fault was mine!
> I set you in a lofty secret shrine
> And sank upon my knees to worship you.
> Within, alone your beauty seemed to shine,
> My inspiration and my deity.

*

In the previous chapter Adam Smith was called in defence of Gerald's wheeling and dealing, for did not Adam Smith hold that "by pursuing his own interest the individual promotes that of society more effectually"? Gerald's methods as middleman, however, beggar anything that the canny Scot dreamt of in *The Wealth of Nations*. Certainly Smith could never have envisaged that the free play of self-interest might lead one to "hobnob with buyable chiefs of police, bloodthirsty bishops, stool pigeons, double agents, blackmailers, hatchet men, secretaries and mistresses of politicians, millionairesses even more ruthless than the husbands they had survived", as was the case with Gerald, according to Christopher Isherwood.

"Gerald," Isherwood continues, "inhabited a world... in which appalling things could happen to you as a matter of course; ruin, prison, even murder, were its occupational accidents." But then risk was the heart blood of the entrepreneurial system, and if Gerald during his lifetime experienced most of these hazards (once he thought he was being followed by a hit-man with a contract to murder him) it showed how much he was an essential part of that system.

Bribery of a judge to drop burglary charges against Skrzydlewski sounds possible – after all, judges can be open to *douceurs* the same as other citizens. The same is true of those customs officials who turned a blind eye while guns destined for the IRA were smuggled past German ports. But Gerald's story of how, as a representative of the Save the Children Fund, he bribed a king's secretary has the ring of implausibility about it. As told by Gerald, the story goes that he obtained Alfonso XIII's signature to "an important document" after slipping "a certain number of 1,000 peseta notes" between the leaves of a copy of Carlyle's *The French Revolution* which the king's secretary borrowed from him. The Maupassant touch comes in at the end of the story, when Gerald claims that the secretary telephoned to complain that he had received only Volume One of a two-volume work.

Six

February 1931: King Zog Survives

In the murky waters of Weimar Germany Gerald, when he arrived there in 1929, was like a tiddler among barracuda. The worst of the inflation, when beggars threw 100,000 Reichsmark notes into the gutter as worthless, had passed, leaving, as in the eye of a storm, an all-too brief period of stabilization before the onset of the Wall Street crash and the Depression. It was a period of stalemate for Hitler and the Nazi Party; nothing moved. However, Germany was still the scene of feverish speculation and profiteering when Gerald arrived. Everyone was on the make, from the war cripple who sold shoelaces on the street corner, and who would throw a realistic epileptic fit if he thought you were likely to give more, to the fantastic millionaire Hugo Stinnes who, operating from a telephone booth, bought up factories, coal mines, and shipping lines; not forgetting Peter Kurten, the child murderer, whose daydreams as he walked the streets of Dusseldorf were of blowing the city sky-high with dynamite. Meanwhile, the unemployed, shivering in the lengthening queues, were offered chess sets to take their minds off their empty stomachs.

"Berlin was full of cabals, and of cabals within cabals," writes one who sat by the Weimar Republic's deathbed. "Soon the webs of intrigue were so enmeshed that... none of the cabalists was sure who was double-crossing whom." While General von Schleicher, whose name in German means "sneak", double-crossed von Papen, only to be triple-crossed by the latter in turn, the Leporellos were busy aping their masters.

Gerald, for example, was spying on Willi Muenzenberg, only to find himself being spied upon by a magus who styled himself The Great Beast 666 – is this intrigue not the comic reverse of the Schleicher-Papen intrigue that brought Hitler to power? Gerald cowering in a closet while his manservant, who is incidentally blackmailing him, tries to get rid of the creditors hammering on the door – is this not the true spirit of the *Weimardämmerung*?

The Gerald Hamilton who arrived in Berlin in 1929 was a changed man from the one who had been swallowed up by Milan's San Vittore prison five years earlier. To begin with, he had acquired a social conscience, or so he would have one believe. At the end of the 1914–18 war Gerald had emerged from Brixton prison with a vague sympathy for the underdog ("I knew... that all was not well with the world; that the poor [were] more often than not exploited by an unscrupulous capitalist system") which had expressed itself on the one hand as a concern for the child victims of war (the Save the Children Fund), and on the other as a fascination with the criminal classes (Georg Skrzydlewski and his pickpocket friends).

In San Vittore Gerald was thrown with men who were not criminals, but anti-fascists whom Mussolini had jailed because of their political beliefs. From them he learned that the underdogs had become something called the proletariat, a force that was feared and courted by politicians and industrialists alike. As a result of the Italian experience, Gerald writes, "I began to take an interest in various social questions... I found myself compelled to do what little I could for the betterment of the conditions of those less fortunate than myself."

Secondly, in preparation for assuming the role of double agent, Gerald had taken a job. He had got himself hired by *The Times* as its sales representative in Germany. "The ease with which I obtained [the position] is only another illustration of the vast scale of hypocrisy upon which the standards of our civilization really depend," writes Gerald, busily biting the hand that fed him. How dare the Old Lady of Printing House Square, that arch moralist, be such a humbug as to hire someone with a criminal record like his? "I was able to provide the usual references," he boasts; "I did not have to tell a single lie, and I found myself suddenly launched into this most respectable and responsible post."

As usual Gerald's memory is faulty, for in his letter of application to *The Times*, dated May 5 1929, he passes himself off as an Old Oxonian as well as an Old Rugbeian, stating that he was educated at St John's College, Oxford (and as a referee he gives none other than his old friend Rudy Stallman, here sheltering behind the dummy corporation 'La Franco-Coloniale Financière'.) What had happened was that Gerald, getting wind that *The Times* intended to appoint a sales representative for Germany, had hurried to London, and had been hired after an interview with C.S. Kent, the general manager. In no time Gerald succeeded in getting the sales office moved from Frankfurt to Berlin, and this brought him into contact with Willi Muenzenberg, a man who, in the Caligari funhouse of Weimar Germany, was as much a victim of his own illusions as the next man.

*

Willi's own particular illusion was that the communists were winning all along the line, a fantasy fed by his own success as a propagandist. Like the combined magician-promoter which he essentially was, Willi could never stand still, but must always be promising new and ever greater attractions; promises which more often than not he fulfilled. In expanding his empire, Willi operated a geometric progression that had a logic all its own. Finding that he could get no publicity for Russian famine relief in the bourgeois press, Muenzenberg started two daily newspapers, *Berlin am Morgen* and *Die Welt am Abend*,[16] which were so successful that he then supplemented them with a weekly picture magazine, *Arbeiter Illustrierte*, which soon attained a circulation of one million. From there he branched out into magazines for women, amateur photographers, and radio hams, and founded a left-wing book club.

Similarly, during the brief respite from inflation and civil war, Muenzenberg, finding that mobile canteens were no longer needed to feed the hungry, switched them to factories where workers were out on strike. From this modest beginning Willi got the idea of sending aid to Welsh coal miners on strike in the Rhondda, and to the mill hands who had been locked out of the cotton mills of Gastonia, North Carolina.

The rumour persists to this day that Willi Muenzenberg was the illegitimate nephew of Kaiser Wilhelm II (is this because his enemies still refuse to believe that such a propaganda genius could have started life as a lathe operator in a shoe factory?). Willi himself never bothered to deny the rumour, which gave him a mythic quality.

Luck played an important part in Willi's early career. He arrived in Zurich while Lenin and the other Bolshevik leaders were still in exile there, and soon came under their influence. He played a leading role in the *Spartakusbund* and its successor, the German Communist Party (KPD), and in 1920, when it was a question of electing a president of the Communist Youth International, Lenin, who had been impressed by Willi's

---

16 *The World in the Evening*, a phrase which achieved its poetic potential when it was borrowed by Isherwood for his 1954 novel of the same name. [Ed.]

potential, tapped him for the job, even though at thirty-one Willi was a bit long in the tooth.

In 1921 Lenin rescued Willi from being typecast as a 'professional youth' by handpicking him to head the International Workers' Aid (IWA), which was set up to relieve the millions of Russians who faced starvation thanks to a combination of war, hasty collectivisation and crop failures. The technique Willi employed was simplicity itself, though it seemed revolutionary at the time. Instead of asking for charity, he called upon workers to give one day's wages as "an act of solidarity with the Russian people", his reasoning being that if a worker is asked to sacrifice for a cause, he becomes emotionally involved with that cause. The response proved that his thinking was correct. Lorries, milk separators, tools, and medical supplies came pouring in from factories all over Germany. By 1926 the value of the goods collected by the IWA and shipped to Russia exceeded 25 million gold marks, according to Muenzenberg, who even persuaded Sidney Hillman, an American garment union boss and no lover of communism, to part with $450,000 for Soviet famine relief. While such contributions were but a drop in the bucket so far as Russia's needs were concerned, their propaganda value was incalculable. IWA even rushed supplies to the victims of the Japanese earthquake of 1923–24. It was when Willi spread his wings internationally that governments, including the French, began to take an interest in him and his activities.

In appearance Muenzenberg resembled a wood carving of a peasant, from his jutting chin and stub of a nose to the spatula-like tips of his fingers, not forgetting the massive shoulders, which were those of a boxer – Willi liked to think of himself as a Dempsey delivering a knock-out blow to oppression. Arthur Koestler, who worked for Willi much later in Paris, likens him to a steamroller and a tank ("Willi sauntered into a room with the casualness of a tank bursting through a wall") yet acknowledges that "his person emanated such authority, that I have seen Socialist Cabinet Ministers, hard-boiled bankers, and Austrian dukes, behave like schoolboys in his presence".

*

Neither a banker, a duke, nor even a convinced socialist was Gerald Hamilton, yet Willi doted on him. Willi was amused by everything that appertained to Gerald from his wig, whose colour if not consistency was that of Shredded Wheat, to the monocle which Gerald affected, and which kept falling out of his eye to give him an air of perpetual astonishment. Nothing escaped Willi, including Gerald's none-too-subtle use of make-up (as Mr Norris remarks "I felt I needed a dash of colour this morning; the weather's so depressing").

At the same time Muenzenberg was quick to perceive Gerald's usefulness. Isherwood professes himself to have been "sentimentally shocked that the Party of the Workers could... stoop to use [such an] unclean instrument" as Gerald Hamilton. But it was precisely because he was an unclean instrument that Gerald was useful. He could be employed at those dirty tasks with which Willi could not afford to soil his hands. An episode which occurred early in 1931 is a case in point.

On the evening of February 20 1931 King Zog of Albania was leaving the Vienna Opera House on the Ringstrasse when shots rang out. The king's adjutant, Major Topola, fell dead with a bullet in the head, and the court chamberlain, Colonel Libohova, was wounded, but the king himself escaped unharmed. The two would-be assassins who had opened fire on the royal party were seized by the crowd and handed over to the police, who soon discovered that they were no ordinary terrorists: one was a former artillery captain, the other a student, both intense nationalists who considered King Zog a traitor for opening their country to foreign exploitation, notably by Mussolini. Sympathy with the would-be regicides was such that the ex-captain was given only a seven-year sentence, while his confederate was let off with three years hard labour.

The shoot-out did not escape Willi's attention and the Comintern was interested in the trial, which was due to open at Ried in Upper Austria on October 3rd. However, the Comintern dare not send a known communist to attend the trial as an observer, for fear of provoking such headlines as "Reds Behind Assassination Plot".

This was where Gerald entered the picture. A *Times* man, his presence as an observer at the trial could easily be explained. After all, who was to know that he was the paper's sales representative and not its Berlin correspondent? So the reasoning went, but Muenzenberg reckoned without the Austrian security police, who had their own sources of information. No sooner had Gerald crossed the frontier at Passau than he was arrested, the pretext being that Gerald was there to organise the prisoners' escape. Nor was he released from custody until the trial was over, when he was sent back across the frontier and into Germany. The mission was a complete fiasco, but it illustrates the type of assignment Gerald could undertake, and for which he was well paid.

Not all of Gerald's work for Muenzenberg was of the clandestine variety, however. Gerald was also employed as a kind of decoy to lure sponsors for the League Against Imperialism, Willi's latest 'front' organization. To Gerald it was a variant of the con-game with which he had been familiar most of his life. He would meet the prospective sponsor by appointment, usually in the type of expensive hotel that has ankle-deep carpets and half-spent cigar butts protruding from its sand urns. Over lunch Gerald would expound on the merits of becoming a league sponsor, much as a broker might advise a client about a certain gilt-edge ("Confidentially, old man, I've got my money in it. Would I invest if it were not a sound thing?"). He would then casually drop such names as Albert Einstein and George Bernard Shaw, whom Willi had already inveigled into becoming sponsors.

Gerald was carried on the League's payroll on a retainer basis, which meant that he was paid directly from Comintern funds. The pay was good, but the Moscow gold was a long time in arriving. As Isherwood explains it, "Gerald found himself up against hard-nosed professionals... [who] demanded results, and they were slow payers even after they got them."

If he had been with Willi during the day then, that evening, before dining out, Gerald would report in writing giving his conversation with Willi, together with any other intelligence he had been able to glean in the course of his rounds, and post the report to Rudolf Stallman in Paris. There was nothing at all personal in Gerald's betrayal of Muenzenberg. In fact, he rather liked the Comintern boss. Sometimes Gerald even found himself swayed by Willi's optimism and actually believing against his better judgment in the "singing tomorrows" which communism was supposed to usher in. At such times he congratulated himself for being on to a good thing.

The moral dilemma involved in betrayal, if it impinged on his conscience at all, was quickly dismissed. A French philosopher (was it Pascal?) pictured the devil as tempting a man thus: "Suppose that every time you pulled a bell-rope a Chinaman would die, but you on the other hand would receive a shiny gold coin – what would you do?" Had Gerald been offered such a choice he would have rationalized along the following lines: "Cathay is far away. There are millions of Chinese. Many of them die of cancer or other incurable diseases. Therefore what harm can it do?" So saying he would have tugged frantically on the bell-rope like some demented campanologist.

*

The irony was that in the early thirties Gerald was relatively solvent, and thus in no need of communist gold. His Aunt May had died in Bath leaving her entire estate, proved at £7,690, to Gerald in the form of a trust fund, the income from which he was to enjoy provided he did not become bankrupt in the meantime. The capital, invested in 3½% Government Stock, was to yield Gerald with an annual income of £300 up to the time of his death.

The second source of his relative affluence is more mysterious. On August 31 1929 at St Jude's Church, Kensington, Gerald married Diana Parker. Aged 21, seventeen years younger than her husband, Diana was the daughter of a captain in the 10th Hussars, and the marriage of course was one of convenience, though the exact nature of the convenience is no more clear than is the size of the *quid pro quo* involved.

In a memorandum he prepared for his publishers in 1968, Gerald, under the heading "My Personal Life", identifies Diana as the mistress of King George II of Greece. Gerald maintains that she married him so that she could appear at court as a respectable matron, but marriage to Gerald would not have gained her an entrée to Buckingham Palace, and as for the Hellenic court, there was none, unless the king's suite at Brown's Hotel could be considered as such. Nearer the truth is Gerald's assertion to Arturo Ewart that he was paid

£10,000 in cash, and given a flat in Belgravia, as his part of the marriage settlement. Asked what happened after the marriage ceremony, Gerald told John Symonds, "Well, we went and had lunch and then dinner... That was all, really. She said that she didn't blame me for what I was doing. She'd do the same herself in similar circumstances."

The marriage lasted two years, during which time neither spouse saw the other. When it was dissolved it was in circumstances as opaque as the original nuptials. One would have expected both parties, in order to avoid scandal, to have opted for adultery on Gerald's part, as grounds for the divorce. But no, when Gerald appeared in court on July 6 1931, it was as the injured party. The co-respondent named was none other than the Baron de Tilleghem. The rigged adultery took place in Paris, to which city all three parties repaired for the farce. "My friend the Baron went through the motions of booking a room with my wife in a Paris hotel," Gerald told Robin Maugham. "I rushed off to the mayor's office to say that my dearly beloved wife was being unfaithful to me... and together the official and I hurried round to the hotel – with the official wearing his sash of office."

The French *constat d'adultère* was admitted as evidence when Hamilton v Hamilton was called before Mr Justice Merivale in the Probate, Divorce and Admiralty Division on July 6th. It was the day of the annual Oxford-Cambridge cricket match. Counsel in the case, knowing the judge to be a great cricket fan, banked on his not probing too deeply but getting the proceedings over in time to get to Lord's. Their surmise was correct. "And I was left with enough money to keep me going for a year or two," Gerald told Maugham.

Gerald, however, always made it a point to live beyond his means. He had left a pile of unpaid bills behind him in

Frankfurt, including one of RM 2,000 owing to a local doctor. In Berlin he proceeded to run up new debts, debts which resulted in complaints being made to *The Times*. Up to that point the paper appears to have had no reason to be dissatisfied with his services. Indeed, by January 1931 Gerald's sales territory had been extended to include Austria, as well as the whole of Germany, and his salary increased to £200 a year, in addition to which he received £360 for office expenses, plus 50 per cent of all subscriptions obtained by him or his agents.

*

According to Gerald, it was his activities on behalf of abortion reform which got him sacked by *The Times*. Early in February 1931 liberal-minded Berliners were shocked by the arrest of two doctors, Dr Friederich Wolf and Frau Dr Kienle-Dacubowitz, who faced ten-year prison sentences. A mass meeting was held at the Sportpalast to rally support for the accused, and at this meeting Gerald sat on the platform as a representative of Willi's International Workers' Association. "I spoke in German to an enthusiastic audience of twelve thousand," Gerald claims, "and next morning's papers were indeed full of nothing else." It is this meeting, or one very like it, which "Comrade" Arthur Norris addresses in *Mr Norris Changes Trains*, except Isherwood has shifted the venue from the Sportpalast to a tawdry hall in the working-class suburb of Neukolln ("On the ceiling, an immense pink, blue, and gold design of cherubim, roses and clouds was peeled and patched with damp") where the workers have turned out to express solidarity with Chinese peasantry.

"Most of the men wore breeches with coarse woollen stockings, sweaters and peaked caps," he writes, going on to describe "the fixed attention of the upturned rows of faces," as though mesmerized, "pale and prematurely lined, often haggard and ascetic, like the heads of scholars, with thin, fair hair brushed back from their broad foreheads." As one of the first speakers, Willi Muenzenberg electrified his audience. "His gestures were slight but astonishingly forceful. At moments it seemed as if the giant energy stored up in his short, stocky frame would have flung him bodily from the platform." When it comes the turn of 'Comrade' Norris to have his say about "the crimes of British imperialism in the Far East", he is accorded the same rapt attention. "They accepted without question this urbane bourgeois gentleman, accepted his stylish clothes, his graceful *rentier* wit. He had come to help them… He was their friend."

In addition to espousing the cause of unmarried mothers, Gerald championed that of borstal reform, which was closer to his heart because of his own prison experience. The brutal way in which borstal inmates were treated was the subject of a play, *Revolte im Erziehungshaus*, by Peter Martin Lampel, a friend of Gerald's, which enjoyed an enormous success in Berlin. On Willi's orders, Gerald attended the trial of the sadist in charge of a borstal at Luneburg, who was convicted of cruelty, but who fled from justice (he was later pardoned by the Nazis).

For a brief period Willi and the German Communist Party also interested themselves in homosexual law reform, notably in the campaign to repeal Paragraph 175 of the German Penal Code which outlawed homosexual acts between males. The repeal campaign dated back as far as 1898, when August Bebel, the Social Democrat leader, had warned the Reichstag, "The number of these persons is so great… that if the police dutifully did what they are supposed to, the Prussian state would immediately be obliged to build two new penitentiaries just to handle the number of violations against Paragraph 175 in Berlin alone." Through the years the repeal petition had gathered the signatures of such prominent figures as Albert Einstein and Thomas Mann.

At first the communists enthusiastically backed Wilhelm Reich's German Association for Proletarian Sexual Politics – "Sexpol" for short – which had repeal of Paragraph 175 as one of its aims; but when the Soviets cooled to the idea of homosexual law reform, the KPD in turn dropped it, leaving Dr Magnus Hirschfeld, pioneer sexologist, almost alone in the field as lance-bearer for the cause. Hirschfeld was to pay bitterly for his advocacy, for when the Nazis came to power one of their first acts was to pillage his *Institut Für Sexual-Wissenschaft*, and to burn his library of over 10,000 volumes, including the works of Havelock Ellis, Edward Carpenter, and Freud.

*

Contrary to what he may have believed, *The Times* was no more aware of Gerald's interest in abortion and borstal reform than it was aware of his sex life (there is no evidence that he was active on behalf of gay rights) or the fact that he had been playing footsie with the communists. Gerald was fired for quite different reasons.

To get sacked by *The Times* in the days when Geoffrey Dawson was editor took some doing because, like the Church of Rome, *The Times* was reluctant to give up one of its own, thereby admitting that it could have been mistaken in judging the character of the anointed. Rather than dismiss a recusant outright, the Old Lady of Printing House Square preferred to transfer him to a less interesting post, according to Claud Cockburn, who recalls two cases where this was done. "One of the unfortunates… had developed 'views' on something or other," Cockburn writes, "and in *Times* language 'viewy' was a dreadfully damaging epithet. The other unfortunate chappie would insist upon passing the girl he was sleeping with off as his wife…"

The *Times* management might have put up with Gerald being "viewy", had it not been for all those complaints from Gerald's creditors. Gerald had also taken to palming himself off as "the *Times* Correspondent in Germany", which was lese-majesty. Gerald's employment by *The Times* was terminated as of April 11 1931 (later extended one month), and he was ordered to close its business office, which was housed in his apartment at Derfflingerstrasse No 2.

The management's troubles with Gerald were only just beginning, however. There was the matter of RM 840, for example. This sum, which works out at about forty-two pounds sterling, was deposited in Gerald's bank account by accident, having been intended for another employee. When Gerald was asked to cough up and refused, it confirmed suspicions entertained at Printing House Square that he was a bounder. Worse was to follow, when it was discovered that nearly £200 paid to Gerald in subscriptions had not been passed on to the circulation department. Alarmed, *The Times* sent to Berlin first John Paulsen, its Copenhagen sales manager, who was given the brush off by Gerald; and then Victor Royle, of its circulation department, who arrived in Berlin on August 10 1931, to make a full-scale investigation of Gerald's tenebrous affairs.

The two front doors of Derfflingerstrasse No 2 might well have reminded Victor Royle of those apertures in a Rathaus clock tower which fly open at intervals, and out of which various allegorical figures appear chased by a scythe-toting

Father Time. Each door had a tiny round peep-hole, and each bore a brass nameplate, the one on the left proclaiming GERALD HAMILTON PRIVATE and that on the right, THE TIMES OF LONDON SALES REPRESENTATIVE.

As Royle hesitated, debating which door to ring, the door marked SALES REPRESENTATIVE was opened by Fritz Thurecht, Gerald's clerk-cum-secretary-cum-valet, who usher-ed the circulation man into the office. Only a beaded curtain separated the office, Gerald's public manifestation, from the apartment, his private persona, as it were. The schizoid personality who was accustomed to flit between the two was absent from Berlin, or so his clerk informed Royle. Gerald was in Moscow, to be exact, and was not expected to return to Berlin until August 28, according to Thurecht. Royle then inquired about repossessing the furniture in the flat, for which *The Times* had paid, but was told that he could not touch a stick of it in Gerald's absence without permission from Gerald's solicitors in London, Messrs Field, Roscoe and Co.

Royle discovered that Gerald, under a hire purchase agreement, had indented with a firm in Leipzigerstrasse for RM24,000 (about £1,200) worth of furniture on notepaper headed *The Times Publishing Company*, and signed by himself as *Times* representative in Germany. Of this amount Gerald had paid only the first instalment. When the furniture firm began to press for more money, Gerald negotiated a loan with the Commercial Investment Trust Company, which took out a bill of sale on all the furniture in the apartment, including the office furniture for which *The Times* had paid. "Under these conditions I am not allowed by law to move one item which is included in the list signed by Hamilton," Royle reported.

But greater revelations were in store. "The young German lad who received Poulsen and told him he was Mr Klein is in fact Mr Thureck [sic], the clerk," Royle writes. "The alleged Mr Thureck whom Mr Poulsen... states was English, about Hamilton's age, is a gentleman who chooses to call himself 'Mr Klein', but whose real name is Spitz... I interviewed this morning a street seller, whose name is Herkstroeter, and who was recently employed by Hamilton to sell *The Times* in Unter den Linden," the report continues. "This lad informed me that he came from Frankfurt with Hamilton, who was also accompanied by his housekeeper, Mr Thureck, and Mr Spitz (alias Klein), and they had all lived, until recently, together at Hamilton's flat..."

"He informed me that Hamilton had not been to Russia, in fact that he had not left Berlin for some months. He was in fact in Berlin when Mr Poulsen was there, and was actually in the flat at the time of the call... To sum up, I am quite convinced that Hamilton has not been to Russia, and that Thureck, Herkstroeter, Hamilton, Spitz (alias Klein) and the housekeeper form a kind of travelling circus, and may move elsewhere at any moment."

Poor Royle, he had yet another name to add to this bewildering array, a "Dr Frommer", who telephoned to state that he understood Hamilton's position was vacant, and that "he would be prepared to take over his duties forthwith, if so desired". "On enquiring who this person was," Royle notes, "I found that he is yet another member of Hamilton's circus."

Royle added a hasty *postscriptum* to his report before posting it to London. "At 11.30 pm on Tuesday, I was sitting in the lounge of my hotel, Central Hotel, Berlin, when I saw Hamilton come down the stairs leading from the restaurant," he writes. "As he got near to the door, I approached him and said, 'Good evening, Mr Hamilton'. As soon as he heard this, he pushed past me, through the swing doors and out into the street. I followed him, and caught him up, but he simply shook his head. I decided that no good purpose would be served by having 'high words' in the street, so I returned to my hotel to write this. Hamilton was dressed in a dark striped suit, light hat, and was wearing his monocle."

As Gerald continued to style himself as the *Times* correspondent, in November 1931 *The Times* was forced to insert the following advertisement in five leading Berlin and Frankfurt newspapers:

> We hereby give notice that we have closed the office, *The Times Agency for Advertisements & Subscriptions*, hitherto conducted by Mr Gerald Hamilton, and that we have dissolved all contractual relations with Mr Gerald Hamilton.   *The Times*

Not that this stopped Gerald – he was to lay claim for the rest of his life to having been *Times* correspondent in Germany. The advertisement did, however, serve as a signal for his creditors to swoop down upon him, foremost among them being the Commercial Investment Trust Company, which proceeded to strip his flat bare of its furnishings. Isherwood set it all down in *Mr Norris Changes Trains* where the narrator and Arthur Norris play sardines behind a locked door while an irate creditor rattles the doorknob, shouting: "You damned swindler! You wait till I get my hands on you!" Afterwards Mr Norris, relieved that his young friend takes it all so lightly, remarks, "In the course of a long and not uneventful life, I can truthfully say that for sheer stupidity and obstructiveness, I have never met anyone to equal the small Berlin tradesman."

Seven

December 1930: The Beast in Berlin

To the young English poets of the thirties, Berlin was "a kind of cure for our personal problems", in Stephen Spender's phrase. Auden, Spender, Isherwood, Lehmann, Brian Howard, their paths crossing and criss-crossing, were drawn there and ended up in each other's books. There was something almost incestuous about the floating colony of literati who preferred Germany to the drab England of Ramsay MacDonald. And not only poets; such oddball characters as Guy Burgess and Aleister Crowley came to Berlin in the Threadbare Thirties to take the cure.

Spender was attracted by the Bauhaus, expressionist painting, atonal music, and nudism, though not necessarily in that order. "It was easy to be advanced," he writes. "You had only to fling off your clothes." His friend Isherwood writes of himself: "To Christopher, Berlin meant Boys." Isherwood was twenty-four when he visited Berlin for the first time, lured there partly by Auden's glowing description of the metropolis, partly by the dire warnings of a cousin, who was British consul in Bremen, that what went on in Berlin exceeded anything "in the most shameless rituals of the Tantras, in the carvings of the Black Pagoda, in the Japanese brothel pictures".

After a brief sampling of Berlin's delights, Isherwood had returned to the Prussian capital for a prolonged stay in November 1929, earning his keep by giving English lessons. It was not until a year later that he met Gerald Hamilton. By that time Christopher had settled in at Nollendorfstrasse 17, in a district which he describes as "middle-class-shabby" with "top-heavy balconied facades, dirty plaster frontages embossed with scrollwork and heraldic devices". It was to be the scene of his Berlin stories. Isherwood was to observe Gerald in all seasons, in the summertime of his affluence when the sun shone on his bewigged head through courtesy of *The Times* and Willi Muenzenberg, and in the winter of his discontent when he had been sacked by *The Times* and his creditors closed in for the kill. In the autumn of 1931 Isherwood writes to Spender, "I spend most of the day laughing with Hamilton over his classic struggles with the bailiff."

Betimes the two friends visited the Cosy Corner at Zossenerstrasse 7, the boy bar to which Auden had introduced Isherwood, and which had photos of boxers and racing cyclists on its walls. Here school-leavers who had joined Berlin's 750,000 unemployed sat around all day playing rummy with greasy cards, "their shirts unbuttoned to the navel and their sleeves rolled up to their armpits", as Isherwood describes them, their *deshabille* due "partly because they knew it excited their clients". They were not professional, but amateur *Lustknabe*, forced to hustle for their next meal. Isherwood, perhaps with a trace of guilt, likens the bartering that went on between the boys and their admirers to jungle trading. Gerald always left his rings and jewelled cufflinks at home when he went slumming with Christopher; even so, he must have appeared to the natives who inhabited this particular jungle less as a trader, and more as a delectable missionary candidate for the stewpot.

Back at Nollendorfstrasse 17, Isherwood introduced Gerald to Jean Ross and Frl Thurau, Christopher's landlady, who were the originals of Sally Bowles and Frl Schroeder of *Goodbye to Berlin*. Gerald referred to the landlady as "La Divine Thurau", while she insisted upon addressing him as "Herr Doktor", and envied him his lavender silk underwear, which she thought was wasted on a man. As for Jean Ross, she received Gerald informally amid soap bubbles ("It's all right, come and talk to me while I have my bath, darling"). It was through Jean Ross that Gerald met Aleister Crowley, whose trail thus snaked its way through the puddles in Frl Thurau's bathroom to join up with that of Hamilton.

Jean had a bit part in Max Reinhardt's production of *Tales of Hoffmann* at the Grosses Schauspielhaus, and Crowley, who had spotted her in the chorus, thought she might do to star in the film version of *Mortadello, or the Angel of Venice*, his comedy written in Alexandrines. Her legs were just right for the part. Crowley had not yet sold the film rights to *Mortadello*, but he reasoned "Royalists want films of this type as propaganda for 'the good old days'." And so they did – Germany at this period was flooded with escapist movies masquerading as historical epics, but with a decided right-wing bias. Snug in the gilt-and-plush splendour of the UFA-Palast am Zoo, while watching an army of Lubitsch extras storm the Bastille or besiege the Tower of London to the accompaniment of a live orchestra, one could forget the angry mobs outside clashing with one another and with the police.

From Crowley's point of view, Jean Ross's star quality was enhanced not only by good legs, but by the fact that she had a banker as her wealthy patron. Besides, Jean had delighted the Beast by remarking when first introduced to him, "But I've known you all my life. You see, when I was a little girl Nurse used to say to me, 'Now, Miss Jean, you behave properly, or I'll fetch Mr Crowley to you'."

Jean's "sugar daddy" agreed to put up RM 30,000 to form the preliminary film company, but by December he had flown the coop, and nothing more was heard of the project. Jean, however, was far from being downcast. She was used to being propositioned by UFA producers who wanted to make a star of her, and so she did not take Crowley too seriously. As she luxuriated in her bubble bath she would regale Gerald with her description of Crowley, who was known to his followers variously as the Mage, the Logos of the New Aeon, and the Great Beast 666 (as foretold in the *Book of Revelations*); of his peculiar dress and the way his fingers were covered with rings engraved with cabalistic and zodiacal symbols; and of his domestic troubles with the woman he lived with. Gradually Jean aroused in Gerald a desire to meet the Mage.

*

However, it was more as a lark that Gerald went with Christopher early in October 1931 to the Porza Galleries in Budapesterstrasse, where Crowley was exhibiting his paintings. The two did not think much of the paintings, typical of which was a nude female monstrosity entitled *Ether* for which Crowley's mistress had posed, the whole being executed, so the catalogue explained, after "both artist and model had inhaled small quantities of the vapour for about an hour". The Beast was fifty-six when Gerald first met him, and owing to dissolute living his looks had lost the poetic quality which so many women had found irresistible. As if in an act of penance he had shaved his head, and cold eyes now stared from a pudding face whose skin was sallow. The two friends came away "delighted at having met this wicked man and thrilled at the welcome he gave us", according to Gerald, though Christopher might not have been so flattered had he read the description of himself as "Hamilton's boy" in the Beast's diary.

Isherwood turned his meeting with Crowley into a short story, 'A Visit to Anselm Oakes', in which Crowley, transfigured as Oakes, is pictured wearing a dirty white terry-cloth bathrobe and a turban to which is affixed a piece of red glass not unlike that which one finds on the rear fender of a bicycle. "As I watched him, I understood that, if a Devil *did* exist," the narrator observes, "the most terrifying thing about him might be simply this: that he wasn't interested in anything, even in damnation."

Crowley for his part found Gerald "delightful", according to his diary, and this despite rumours relayed to him by his German disciple Karl Germer that Gerald was a fraud. ("Germer rings up that Hamilton is a crook pretending to be on *The Times*"). "The maniac must have rung up all the old cats in Berlin the moment I left him, having let his [Hamilton's] name slip out." Crowley was at heart a snob, and having been given to understand that Gerald was "Berlin Correspondent" of *The Times* was loath to acknowledge that his new-found friend could be anything less.

The Great Beast, too, had come to Berlin to take the cure for personal problems. Expelled from France as undesirable, barred from returning to England by a wife who was waiting for him with a writ for maintenance, Crowley had holed up in Berlin with Bertha Busch, whom he called "Bill", when not referring to her as the Scarlet Woman. When she was sober Bill was an excellent cook, and made him a comfortable home. When drunk, which was more often than not, she was given to throwing plates. Crowley's flat in Charlottenstrasse was littered with broken crockery.

Though absent from England, Crowley was never out of the headlines. Whenever they were hard up for copy, Fleet

Street hacks would dredge their piles of Crowley cuttings for yet another series of articles on "The World's Most Evil Man". These told how Crowley drugged otherwise respectable matrons, initiating them into the Eleusinian mysteries and inducing them to indulge in 'unspeakable practices', preliminary to photographing them for blackmail purposes. The suicide of more than one distraught disciple was laid at Crowley's doorstep by the Sunday Dreadfuls, though the only case cited was that of an Oxford graduate, who apparently threw a fit while sacrificing a cat at one of Crowley's midnight orgies. Witnesses were produced to testify to Crowley's feats of magic (which he spelt "magick") – how he had made flames shoot up through the floor of Nina Hamnett's studio ("If that's not sinister, my dear, I'd like to know what is") and books vanish from their shelves in John Watkins's bookshop off the Charing Cross Road.

Indeed, there is something mystifying about the following entry in the diary Crowley kept in Berlin in 1931: "Arose in my might & stopped a gramophone in the Terminus by threatening all present with immediate death". Is one supposed to infer that Crowley went in high dudgeon to complain to the station-master at a nearby railway terminus that his peace was being disturbed by the infernal racket made by a gramophone? Or, as he implies, that he was able to silence the offending machine by means of occult powers?

*

Crowley wasted no breath in talking of magick to Gerald, "because he knew I was a disbeliever", as Gerald told John Symonds. Hamilton preferred to look upon him as "a typical *bon bourgeois* fond of good eating, rare wines, ladies and fine cigars". Whenever he set out for London Gerald was given a shopping list by Crowley of delectables to bring back to Berlin, including his special brand of tea, obtainable only from Fortnum and Mason, and the Pure Perique Medium Cut pipe tobacco purveyed by Fribourg and Treyer in the Haymarket.

As for the Beast himself, he looked upon Gerald as a meal ticket. As far back as May 1929 Crowley had begun to fancy himself in a new role, that of secret agent. That month Crowley had been invited to London with all expenses paid as the guest of Colonel J.F.C. Carter, of Scotland Yard's Special Branch, whose multifarious duties included keeping tabs on secret societies. Over dinner at the Langham Hotel, Colonel Carter had the Magus in stitches as he told him how he instructed his adolescent sons to masturbate on Saturday nights so that it would not interfere with their studies. Afterwards, over coffee and brandy, the colonel sought to recruit Crowley to spy on Annie Besant's Theosophical Society, which just at this moment was giving the British government headaches by stirring up trouble in India.

The employment of Crowley on such an assignment appears incredible, but it should be borne in mind that the Beast himself had once been the subject of an investigation by MI5, whose agents infiltrated his midnight soirees. "MI5 agents who attended these functions disguised as witches and wizards wrote long memoranda about the consumption of goat's blood," according to the authors of a recent book on Kim Philby. In the present instance Crowley was too well-known in masonic circles to spy on Annie Besant himself, but his secretary Israel Regardie did join the Esoteric Section of the Tingley Theosophical Society on Crowley's instructions, and his subscription was paid by the Special Branch.

Crowley took on the role of Colonel Carter's man in Berlin,

keeping the Special Branch officer supplied with running commentaries which, like the Mage's paintings, sounded as though they had been concocted while Crowley was under the influence of ether. Thus in October 1931 Crowley predicts that the Hohenzollern monarchy would be restored by Christmas, with the backing of what he calls the Hitler-Hugenberg crowd. "This means utter smash all round... French intervention, also revolution ending in anarchy with a probable attempt of the Soviets to capture the country."

Crowley was no friend of the Soviets, though earlier he had swallowed his anti-communist bias long enough to suggest that the Bolsheviks should adopt his Gnostic Mass as a State religion ("The Russian temperament demands something in the nature of spiritual debauch," he explains in a letter). In Berlin Crowley had distinguished himself for his anti-Red militancy, and in doing so had become a hero in the eyes of his wealthy disciple Karl Germer. Crowley was out motoring with Germer one day when the latter's open-top Mercedes was blocked by a column of communist youths marching under red banners. Germer describes what happened: "The Beast, springing to his feet with a superb gesture, gave the order to charge. My chauffeur, a hard-bitten soldier of the *Reichswehr*... stepped on the gas... Realizing from the light in the Beast's eyes that he meant business and halted by the roar of the rushing engine of destruction, the ruffians broke and fled."

Crowley had not been friends with Gerald for long before he saw his opportunity to cover himself with glory in the eyes of the Special Branch as a spy. For Gerald, of course, could not keep quiet about his communist connections, but boasted of his influence with the Comintern through its Berlin boss Willi Muenzenberg. Late in 1931, super-spy Crowley's strategy was directed towards persuading Gerald to come and live with himself and Frau Busch as a paying guest. Once Hamilton was installed under his roof, Crowley would be able to report on his movements, or so he reasoned. To Gerald, who was virtually under a state of siege from his creditors at the Derfflingerstrasse apartment, the offer appeared attractive, especially as Frau Busch was an excellent cook ("Hamilton starving!" Crowley exults in his diary entry for December 29th). Before Gerald could make up his mind, however, an incident occurred which considerably dampened his desire to become a part of the Crowley ménage.

The incident is recorded in Crowley's diary for December 15th as follows: "Bill went to kitchen, I to study. Suddenly she walked in on me and stabbed me with the carving knife. She then became violent. I had to hold her down. So bled till Marie [the landlady] got a doctor, about two hours later." Crowley had been stabbed below the shoulder blade, the knife missing an artery by millimetres, he claimed. Afterwards he tried to make light of the matter, writing to Brother Volo Intelligere [Gerald Yorke], "Surely a lady has a right to stab a pal in play." But it was no laughing matter to Gerald, who had dinner with Crowley and his lady-love shortly after the stabbing. Gerald was "totally incredulous when told of the stabbing, and made quite ill when he pictured the blood", Crowley notes in his diary, adding, "This is all his complex – homosexuality and pacifism."

Crowley recovered sufficiently to celebrate Christmas in high style, with Gerald, Karl Germer, Christopher Isherwood, and Stephen Spender as his guests. Bill was in fine form, too, threatening the Beast with whatever kitchen implements came to hand. The climax of the Christmas dinner was like the scene in *Alice* when the cook goes berserk in the Ugly Duchess's kitchen and starts hurling objects ("the fire-irons came first; then followed a shower of saucepans, plates, and dishes. The Duchess took no notice of them even when they hit her…"). Gerald himself was saved from possible mishap by the presence of one of Britain's leading young poets. "I remember Stephen Spender… interposing his great height between me and a flying missile," Gerald records, adding that Crowley "alone was serenely unconscious of anything untowards happening."

Despite misgivings, Gerald moved in with Crowley early in January 1932, and soon found himself embroiled in domestic drama. One wintry night Gerald returned to the flat late to find the fire had gone out and Bill was lying on the floor stark naked. When he roused Crowley to enquire if Bill was sick, the latter roared, "What, hasn't that bitch gone to bed yet?" Whereupon the Beast kicked her, the Scarlet Woman sprang up wild-eyed, and Gerald ran for the doctor as the two resumed their struggle. When the medic arrived, he gave Bill a shot in the arm to calm her, while Crowley upbraided Gerald for having incurred the expense of the doctor's visit. On another occasion Gerald came back to find Bill drugged and trussed up like a Christmas turkey, with a "Do Not Touch" note in Crowley's handwriting pinned to her clothing.

Isherwood made the mistake of introducing Crowley to the Cosy Corner bar. Boasting "I haven't done anything like this since I was in Port Said," the Beast "walked up to a very tough-looking youth in an open shirt, standing by the bar, and scratched the boy's chest deeply with his nails"; "Only a sizeable gift of money succeeded in restraining the boy from beating him up on the spot." Crowley was drugging himself heavily with morphine during this period, and was perhaps not fully responsible for this and for another incident which is recorded in his diary for February 29: "A really wild night at Maens [a Berlin nightclub]. I bust up the whole café over a Jew who would wear his hat. I disliked the shape." When a month later the Beast himself was beaten up in the street by Storm Troopers it may have seemed to some as though a poetic justice was in operation.

*

Now that he had Gerald under observation, Crowley was alarmed by what he saw as his paranoia getting the better of him – the irony is that it was the Beast himself who was accustomed to strike terror in the hearts of his disciples, employing curses and incantations to this end. For example, in the case of Norman Mudd, the Master cursed him as a "traitor", predicting that he would die "by water and the rope". Some years later the renegade Mudd obliged by drowning in the sea with a rope round his neck.[17]

Now the tables were turned, and Crowley spent sleepless nights wondering what his guest would be getting up to next. With the Comintern behind him, Gerald's whammy was clearly more potent than Crowley's "Fiery Trigons and Aquatical Trigons".[18] Crowley's fears fed on distrust of Gerald over money matters. For inevitably Gerald was drawn into a scheme to con Frater Volo Intelligere, Crowley's English disciple Gerald Yorke, out of £500, which was to be paid in six monthly instalments. Brother V.I. was to put up the money on

---

17 Norman Mudd, a mathematician and something of a lost soul, came from modest Manchester origins and won a scholarship to Cambridge. He had been one of Crowley's most earnest disciples, but they fell out and in 1934 he drowned himself in the sea, his bicycle-clipped trousers filled with stones. The rope seems to be a myth. Crowley's characteristic comment was "I feel sure that he must have left a long, elaborate mathematical proof as to why he had to do this." [Ed.]

18 Cullen's allusion is to Congreve's *Love for Love* (1695), Act II Scene V, and the speaker is the superstitious old astrologer Foresight. [Ed.]

the understanding that it would be used to finance an edition of the Master's magical writings. But no sooner had Gerald departed for London to sell the idea to the intended victim than Crowley began to entertain doubts. "Hamilton seems the sort of man that might pull off a deal for a million and go reasonably straight, but at the same time capable of pawning his best pal's overcoat during a cold snap," as Crowley expressed it in a letter to Brother V.I. himself.

Crowley had been using the I Ching to work out his relationship with Gerald, and, after casting the yarrow stalks, had come up with the symbol "IX Hsiao Khu", meaning "Very good after preliminary struggles. But it is not permanent. If good luck… turns to bad, don't try to keep on." Early in 1932 it looked as though this turning-point had been reached. Gerald's sexual morals did not cause Crowley to turn a hair. After all, the Beast had indulged in almost every form of sex. No, it was Gerald's business ethics, or lack of them, which shocked Crowley. "I wouldn't trust H to push any honest project," he confides to Brother V.I. "All he wants is a 'coup': 50–50 (if you can get your share) and a quick get-away. I vomit. I repeat: I only tolerated the animal in hopes of helping England against communism. *Genug*!" ["Enough!"]

In the last sentence the Beast touched on the real source of his fear: Crowley was afraid that Gerald would discover that he was being spied on. Specifically, the Master was fearful that Brother V.I., whom Gerald had been seeing in London, might unwittingly spill the beans. "If Gerald should even suspect that I have any relations with [Carter] beyond pulling his [Carter's] leg, there would be work for you within a week or two with the embalmer," Crowley warns the patient V.I. "So please avoid discussing my politics, or, if forced to do so, say that you regard me as at least 80% Bolshevik." Again, in the same letter, he writes "You can talk freely to Hamilton about my notions of the Law of Thelema... Only avoid politics like poison. He thinks that I want to use the TS [Theosophical Society] to help communism. Encourage that idea."

By the time V.I. was due to arrive in Berlin on a visit Crowley had worked himself up to the pitch where he believed that his flat had been bugged, presumably by the OGPU, on Gerald's orders. "Be even more careful when you arrive," he cautions. "On no account talk about anything that might in any way be serious until we have had a long private talk together in the open air. *Be bloody careful*!" [Crowley's emphasis]

Crowley must have been steaming open Gerald's letters, for by March 27 1932 he had discovered that Gerald was a double agent. "H (I am pretty sure) has sold out to the French Secret Service," he writes to his disciple in London. "This may make my relations easier or harder with [Carter] – can't tell till I see Ham." Shortly afterwards Gerald moved out of the Crowley flat. "We decided not to have him live with us. Whether as a friend or as an enemy, he will be easier to deal with if he is not in the house." "Be careful, please," Crowley cautions, "not to assume that any letter or telegram from him has our approval. Also, in case of telegrams from me or Bill, we shall not (in future) sign Crowley, 666, Bill, etc. but the initials of the last five words of the telegram itself. Never forget for one moment that H is capable of getting us £100,000, or doing us out of a fiver."

Crowley's paranoid fears came full circle in September 1932 when he broke with Brother V.I., who had begun to suspect that the money he sent to Berlin was being used to subsidize the Beast's drug habit rather than his collected works. When the rupture occurred Crowley, in a spasm of vindictiveness, turned to Gerald and asked the latter to put his whammy to use to discipline the recalcitrant disciple: would Gerald please arrange with his Soviet masters to have Brother V.I., who was on the verge of fleeing to China in an effort to escape the Beast's clutches, removed from the Trans-Siberian Express? Crowley wanted him yanked off the train so that he could be returned to London to face a suit for £15,000 damages alleging breach of contract. Loathe to disabuse Crowley about the extent of his powers, Gerald blandly replied, "As to the ex-adept now on his way to the Middle Kingdom, I have duly taken the steps you wished me to take."

*

But before anything happened Willi Muenzenberg took pity on Gerald, and removed him from Berlin. Specifically, Willi arranged for Gerald to accompany a delegation headed by the distinguished writer Ludwig Renn on a fact-finding mission to Ruthenia in the Carpathian mountains, where half a million peasants were slowly starving. Gerald was supposed to act as press officer for the Renn deputation, using his journalistic contacts to get them maximum publicity. But it was as much to rescue Gerald from his creditors as from the flying crockery of Frau Busch that Muenzenberg acted.

The bulk of Ruthenia's population were descendants of Ukrainians who had fled to Eastern Czechoslovakia at the time of Ivan the Terrible, and who had since made their living felling trees. "This province had belonged to Hungary before the Versailles Treaty," Gerald points out, "but… had been lapped off Hungary and added to Czecho-Slovakia, with the most disastrous economic and social results." Notably the customs barrier between the two countries prevented the woodcutters from selling timber to Hungary, their traditional buyer. The Czech government had done nothing to alleviate the resulting hardship because the woodcutters' loyalty was suspect, having retained a strong fellow feeling for the forty-five million Ukrainians of the Soviet Union.

With Gerald handling the press relations, the Renn deputation, which comprised a woman senator, several doctors, and journalists, left Prague en route to the capital of Ruthenia early in March 1932. As their train snaked its way in and out of Germany, Hungary, and Romania, they began to appreciate the havoc created by the Versailles carve-up. Finally they had to leave the train and travel for seven hours by bus over roads pocked with holes.

Gerald found Ludwig Renn to be "an ideal companion on this most difficult journey", as he records. A Saxon aristocrat by birth, Renn, whose real name was Arnold Vieth von Golssenau, had gone over to the communists as a result of his experiences in the 1914–18 war, from which he had emerged a captain; post-war disillusionment is the subject of his novel *Krieg* and of its successor *Nachkrieg*, which became bestsellers. As the deputation lurched by bus through the Carpathian mountains Gerald found Renn's "patience and gentleness, besides his knowledge of Russian, were often most soothing".

Once arrived at Uzhorod, the capital of the Ruthenian province, there was the question of accommodation. Visiting the capital a few years later, a British journalist reports that in Uzhorod's premier hotel, which boasted twenty bedrooms, the bed sheets were of a "grubby, grey tint", while the towels looked as though "recently used for polishing black boots". As for the food, it was served "dimmed and blurred, like an old painting under its varnish, by the grease which submerged everything". One can imagine the effect such amenities would have had upon Gerald, with his love of gourmet cooking and his obsession with personal hygiene. Fortunately, his attention was distracted by the pitiable condition of the Ukrainian women and children whose only nourishment was bread made from bran and half-rotten potatoes, and who walked barefoot in the snow.

The deputation toured the region for six days, after which they returned to Prague and held a press conference. At this conference Gerald talked as much as Renn, and was as widely quoted. The story got a good play not only in *Rudé Právo*, the communist newspaper, but in the *Prager Tagblatt*, which identified Gerald as "a descendant of an aristocratic family", who had been until 1914 "in the British diplomatic service", and more recently "general representative of *The Times* for Germany and Austria". Gerald then telephoned the story to the Vienna correspondent of the *Daily Express*, which ran it on March 12 under the bold headline LAND OF DYING PEOPLE: FAMINE IN CARPATHIA. Describing Gerald as "an ex-official of the British Foreign Office", the *Express* reporter quoted him as saying, "I have seen famine in India and China, and was in Germany during the starvation blockade of 1918; never have I seen hunger and want so appalling."

The official reaction was swift. In an interview in the *Prager Presse*, Dr Slavik, the Minister of the Interior, sought to denigrate the Renn deputation by pointing out that it had spent only six days in the province "escorted by a number of well-known communists". The Czechs had done more for Ruthenia in one year than the Hungarians in ten, he said. Further, "the distress, which is largely due to ignorance, a low standard of culture, and alcoholism, cannot be eliminated in a few generations."

Joseph Addison, the British Ambassador at Prague, in a report to the Foreign Office, grudgingly admitted that the

Renn-Hamilton press conference had "focused the attention of the whole country on the Ruthene Territory and forced the Government to give immediate consideration... to the problem of alleviating the distress there". Muenzenberg, for his part, had reason to be proud of his protege. Gerald had indeed achieved maximum publicity. Willi was in need of all the cheer he could get, for in the March 13th Presidential election Hitler had polled eleven million votes to Hindenburg's eighteen million, thus doubling the Nazi vote, and leaving the communist Thaelmann, with five million, trailing as a poor third.

As for Ludwig Renn, shortly before Hitler came to power he was to be arrested for "literary treason", then amnestied, only to be arrested again. He would escape to Spain to command the famous Thaelmann Battalion in the Spanish Civil War, and later became Chief of Staff of the XI International Brigade. It only remains to be added that he did not reciprocate the esteem in which Gerald held him. When I contacted him in East Berlin shortly before his death, the 89-year-old Renn told me "I never trusted [Hamilton's] tales and his left-wing sympathies. In Berlin he probably played a double game..."

Eight

August 1932: The World Congress Against War

A tiny hotel room in Amsterdam on one of the hottest nights of the year, with the queasy smells of garbage and diesel oil floating up from the canal, is scarcely conducive to clear thinking. The room's occupants – four men and a woman – could only hope that the electrical storm which had been threatening all day would break and clear the muggy atmosphere. Meanwhile, in deference to the heat, the men – chosen from among the British delegates to the World Congress Against War – had removed their jackets and draped them over the backs of their chairs. The woman, who was from Hungary, wore a sleeveless dress and perspired freely, much to Gerald Hamilton's distaste.

On the face of it, their task was simple; to translate from German into English the manifesto adopted that afternoon by the congress. However, the translation had to be "as rigidly exact as the Athanasian Creed", in the words of Claud Cockburn, who was there to give it the popular touch. Then there was the woman from Buda (or was it Pest?) whose capacity for creating difficulties appeared to be limitless. Because her German was letter-perfect she supposed that her command of English was even more masterful, a proposition vigorously contested by Evelyn St Loe Strachey. "*Nein, nein,*" Strachey shouted at her, "you cannot translate *demagogischer Mystizismus* literally into English – not without causing a red mist to rise and float before the eyes of the reader."

If anyone should know about such matters it was tall, dark, stoop-shouldered Strachey, who looked as though he had stepped from an El Greco canvas. Strachey had already gained a reputation as a popularizer of Marxist thought. His forthcoming book *The Coming Struggle for Power* would become a classic, read by well-intentioned ladies under the hair-dryer and, in its 3/6 paperback edition, finding a place in the rucksack of many a British volunteer setting out to fight for the Loyalists in Spain.

This left only Gerald Hamilton's presence to be accounted for. Certainly his literary ability had no part in it. His writing style was as baroque as his speech and would prove a hindrance, rather than a help, to the translators. He was there as Willi's protege, perhaps, since Willi, as Comintern boss, was running the Amsterdam show.

*

Writing about the Amsterdam congress later Willi was to draw a parallel between it and the congress he had attended in Basle in November 1912. That was two decades earlier, when the leaders of European socialism were more confident of their ability to halt the spread of the war then raging in the Balkans. Bareheaded, Jean Jaurès had walked through the streets of Basle on his way to the cathedral, flanked by those triumvirs of German socialism, Karl Kautsky, Rosa Luxembourg, and August Bebel. With the cathedral carillon ringing in his ears, Jaurès had mounted the pulpit and in words that seemed graven on stone invoked the spirit of the bells:

> *Vivos Voco*: I call on the living to resist the monster which would ravage the land. *Mortuos Plango*: I weep for the countless dead, now buried in the east, whose rotting stench fills us with remorse. *Fulgura Frango*: I will harness the thunderbolts of war now breaking across the skies.

The thunderbolts, however, had not been harnessed. Now, two decades later, the monster was set once more to ravage the land, and there was little the two thousand delegates could do to stop it.

Later, more than one delegate was to confess to an eerie feeling of being turned around so that they were facing the wrong targets, for which manoeuvre the presidium, packed by the communists, was held to blame. Instead of pointing the delegates in the direction of the greatest menace, Hitler and his brown-shirted followers, the speeches and resolutions diverted attention to the defence of the Soviet Union "whose very existence constitutes… a hope and example to exploited peoples". In place of calls for the broadest possible unity against Japanese aggression, the RAI Gebow rang with catcalls aimed at the "social fascist" leaders of the Second International who had boycotted the congress in France, Denmark, and Switzerland.

Finally, the congress had cobbled together a manifesto which placed the blame for war on "the conflict of imperialist ambitions", declared that mankind's future "lay at the mercy of diplomatic disagreements, political crimes and frontier incidents", and, as a sop to the German revisionists, condemned the Treaty of Versailles for having "saddled Germany with war guilt". It was with this manifesto that the four occupants of the hotel room grappled in an effort to translate it into an English readily accessible to a tabloid reader.

*

Inside the room, that task was going anything but smoothly, with Strachey still arguing the toss with the Hungarian woman as to how certain of the manifesto's key phrases should be translated. Finally, in desperation ("I couldn't bear the heat and the argument any longer") Gerald whipped off his wig and sat dandling it upon his knee, a gesture designed to create a diversion as much as anything else. This brought the squabbling to an abrupt halt. "Good God," exclaimed Strachey, "you're as bald as an egg," to which Gerald, drawing himself up with dignity, replied, "I think you'd be sorry to eat an egg which has as many hairs on it." Cockburn was possibly alone that night in sensing that there was something not quite kosher about Gerald, whose presence, Cockburn writes, "introduced into the proceedings a peculiar flavour of somewhat sinister farce… [like] some curious ingredient in a curry".

It was only much later that Cockburn was able to identify that ingredient and to recognise that on the night in question Gerald had been acting as a double agent, "or at least marking time among the communists while preparing to act as an agent of a French armament manufacturer". Cockburn was wrong in one respect. Rudolf Stallman, to whom Gerald had been sending full reports on the Amsterdam congress, dabbled in mining shares, not armaments, though he used La Franco-Coloniale Financière chiefly as a blind for espionage on behalf of French intelligence.

When the electrical storm which had been threatening finally broke over Amsterdam the next morning it was as nothing to the political storm which broke over Berlin: Willi Muenzenberg, who had travelled all night by train, arrived in the Prussian capital in time to cast his vote in the Reichstag, where he was a communist deputy, against the election of Hermann Goering as Reichstag president, but in vain – Goering was swept into office. Now the Reichstag would be dissolved, and there would be fresh elections. Hitler's advent to power was only five months away.

*

None scampered before the storm faster than Gerald, who returned to Berlin determined to switch political alliances and ingratiate himself in right-wing and nationalist circles. Irrationally, he blamed Willi Muenzenberg for having let him down; for Gerald, against his better judgment, had allowed himself to be persuaded by Willi's infectious optimism. He had found himself half-believing in the latter's vision of a workers' republic in which there might be a niche for an old *kulak* like himself. Now he saw that prospect lying in ruins, and Willi, whom he had looked upon as a prophet, as less than infallible.

Mr. Norris changes trains, yes, but not even Buster Keaton could have managed the death-defying leap which Gerald was required to make from one to another, considering the trains were speeding in opposite directions. But first a practice jump. On October 20 1932, less than two months after his return from Amsterdam, Gerald wangled an invitation to that miniature Nuremberg rally, the marriage of Princess Sybil of Saxe-Koburg-Gotha to Prince Gustav of Sweden, at which all the Nazi big-wigs were present with the exception of Hitler (he sent regrets).

Gerald obtained his invitation from ex-Tsar Ferdinand of Bulgaria, Foxy Ferdy, who shared Gerald's partiality for page boys in cornflower blue uniforms. Not since the 1918 armistice had so many royal has-beens been assembled under one roof as at Koburg, the Schleswig-Holstein-Sonderburg-Glucksburg crowd who looked to a Nazi victory to restore their privileges, having turned out in full force. At the wedding itself, according to Gerald, there was much jockeying for position on the part of Foxy Ferdy, who did not hesitate to use his walking-stick to assert his precedence; however the Grand Duchess Cyril of Russia one-upped Ferdy by getting herself announced as the Tsarina of All the Russias. That night there was a firework display, and four thousand brown-shirted youths marched through the streets of Koburg in torchlight procession.

Gerald realised he had left it too late, and that it would take more than a Koburg wedding for him to get into the good graces of the new masters of Germany. Crestfallen, he returned to Berlin to find that it was *sauve qui peut*. His left-wing friends were leaving the capital as though an epidemic of plague had broken out. Gerald's turn was not long in coming. "Very soon," he writes, "I received a *Vorladung* from the political police, who questioned me closely about my former activities." When Gerald produced a letter written in 1919 by Friedrich Ebert, the Weimar republic's first president, thanking him for his work with the Save the Children Fund, the Gestapo official to whom he showed it merely glanced at it. "*Das ist fur uns gerade kein Empfehlung.*" [That's just no recommendation for us]. "I felt... this new Germany was no place for me," Gerald writes.

Arthur Norris, too, had to get out of Berlin in a hurry, it will be recalled, but at least Mr Norris had his train fare. Gerald had to borrow his from John Lehmann. "Christopher Isherwood told me Gerald was in danger of arrest unless he left Berlin immediately," Lehmann explained when I spoke to him. "So I loaned Gerald enough money to get to Paris with the understanding that he would repay me when he arrived. But of course he never did." Instead Gerald persuaded Lehmann to invest the loan plus two or three hundred pounds more in one of Rudolf Stallman's bogus mining schemes. "Most of the money I never saw again," Lehmann told me.

As for Willi, he escaped from Berlin on the night of the Reichstag fire in February 1933 despite a police alert for his arrest. The day after his arrival in Paris at the Gare du Nord he had opened for business in the rue Mondétour near Les Halles, from which he later transferred shop to 83 boulevard Montparnasse. From dingy rooms at the latter address Willi proceeded to organize the world crusade against fascism, producing "popular front" committees "as a conjurer produces rabbits out of his hat", in the words of Arthur Koestler, who worked for him for a time.

At Willi's headquarters in Montparnasse Gerald met Henri Barbusse, Romain Rolland, and Ellen Wilkinson, a Labour MP who was a frequent visitor from London. Guy Burgess was another who turned up at 83 boulevard Montparnasse, according to Andrew Boyle, who writes that Guy, who was then working for the BBC, came "for secret exchanges with Willy Muenzenberg and Otto Katz, the chief manipulators of the Comintern's propaganda apparatus in western Europe".

When John Lehmann visited the Montparnasse office he found "dishevelled, overburdened political workers [who] struggled with bursting files, broken-down typewriters and a dozen different languages, Gauloises forever drooping from their mouths..." Eventually Lehmann was taken into an inner office to shake hands with Barbusse and to receive his blessing "to act as their secret correspondent in Vienna". "The idea of this work acted like an aspirin on my rentier-guilt," he concludes.

*

Gerald showed no signs of rentier-guilt nor any other kind when, in July 1933, he jumped at the chance to accompany Lord Marley, a socialist peer, and a delegation of French and Belgian anti-fascists to Shanghai as a spin-off of the Amsterdam Congress. Apart from Marley and Hamilton, the delegates were Paul Vaillant-Couturier, French communist deputy, Dr Jean Marteaux, Belgian socialist deputy, and Georges Poupy, a French writer. Ellen Wilkinson, who was to have accompanied them, had been detained in London at the last minute. Willi arranged that Gerald should act as the delegation's press secretary, arguing that since Gerald had been born in Shanghai, he must know the Far Eastern situation from inside out. Lord Marley was perhaps naïve in accepting this argument.

The Comintern's interest in the Far East in 1933 stemmed from the Kremlin assessment that war was far likelier to break out there than in Europe. Earlier Japan had walked out of the League of Nations after Japan's conquest of Manchuria had been censured. The Truce of Tangku, which China and Japan signed in May 1933, heralded an uneasy peace which the slightest incident might disturb. But Lord Marley and his delegation appeared to have been blissfully unaware of the explosive situation as they arrived at Shanghai on the French liner *André Lebon* on August 15.

Gerald, looking immaculate in his white tropicals, had his photograph taken standing alongside Mme Sun Yat-sen, widow of the founder of the Chinese republic, and afterwards gave an interview to the *South China Morning Post* in which he declared that "if a war developed in the Far East it would have a world-wide effect and be of even greater dimensions than the Great War". Carefully toeing the Comintern line, Gerald then went on to condemn the "inadequacy" of the Disarmament Conference and the "futility" of the League of Nations.

But the delegation had put its head inside a dragon's mouth. One by one, at the behest of the puppet Chinese government at

Nanking, the Greater Shanghai Municipality, the International Settlement, and the French Concession refused permission for the anti-war conference to be held within their respective jurisdictions. While the other delegates sat around dejectedly in the lobby of the Cathay Hotel, Lord Marley sailed for Japan to stir things up there, only to be refused permission to land when his ship docked at Kobe.

Meanwhile, in the Cathay Hotel bar, Gerald scraped an acquaintance with a drunken German arms dealer, who explained the ins and outs of his trade. The crates labelled "Bibles", which Gerald had seen on barges in the Whangpoo River, contained revolvers; the ones marked "Pianos", machine guns, while "Umbrellas" referred to rifles. Germany, which was not a signatory to the international arms embargo, obligingly supplied arms to everyone except the Reds, who got theirs from Kuomintang army deserters, Gerald learned. "When a prisoner is taken [by the Reds], it is quite usual for the captor not to shoot him, but to take his rifle and give him five dollars for it," the dealer explained. "He rushes back to his comrades with this unexpected gift, and the next morning hundreds, if not thousands, of rifles are brought for five dollars – expected, but not always paid." If only things had been as simple back in the twenties, Gerald thought, when he was engaged in supplying guns to the IRA.[19]

A representative of the 19th Route Army, whose soldiers had defected to the Reds, addressed the Anti-War Conference which met secretly on September 30 in defiance of the official ban. The sixty-odd delegates from various parts of China had assembled stealthily the night before, keeping vigil by the

---

19 In fact, even while travelling to Shanghai on Anti-War Congress business, Hamilton had been instructed by Soviet agent Otto Katz to supply rifles and machine guns to Vallabhbhai Patel, the anti-British "Iron Man of India": see Jonathan Miles, *The Nine Lives of Otto Katz* (Bantam, 2010) pp.127-28. [Ed.]

light of candles stuck in bottles, according to the *North China Daily News*. Lord Marley presided, and Mme Sun Yat-sen was the principal speaker at the conference itself. In a memo to his superiors in Whitehall, the British Acting Consul-General comments sourly that the visit of the European delegation had "accomplished little beyond acting as the focal point for the activities of all the local radical and communist elements".

The delegation left Shanghai aboard a Norwegian steamer early in October, returning to Europe via Vladivostok and the Trans-Siberian railway as guests of the Soviet government. En route Gerald had a close call when the coach in which he was travelling overturned in the night, pitching him out of a window. He was rescued by some Red Guards who were travelling on the same train. Characteristically, it was not the accident but the excellent food which lingered in Gerald's memory: "I have never had an opportunity before… of having caviar three times a day."

In Paris Gerald discovered to his horror that he was billed to speak at a mass meeting at the Salle Bullier on "Imperialism and Indo-China", a subject about which the French government was extremely touchy. A friend advised Gerald to absent himself from Paris for a time, so he went to Brussels, where he took a lease on a small villa in the suburb of Uccle. He remained there until the outbreak of the 1939–45 war forced him to return to London. Though he made Brussels the base of his operations, Gerald continued to work for Muenzenberg.

One searches Gerald's memoirs in vain for any mention of his having visited Malaga during the Spanish Civil War at Willi's behest, the omission being understandable perhaps in view of Gerald's later admiration for General Franco. Yet in the Foreign Office files there is a curious letter from Gerald recounting such a visit on an errand of mercy. The letter is dated February 20 1937, addressed to Viscount Cecil of Chelwood, and posted from the Palais Jamal at Fes, Morocco. In the letter Gerald congratulates Lord Cecil on a protest His Lordship has made to *The Times* against the "indiscriminate bombing" of Almeria by Franco forces, and goes on to say: "I myself have lately been helping some of the Malaga refugees to reach Morocco and was a witness of some of the most terrible atrocities that it is possible to imagine, which were committed by Franco's troops with the full approval and encouragement of the officers." The officers themselves "directed fire from aeroplanes on the wretched fugitives, who were mainly women and children", according to Gerald. "There can be no doubt," he adds, "that horrors and cruelty are the order of the day on both sides, but there can equally be no doubt that the so-called 'Whites' display a barbarity and cold-blooded cruelty that the so-called 'Reds' have not yet shown."

In later years Gerald would reverse this judgment, describing the so-called Reds as "Red murderers", and hailing Franco as "the saviour of western civilization against advancing barbaric hordes". He would go further in a letter to *The Sunday Times* in February 1958, defending the murder of the distinguished Spanish academic, Dr Jesus de Galindez, who, though no communist, had cast his lot with the Loyalist government, writing without a trace of irony, "Sometimes fellow-travellers who pretend not to be Communists, but are ready and eager to do the dirty work for their associates who are Party Members, can be more dangerous than the Communists themselves."

*

Gerald saw Christopher Isherwood from time to time when their travels brought them together. In March 1935 Isherwood had published *Mr Norris Changes Trains*, after first sending the manuscript to Gerald who was then in Paris. Gerald in fact took a proprietory interest in the novel, reporting to Isherwood, when the book was favourably reviewed, "we got a very good notice in the *Telegraph*". Mr Norris was to change Gerald's life profoundly, transforming him overnight into a legend.

His ability to incarnate the legend was severely taxed when on the occasion of Isherwood's thirty-first birthday in August 1935, Gerald played host to a number of Isherwood's friends at a luncheon party in The Hague. The group included Stephen Spender, Klaus Mann, Brian Howard, E.M. Forster, Bob Buckingham, and of course Isherwood and his German friend Heinz. Unfortunately for Gerald, a storm broke soon after the arrival of his guests, forcing them to take shelter in a prison which had been converted into a museum. "This was an emergency which demanded all Gerald's art as a host," Isherwood comments. "He had to entertain his guests without benefit of alcohol or even chairs, amidst a depressing display of antique torture instruments." Isherwood notes the various reactions: "Gerald himself sparkled with jokes [though] he had an air of nervously expecting the police to appear. Stephen simmered with sly giggles, aware of the Joke behind the jokes... Brian Howard's dark heavy-lidded keenly searching and testing eyes missed no nuance of the situation but were made restless by his need for a drink."

At lunch the group became aware two men sitting at a nearby table, who were obviously plainclothes detectives, were intent upon listening to their conversation. Nor did they succeed in shaking the two gumshoe artists that afternoon until Gerald had caught the train for Rotterdam, when the detectives disappeared in his wake.

Gerald, wearing a fur-lined greatcoat and giving off a strong scent of Lily of the Valley, which he had specially made up for him by Floris of Jermyn Street, was on the dock at Antwerp to wave goodbye to Isherwood, Spender and their partners when the quartet left for a Portuguese holiday in December. Later Gerald joined them at Sintra, where he caused a grotesque plumbing accident by trying to use a wash-basin as a bidet.

Contrary to Claud Cockburn, Gerald did not attend the famous party in Brussels on the eve of New Year's Day 1939 when Wystan Auden read rhymed toasts dedicated to friends present and absent. Auden's 'Ode to the New Year' was prefaced by an invocation to the host city:

> O beautiful city of Brussels
> With your parks and statues and *boîtes*,
> Where they really know how to cook mussels,
> And there's fucking *à gauche et à droite*.

The verse dedicated to Gerald, who was celebrating New Year's Eve in London, reflects the ambivalent attitude of the Isherwood circle towards this "darling dodo" and indicates that they were not wholly in the dark concerning the nature of his activities.

> Uncle Gerald, your charm is a mystery
> I shall not attempt to define;
> It concerns your appearance, your history,
> And your knowledge of servants and wine;
> Do you think if I summoned the waiter,
> He could tell us instantly why
> The Embassy thinks you a traitor,
> And Olive thinks you a spy?
> Now it's you that I raise my cup to,

Though I haven't the slightest idea
What on earth it is that you're up to,
I wish you a happy New Year.

Auden gave the manuscript of this poem to Jack Hewit, who was present at the party. Hewit then lent it to Gerald to copy and never got it back. In both *Mr Norris and I* and *The Way It Was With Me* Gerald quotes the stanza about himself, but leaves out the four lines having to do with him being considered a traitor and a spy.

The friends present and absent may not have realised it, but the Brussels feast marked the end of an epoch, an era of shared assumptions as well as shared guilts, of flirtations with dangerous causes that were now lost. Gerald had his first intimation of the new dispensation when, early in January 1939, arriving at the Auberge de France restaurant in London to host a dinner of the Wine and Food Society's Lucullus group, he found the restaurant picketed by demonstrators whose banners proclaimed, "We are starving and have no work." After some of the protesters had forced their way into the restaurant Gerald graciously consented to see a deputation. "I said that if any member of their party was really hungry, I would be delighted if he or she would be my guest... I then went on to try to explain that a great many of my friends spent large sums of money on buying valuable paintings. I personally had only one weakness and that was my love of food and drink." Gerald felt it was this "frank approach" which pacified his visitors, but more likely it was the news that the restauranteur had sent for the police which caused them to disperse. Gerald and his twenty guests then tucked into a banquet which included salmon that had been swimming in the Shannon that morning, and truffles which Gerald had had specially flown from the

Perigord, washed down by wines including a Chateau Lafite 1924 and an Oloroso 1845.

That same day Isherwood and Auden sailed for Manhattan aboard the French liner *Champlain*. On deck a few mornings out Christopher found himself confiding, "You know, it just doesn't mean anything to me any more – the Popular Front, the party line, the anti-fascist struggle. I suppose they're okay but something's wrong with me. I simply cannot swallow another mouthful." To which Wystan replied, "Neither can I."

*

In October 1939 Gerald received a letter from Isherwood in Hollywood retailing news of other British expatriates living there, and making some indiscreet references to German refugees who likewise had taken up residence in California; the letter, of course, was not intended for publication. Gerald promptly rushed around to the *Daily Express* and sold the letter to Tom Driberg who wrote the paper's "William Hickey" gossip column, where it duly appeared on November 27.

The letter as quoted by Driberg read in part: "The studios here are very cagey about producing anything about the war, so I am working on a Chinese story [for Goldwyn]... Huxley lives in the same street; I see him daily. Also Gerald Heard. I have got very absorbed in Yoga... I have no intention of returning to England." Referring to the anti-Nazi refugees, Isherwood claims that they are "already squabbling over the future German government"..."God help Germany if some of them ever get into power," he continues. "Others are interested apparently, in reconquering the Romanisches Café, and will gladly sacrifice the entire British Army to make Berlin safe for night-life."

Earlier Gerald had tried to sell a number of other gossip items to Driberg, including the rather stale story of Hitler suppressing that part of von Hindenburg's will in which the aged German president had called for a restoration of the Hohenzollern monarchy. Arthur Christiansen, the *Daily Express* editor, had agreed to pay £25 for the von Hindenburg story, expecting it to be supported by a wealth of substantiating evidence. When this latter was not forthcoming the Beaverbrook paper decided not to publish, whereupon Gerald put the collection of the £25 in the hands of his solicitor. In the event Gerald was happy to settle for £10. To dispel any notion that he was being greedy he told Driberg "I had to write a cheque yesterday for a trifle more than £25 for two dozen Chateau d'Yquem '21."[20]

To return to the Isherwood letter, its tone sounded flippant to Britons digging in against bomb raids, while its references to the British Army being sacrificed to make Berlin safe for irresponsible Germans smacked uncomfortably of the type of propaganda with which Lord Haw-Haw's name was later to be associated. With the publication of the letter, the anti-Auden-Isherwood campaign went into full hue and cry, with fellow-writers like Cyril Connolly and Harold Nicolson adding their two shilling's worth. Connolly, in *Horizon*, accused the two poets of opportunism in deserting "the sinking ship of European democracy", while Nicolson confessed himself puzzled that four of our most liberated intellectuals refuse to identify themselves either with those who fight or with those who oppose the battle. (He was referring not only to Isherwood and Auden, but to Aldous Huxley and Gerald Heard, who likewise were living in America.) Then in June 1940 Auden and Isherwood were mentioned by name in the House of Commons in a parliamentary question tabled by a

---

20 About £1250 today, by relative prices, or £5000 by relative earnings. [Ed.]

Major Sir Jocelyn Lucas (Conservative), who wanted to know "whether British citizens of military age, such as Mr W.H. Auden and Mr Christopher Isherwood... will be summoned back for registration and calling up in view of the fact that they are seeking refuge abroad."

Gerald's role as a catalyst in this affair was perfectly consistent with his previous record of betrayal, his earlier intervention allegedly on behalf of Isherwood's German friend Heinz being a case in point. The Heinz story has been told so fully in *Christopher and His Kind* that there is no need here to give more than a summary of it. Isherwood was twenty-seven when in Berlin in March 1935 he met Heinz, who was ten years his junior. They became lovers, Isherwood adopting a protective attitude towards the German boy which translated itself into a determination to keep Heinz out of Hitler's army. The two were on holiday in Sintra in June 1936 when Heinz's call-up papers arrived. By refusing to return to Germany for his military service Heinz automatically placed himself outside the law. A year earlier Isherwood, foreseeing that this crisis would arise, had appealed to Gerald for help, and Gerald had suggested that Heinz should acquire Mexican nationality by means of a little judicious bribery, which would necessarily be expensive. A thousand pounds was to change hands in the next two years, part of it allegedly going to various Mexican consular officials, and part of it to Furnival Salinger, the Brussels solicitor whom Gerald brought in on the deal, with Gerald's well-manicured hands in the middle.

"What the authorities were supposed to do," Isherwood explains, writing from Santa Monica in response to my query, "was stretch the regulations a bit, in return for a bribe; this made it possible for you to become a citizen of a country before you actually entered it." But in return for the thousand pounds

Isherwood was given no guarantee that the naturalization papers would be forthcoming, "or if obtained, would prove to be valid".

The tragi-farce played itself out to the bitter end. On May 12 Heinz, acting on Salinger's advice, took the train to the German border city of Trier, where Salinger was to meet him and go with him to the Belgian consulate to obtain a Belgian visa. That same afternoon they were to drive back to Brussels, where Christopher would be waiting for them. That at least was the plan. Heinz got his Belgian visa, but he was arrested by the Gestapo as a draft evader as he sought to re-enter Belgium. Isherwood hired a German lawyer to defend Heinz, and sent money to him via Jack Hewit, Christopher himself being *persona non grata* in Germany as Heinz's "corrupter". "I don't know how much money was in the packet Christopher gave me," Hewit told me, "but it was a sizeable amount."

As for Heinz, he served on both the Russian and Western fronts during the 1939–45 war, and, after surrendering to the Americans, escaped from a POW camp to go home and look after the wife he had married in 1938 and their five-year-old son. When Isherwood returned to Berlin in May 1952 he found that Heinz had become "a very solid citizen, working to support his wife and son", as he writes to Gerald adding, "I greatly admire his lack of self-pity and general calm."

In the aftermath Isherwood was inclined to exonerate Salinger, whom he refers to as "the lawyer" in his account of the episode, but his intuition told him that Gerald was guilty. "When Christopher said to himself that Gerald was somehow guilty," he writes, "what he actually meant was that Gerald was *capable* of this crime. Gerald's dishonesty… was pathological. There was no question, in his case, of the sum at stake being too small, or of the risk of losing a friend too great.

He would betray a friend without hesitation and immediately feel terrified of being found out and punished for it, in this and the next world."

From that moment onwards Isherwood harboured a strange fantasy, he tells his readers. It was of being present at Gerald's death-bed, and of kneeling beside him to ask, "Gerald, did you do it?" "If Gerald answered, 'Yes', Christopher would forgive him; if 'No', Christopher would believe him but would feel subtly disappointed."

Nine

July 1941: Interned Again

In later life Gerald never travelled without the photograph portraits of the two individuals he designated as "My Wife" and "My Husband" – Suzy Renou, whom he married at Chelsea Town Hall on April 29 1933, and Ken "Snakehips" Johnson, his lover from British Guiana. Like household gods these two in their silver frames adorned the mantelpiece of every Hamilton dwelling, Suzy looking demure like the ingenue of a 1930s musical comedy, and Snakehips in a white tuxedo with white satin facings.

That Gerald should venture into matrimony a second time need occasion no surprise. In the thirties many of his homosexual friends with left-wing sympathies married German girls to keep them out of Hitler's concentration camps. In 1935 Michael Davidson, for example, readily consented when asked to confer his British nationality upon a German girl who was considered valuable to the anti-Nazi cause, and they were married at the St Pancras Town Hall. That same year Wystan Auden married Erika Mann, eldest daughter of Thomas Mann, whose German citizenship was about to be taken from her. Isherwood was first approached by Erika, but while he felt "honoured, excited, amused", he passed the proposition along to Auden, who wired back, "delighted". Auden in turn persuaded another of their circle, John Simpson, to marry Erika's German actress friend, Therese Giehse, with Auden wearing a carnation and standing in for the bride's father. "After all, what are buggers for?" he is often quoted as saying.

There was nothing selfless or altruistic about Gerald's marriage to Suzy Renou, however. With Gerald, it was strictly cash on the nail. Suzy was Rudolf Stallman's mistress and seven months pregnant when Gerald married her. "A more solicitous fiance than Gerald was never seen," writes Claud Cockburn, who apparently attended the marriage ceremony at the Chelsea Town Hall. "He would scarcely let Susie [sic] cross Sloane Square for fear she might be bumped by some vehicle," he adds, quoting Isherwood, who served as Gerald's best man, as saying, "Well, it's natural. There are several thousand quid for Gerald in that girl's belly." How many thousand quid is anybody's guess. Gerald told Arturo Ewart that he asked for a marriage settlement of £20,000 and got it, but this sounds like a Hamilton exaggeration. Stallman, on the other hand, was a wealthy man, thanks to a lifetime of crooked dealings. Two months to the day after her marriage Suzy gave birth to a son, whom Gerald recognised as being his own. In due course the child was baptised Francis Gerald Rodolphe Hamilton, the "Rodolphe" being a reminder of the child's real paternity.

Apart from any marriage settlement, the match was to prove decidedly to Gerald's advantage. Thus at his public examination in bankruptcy in 1941 Gerald claimed that his financial troubles had started when the Nazis invaded France and Gerald's income from his wife had consequently been cut off. Up to that time he had been living on the £600 yearly allowance made to him by Suzy, who was "a very rich woman", with a house in Paris and "a large estate" at Beauvallon in the south of France, he told the examiner.

Suzy became a useful counter in Gerald's battle with his cousins, the Haltons, who took him to Chancery Court in the early 1950s in an effort to break the trust fund set up by Gerald's Aunt May for his benefit (the trust would devolve to the Haltons if they could prove that its terms had been violated). The Chancery action precipitated a blizzard of affidavits dealing with such questions as Gerald's sexuality, whether or not he was the father of Suzy's son, and whether by marrying a Catholic he had forfeited his right to the trust. The court action was dropped only after it had been allowed to drag on for more than five years, and the legal expenses incurred by the Haltons threatened to gobble up any estate they might have hoped to inherit.

Suzy remained loyal to hubby throughout these legal battles. Gerald for his part was genuinely fond of her, as is evident from the prominent place her photograph occupied on his mantepiece. And when Gerald died "Mme Hamilton, veuve" made just one last, brief appearance to claim his estate, only to discover that it was non-existent.

*

As for Ken "Snakehips" Johnson, he had come to London from British Guiana and studied medicine, but soon abandoned it for jazz. In 1940 when Gerald first met him, Snakehips had formed one of the best dance bands in Britain with Yorke de Souza on piano, Carl Barriteau on clarinet, and Leslie Hutchinson on trumpet, and they were playing the Café de Paris in Piccadilly Circus.

It would be difficult to imagine two more different personalities. Ken, who was Gerald's junior by twenty years, was never more at home than when sitting in on some all-night jam session, which Gerald would have abominated because of the smoke and the noise (Gerald was tone deaf, and the only person I talked to who can remember having heard Gerald sing is Ivor Powell, who tells me Gerald on one occasion gave an off-key rendition of an American ditty entitled 'The Iceman was a Nice Man'.) But Ken, like many others, was amused by Gerald's Edwardian airs and malicious anecdotes, and considered him to be "a real cool cat"; while Gerald, for his part, undertook to educate Ken's palate in the mysteries of wine ("I can conceive no greater pleasure than that of instructing a willing pupil in the glories of a worthwhile cellar," as Gerald expresses it).

The two set up house together, first at 91 Kinnerton Street, near Belgrave Square, then, when the bombs began to fall on London, at a Thames-side cottage called "Little Basing" at Bray in Berkshire. It was Ken's love of the river and of sailing, as much as the desire to get away from the Blitz, which dictated the choice of Bray. After he had finished at the Café de Paris Ken would motor down to the cottage, arriving at two or three o'clock in the morning. He would be out on the river the next day until late afternoon, when it was time for him to set off for London.

Night after night the Café de Paris was packed, the khaki and navy-blue uniforms of the armed services outnumbering more formal dinner jackets on the dance floor. The fact that the Café de Paris billed itself as "the safest restaurant in London", its dance-floor being located forty feet underground, had much to do with its popularity. One writer describes it thus: "You walked off Coventry Street out of the black-out and, suddenly, you emerged in the pink-and-plush atmosphere of a pre-war nightclub."

It was a few minutes before 9.30 on the night of Saturday March 8 1941 when Ken, tall and elegant in his white evening clothes, and with a gold bracelet Gerald had given him dangling from his wrist, walked to the front of the bandstand. As band leader, Ken played no instrument. Instead, with an ivory baton in his hand, he danced, undulating to the rhythm of the music in the manner which had earned him the nickname "Snakehips". The band started to play "Oh, Johnny", and with the first bars of this 1941 hit song people put down their drinks and began to flow down the curved staircase from the balcony onto the dance floor.

> Oh Johnny, Oh Johnny, how you can love
> Oh Johnny, Oh Johnny, heavens above...

Suddenly, having crashed down the ventilation shaft of the building above, a bomb exploded on the dance floor. Among the eighty-four bodies pulled from the nightclub's smoking ruins was that of the manager, Danish-born Martin Poulsen, who used to assure patrons "It's the safest restaurant in London", and Ken Johnson, who had been decapitated.

Early on Sunday morning Gerald was awakened by a telephone call from the police in London asking him to go to the mortuary in Lupus Street, near Victoria Station, to identify Ken's body. "Again that awful feeling of nausea which I had felt when France fell, and again the sensation of the ground slipping from beneath my feet," he writes. This is Gerald's only recorded comment on Ken's death; yet in the Birthday Book, which was as sacred to Gerald as the Bible, among the anniversaries which he observes – those of Charles I, Mary Queen of Scots, and Roger Casement – is enshrined that of Ken Johnson, March 8 1941.

*

Gerald stayed on at Bray after Ken Johnson's death, but that event heralded a succession of mishaps which added up to what Gerald describes as the unhappiest year of his life. To begin with, thieves broke into his Kinnerton Street house while Gerald was at Bray, and looted his wine cellar of vintage burgundies, clarets and champagnes, and some bottles of 1906 Chateau Mouton Rothschild with which he had been hoping to celebrate V-E Day. Gerald hurried up to London in a rage, and took a room at the Alexandra Hotel. That night the hotel received a direct hit, and Gerald was one of the lucky few to crawl from the wreckage (the same raid gutted the House of Commons, and damaged Westminster Abbey and the British Museum).

Gerald must have had the feeling of history repeating itself when two months later he was arrested "for acts prejudicial to the public safety" and interned in Brixton prison under Clause 18B of the Defence of the Realm Act. The unhappiest year closed with the death of Frank Souter, who cut his son off in his will without even the proverbial trouser button. Instead, Gerald's father left his entire estate, proved at £437,697, to Gerald's Aunt Helena "Dolly" Souter.

*

Gerald's arrest and internment as a result of what he called "My Peace Bid" must rank as one of the most bizarre episodes in a bizarre existence. It was one which can best be summarized as a five-act extravaganza, whose cast included:

Monsignor Barton-Brown: a loud-mouthed Yorkshireman with a taste for port wine, a face the colour of his purple soutane, and the eccentricities of a Cardinal Pirelli.

The 12th Duke of Bedford: a dotty peer whose hobbies included birds (he kept a pet owl at Woburn Abbey), insects (he fed steak to his favourite spider), peace, and monetary reform.

Cardinal Maglione: Secretary of State to Pope Pius XII.

The 10th Duke of Berwick and Alba: Spanish Ambassador at the Court of St James.

Dr. George Kennedy Allen Bell: Bishop of Chichester.

In addition, the comedy featured in walk-on parts such notables as David Lloyd George; Rudolf Hess, No. 3 Nazi; Detective-Inspector G.G. Smith of Special Branch, Scotland Yard: the Mother Superior of the Little Company of Mary Convent, on Sudbury Hill, Harrow; and the de-coding clerk of the Spanish Embassy.

Act One

Time: summer 1940. The scene: Visitation Lodge of the Catholic convent on Sudbury Hill where Monsignor Barton-Brown is chaplain. The port-loving monsignor, who keeps crates of the stuff under his bed, listens patiently as his old friend Gerald Hamilton pours out his fears and apprehensions, now that the phoney war had turned into a real one. "I feared Russia and felt that England and Germany should be allies," Gerald explains, adding, "So I moved from thoughts in World War I of 'Save the Children' to thoughts in World War 2 of 'Save the World', and though by no means seeing myself as a Saviour, I did see myself as a man with an idea." The idea? To turn the war around so that England and Germany are fighting Russia and not one another. "I realised the impossibility of bringing this about except through a powerful catalyzing agent in the form of the Vatican."

Act Two

Time: shortly after the foregoing. Scene: Spanish Embassy, Belgrave Square. The Man With An Idea renews his acquaintance with the 10th Duke of Berwick and Alba, reminding H.E. of his, Gerald's, long friendship with Queen Ena, and how he had been received at court as a representative of the Save the Children Fund. Gerald has a favour to ask. There is this little peace plan of his which he would like to transmit to Cardinal Maglione for the eyes of the Holy Father. The British censor's office had refused him permission to communicate directly with Rome. Would H.E. mind awfully slipping his letter to Cardinal Maglione into the Embassy's diplomatic pouch? Gerald was vague as to the nature of his peace proposals, except to say they provide "that the integrity of the British Empire should be respected". In the event, "Telegrams were exchanged and I found myself embarked on a course of action which might have changed the History of the World," as he modestly remarks.

Act Three

Time: early spring 1941. Scene: the Bishop's Palace, Chichester, where Dr Bell is entertaining Gerald and the 12th Duke of Bedford. "The late Duke of Bedford was very enthusiastic about my attempts to establish contact [i.e. with the Vatican] with a view to a possible peace," Gerald claims, adding that the Duke was in touch with Bishop Bell and "a meeting was arranged between the three of us."

Act Four

Time: May 1941. Scene: a lonely glen near Newton Stewart in Scotland where the Duke of Bedford has a fishing lodge, and where Gerald is staying as the duke's guest. There is a news flash on the wireless that Rudolf Hess, Hitler's deputy, has just been arrested after parachuting on to the Duke of Hamilton's estate. "I had met Hess in Germany before the war," Gerald observes, "and I have no doubt in my mind that he, although not a Catholic himself, had heard of my plans, and... hoped for an opportunity for Peace discussions with me." Obviously, Hess had simply got the wrong Hamilton. It is while Gerald is the Duke's guest that it is decided "that I should go to Ireland to continue negotiations (i.e. with the German Legation in Dublin) which had begun quite favourably". Expressed another way: "The Duke of Bedford seems to have thought Mr Hamilton might succeed where he had failed and offered to finance him to the extent of £1,000 once he arrived in Eire en route for the Vatican."

Act Five

Time: summer 1941. Scene: the same as Act One, Visitation Lodge, Sudbury Hill. Hitler's invasion of Russia in June would seem to have put paid to Gerald's scheme to turn the war around, but no – Gerald, with all that money waiting for him in Dublin, intends to get to Ireland disguised as a nun in a party of Irish nuns from the Sudbury Hill Convent. "The Reverend Mother was... used to the 'troubles' in our country," he explains, "and one nun, who was in weak health, was ready to yield her place to me. Suitable attire was found for me in the convent and it was felt that a party of six nuns, prayer books and rosaries in hand, would not be interfered with." But before Sister Hamilton could get into her suitable attire,[21] enter Detective Superintendent G.G. Smith with a posse of Scotland

---

21 Subject of a Ronald Searle cartoon, 'Sister Hamilton', in *Mr. Norris and I* facing p.149. There are further Searle cartoons of Hamilton in Richard Lane [pseud. Maurice Richardson], 'Portrait of a Fisherman in Troubled Waters', *Lilliput*, September 1948. [Ed.]

Sister Hamilton: a drawing by Ronald Searle

Yard men and a warrant for Gerald's arrest under Clause 18B of the Defence of the Realm Act. It appears that he has been betrayed by a de-coding clerk at the Spanish Embassy. On the 25 July 1941 Gerald is led away in handcuffs by Smith, who consoles him with "At Brixton, you'll be able to play tennis with Sir Oswald Mosley."

There is an optional scene omitted which has to do with an interview which Gerald "in my wild anxiety to have the war stopped" had with Lloyd George. "I was gratified by this statesman's agreement with much of what I said," he adds. However, I have examined Lloyd George's engagement diaries for the years 1939 through 1941, and can find no record of such an interview taking place.

*

Where does the truth leave off and the fiction begin? Unfortunately, Gerald's diary for 1941 is missing, so it is impossible to check his movements during this period. Nor are Gerald's various narratives of events helpful in pinning down dates. If short on dates, Gerald's narratives are long on names. How many of these people did he actually know? Certainly, Gerald and Mgr Barton-Brown were old cronies, having met first in Rome. Barton-Brown's assistance to Gerald in obtaining papal honours for various of Gerald's clients has already been touched on. In fact, Gerald exploited his friend shamelessly, as is evident when Barton-Brown begs off helping to get a further papal title for a viscount. "It is not a matter which can be effected by simply going to Rome and asking for it, even with a 'quid pro quo'," the ecclesiastic writes. "It is not like a K.S.G. *con placa*, or even the post of *Cameriere di Spada e*

Cappa. I could not really do anything very much to help."

Gerald knew Cardinal Maglione, whom he first met in 1919 when the latter was Papal Nuncio at Berne, and he knew the Duke of Berwick and Alba, to whom he once tried to sell some Constable paintings of doubtful provenance. On the other hand, there is not a scintilla of evidence to link Gerald with Bishop Bell. Dr Bell was too astute to have anything to do with any hare-brained scheme for a negotiated peace which Gerald may or may not have concocted. (Though pressed to do so by James Graham Murray, Gerald was unable to produce any draft of the peace proposals he allegedly forwarded to Cardinal Maglione). In a speech to the House of Lords as early as December 1939, Dr Bell made his position clear. "I am not a pacifist," he declared, "nor am I one of those who ask that peace should be made at any price." Courageously, throughout the war he appealed to the German churches, seeking to put an end to the conflict. As for Rudolf Hess, when asked by Robin Maugham whether he had ever met him, forgetful Gerald replied, "No, I never met him, but I always admired him." So much for the myth of Hitler's deputy trying to renew contact with Gerald when he parachuted into Scotland.

This leaves the 12th Duke of Bedford. Among Hamilton's papers are four brief notes from Bedford. The earliest, dated December 27 1944, reads: "Dear Sir, I have read with interest your letter in the *Catholic Herald*. Possibly you may care to have the enclosed as the subjects dealt with, though controversial, are of great importance." (The enclosure is missing, but his son says that in the latter stages of the war the duke became zanier and zanier, "deluging all sorts of people with a series of pamphlets, with such titles as *Don't be a Gull*; *Why Blunder On*; *The Financiers' Little Game…*") The other notes all use the salutation "Dear Sir", and are equally formal in tone. Either the duke had never met Gerald personally or, in the three or four years that had elapsed since 1941, had forgotten that he once entertained Gerald at his fishing lodge at Newton Stewart, or offered him £1,000 if he could get to Dublin en route to Rome.

All of which did not prevent Gerald from stealing the duke's clothes, so to speak. The closer one examines the farrago which Gerald puts forward as his peace initiative the more apparent it becomes that the Invisible Mender is at work once more. What Gerald has done is to stitch together two narratives, his own and that of the 12th Duke of Bedford, in the hope that the join will not show. For the duke, who was pro-Hitler, did have a peace plan. During the so-called phoney war, while Chamberlain was still prime minister, the duke (he was then the Marquis of Tavistock) wrote to Lord Halifax, the Foreign Secretary, to say that while "Ribbentrop does seem to be a decidedly unpleasant customer and Goebbels no angel either", Hitler and Goering might be managed "if handled with sympathetic imagination". Thereafter the duke visited Dublin and made contact with the German Legation there in an effort to extract some sort of assurance from the Nazis concerning the future of Poland, an assurance which could be used "to encourage the peace movement in England". Furthermore the duke was in touch with Lloyd George whom he looked upon as the nation's possible saviour. ("There is only one man to whom, by reason of his reputation and record, they [i.e. the Chamberlain government] could with any semblance of dignity, hand over the task of forming a peace government – and that is yourself.")

The man best qualified to evaluate Gerald's peace initiative is James Graham Murray, whom Gerald conned into including a brief account of it in his 1964 book *The Sword and the*

Umbrella. Primarily a study of patriots who sought to end the war at the risk of their own lives, *The Sword and the Umbrella* deals with heroes such as Count von Stauffenberg, Adam von Trott, and Captain S. Payne Best, who was kidnapped by the Gestapo on Dutch soil and dragged across the German border. In such brave company Gerald was singularly out of place, as Graham Murray realized when he came to describe the latter's escapades. "You won't like it much," Graham Murray warns, referring to his account of Gerald the Peacemaker. "All along I said I didn't want to do it because it wasn't a genuine peace move... but a piece of disguised spivvery," the "spivvery" being "to get money out of Bedford", as the author amplifies in a follow-up letter. "As a con-trick I'm not very against it, and only sorry you didn't make Ould Oirland and the lolly. But... it has an unmistakable aura of Jiggery-Pokery." Finally, Graham Murray felt that he must make his own position clear: "I must again tell you, without the slightest animus, that to me your politics are an abomination. Pro-Nazi, pro-Vichy, pro-Verwoerd, pro everything that I regard with horror."

What Gerald failed to disclose to Graham Murray was the real reason for his urgency to get to "Ould Oirland", which was to foil the receiver in bankruptcy. On December 12 1940, a petition for a receiving order in bankruptcy had been filed against "Hamilton, G (Male)", described as a "journalist", of 91 Kinnerton Street, the petition being granted the following May. Gerald's unsecured debts totalled £3,560, including two bank overdrafts; £525 worth of furniture obtained from Liberty's under a hire-purchase plan but since re-possessed; £112 in back rent on Kinnerton Street as of September 1940, when Gerald moved to Bray; £333 owing to shopkeepers in the Bray-Maidenhead area; and £70 claimed by G.A. Dunbar Axtell, whom Gerald, in disputing this debt, described as "a convicted criminal now in prison". In a "Statement of Affairs" sworn to by Gerald he listed assets totalling £2,500, including £1,250 allegedly held in an account with the Credit Anversois of Brussels, and £1,000 worth of jewellery in a safety deposit box at the same bank. Subsequently it developed that the £1,250 had vanished in thin air, or rather it had vanished in payment of debts which Gerald had left behind him when he quit Brussels for London. As for the jewellery, when the safety deposit box was eventually opened there was nothing inside but empty jewel cases.

During the five months he spent at Brixton Prison Gerald came under the influence of Sir Oswald Mosley, leader of the British Union of Fascists, just as a quarter of a century earlier he had submitted to the influence of the unseen Sir Roger Casement in that same prison. In fact, there are parallels between the Mosleyites interned during the 1939–45 war and the Sinn Feiners jailed during the First World War insofar as party discipline and morale are concerned. Just as in 1916 Eamon de Valera, locked up in Dartmoor, was undisputed boss of the Irish rebels with him there, so in 1940 Mosley's word was law among the eighty Blackshirts with him at Brixton. Shortly after Gerald's arrival he got an insight into the respect in which Mosley's followers held him when Sir Oswald's mother came to see him and the warder bawled out to the top landing, "Mosley, come down, there's a visitor for you." This set off a chorus of "Call him Sir Oswald, you bastard!"

Besides Mosley, Gerald's fellow internees in F-Wing at Brixton included Captain Ramsay, the Conservative Member of Parliament for Perth; Admiral Domville, the one-time Director of Naval Intelligence; the former Mayor of the London Borough of St Pancras; several Old Etonians; a zealot whose chief claim to fame was that he had once removed the

Mace from the House of Commons; and Cahir Healy, the Irish rebel, who was the cuckoo in this nest of fascists. Less than a fortnight after Gerald's arrival he and Healy succeeded in getting a Requiem Mass said in the prison chapel to mark the twenty-fifth anniversary of Roger Casement's execution.

Clause 18B prisoners were treated as though they were on remand, and were allowed certain other privileges, including their own furniture, food, cigarettes, and typewriters. Visitors were allowed once a week, and there was no limit to the number of letters they could send out or receive, though the letters were subject to censorship. There was a recreation ground where the internees could exercise or play games, the row of lavatories there being designated as Lenin's Tomb. (Captain Gordon-Canning's ability to lift a half-volley from his cricket bat over Lenin's Tomb earned this Old Etonian the admiration of all, being "quite as good as one over the Pavilion at Lord's" in the opinion of Admiral Domvile.)

Clause 18B internees were also allowed a drink ration of a bottle of beer per day, or a half-bottle of wine, leading to an amusing contretemps when Tom Driberg sent Gerald a bottle of Gevrey Chambertin 1916. Gerald turned livid when he discovered that this fine burgundy had been decanted into his tin mess cup. The following morning he complained to Captain Clayton, the prison governor, who thought it was the most frivolous complaint he had ever received in all his years at Brixton. "I myself can't afford to drink Chambertin 1916," he said.

On the recommendation of the Home Office Advisory Committee, which had interviewed him, Gerald was released from Brixton in January. No doubt Captain Clayton was glad to see the back of him, echoing the verdict of the MI5 official who, after hearing Gerald protest for the umpteenth time that he was neither a communist nor a fascist, remarked "I don't know what you are politically, but I do know that you're a damned nuisance." On January 2 1942, five months after his internment, Hamilton had just sat down to a game of poker with Admiral Domville and Captain Ramsay when the warder entered and tapped him on the shoulder. "Ere, 'Amilton," he said, "You're for outside."

Ten

March 1948: Business In New York

Gerald was free for just six months before being taken into custody again, this time for offences under the 1914 Bankruptcy Act. What had happened was that the Official Receiver, following Gerald's public examination in bankruptcy, had referred his case to the High Court of Justice for prosecution. May 7 1942 proved to be a highly charged day for Gerald. Arrested at 9 a.m., he persuaded the wealthy arts patron Peter Watson to put up bail, and was released in time to keep a lunch date at Frascati's with Tom Driberg.

During the brief interval he was at large, Gerald became friends with Mary Seaton who, like many before her, fell captive to his old world charm. Certainly there was nothing about Gerald to suggest a man in dire straits when, early in June, he turned up at the National Gallery in Trafalgar Square to keep an appointment with Miss Seaton. They were meeting to discuss the possibility of Gerald becoming a regular contributor to *Ridley's Circular*, a periodical for the wine and spirit trade which Miss Seaton edited. Gerald looked his usual spruce and debonair self, wearing a pearl-grey homburg and carrying a malacca cane with an agate head. "I chose the porch of the National Gallery," Miss Seaton says, "because the view from there down Whitehall was supposed to be one of London's finest, and I wanted Gerald to admire it. Anyway, we were sitting there... when suddenly Gerald turned to me and confided, 'I think you should know, dear lady, that I've been bankrupt twice. Moreover I have run up a wine bill for

£29 with Hedges and Butler, and if this is not paid by this time tomorrow I shall be in schtuck. I don't suppose, dear lady, you could drop round to Hedges and Butler and ask for an extension. I shall be eternally grateful to you if you do.' " "Well," says Miss Seaton, "how can one resist such an appeal? Not only did I get Gerald his extension, but in the end I loaned him the money to pay the bill."

On June 16 Gerald lunched at the Piccadilly Hotel with Miss Seaton and Mrs Deborah Hogg, a friend of Aleister Crowley, before setting out in Mrs Hogg's Rolls-Royce for Newington Butts, where Gerald's hearing was scheduled to take place before the London Sessions. Gerald was in a jaunty mood, having been assured by his solicitor that, in pleading guilty, the worst that could happen to him was that he would be bound over. The judge, however, took a different view, and sentenced Gerald to three months. "When Gerald followed his gaoler down the steps leading from the dock to the cells below it was a little like the last act of Don Giovanni, where the *Commendatore* summons his fellow diner to hell," Miss Seaton recalls. "One moment there was Gerald bubbling over with confidence, the next he had vanished."

This time Gerald was locked up in Wandsworth Prison, which he disliked intensely, and where as a common felon he had none of the privileges that had been accorded to him as an 18B detainee at Brixton. What is more, his arrival at Wandsworth coincided with the height of the Blitz, and the walls trembled under the impact of bombs falling nearby. "It is an extremely unpleasant sensation to be shut in a cell when a dangerous air raid is in progress," he recalled. Once he was awakened by ack-ack fire and the crash of an enemy plane being brought down on Wimbledon Common.

While Gerald was in Wandsworth a man named Gordon

Frederick Cummins, "the Black-Out Ripper", was executed. Cummins, an RAF cadet, was hanged for the murder of four women whom he strangled for the contents of their purses. On the morning of such an execution, "even the most hard-baked and callous of prisoners feels more miserable, unhappy and lonely", Gerald writes. "He is more conscious than ever… that he too is an outcast of society."

Gerald was somewhat cheered when Miss Seaton and Mrs Hogg visited him in July: "I forgot that I was clad in the coarse grey suit of a convicted prisoner… and for a few brief minutes had the illusion that I was sitting with my friends once again at the Abri Bar at the Ritz." Released from Wandsworth in August, Gerald met Mary Seaton at Brown's Hotel, and she took him to dine at Czardas. "He claimed he hadn't touched any of the prison food," she recalls. "Indeed, he looked very thin."

Gerald suffered from old lag's jitters for some time afterwards. Nearly two years later, when Gerald accompanied Sergeant Pat Kenneally to Buckingham Palace, where the latter was to be decorated with the Victoria Cross, he was extremely apprehensive. When the Lord Chamberlain asked those in Kenneally's party to stand up Gerald was certain that his prison record had been discovered. "They intend to turn me out," he whispered to Kenneally. But no, His Majesty simply wanted the sergeant to have a front row seat as befitted a hero of the North African campaign.

Gerald had met Kenneally at Ward's Irish House in London a year before the heroic incidents which resulted in him being awarded the VC. In April 1943, before the final assault on Tunis, Kenneally, who was a lance corporal with the Irish Guards, charged the enemy single-handed, firing his Bren gun from the hip, and thereby "unbalancing the enemy company, which broke up in disorder", according to the VC citation. He repeated this exploit the following day, inflicting many casualties and being wounded himself. Gerald, as a pacifist, did not approve of all this carnage, reminding Kenneally that the Germans he had killed all had mothers and fathers. When King George VI, in presenting the VC, remarked "Your family and friends must be very proud of you," the Irishman replied, "One of those with me here today considers me to be no better than a murderer."

Returning to Gerald's release from Wandsworth in August 1942, he soon afterwards moved into a studio flat at No 56 Glebe Place, Chelsea, which belonged to Sir Frederick O'Connor, the Tibetan explorer, who had retired to Tunbridge Wells. The studio was somewhat derelict, but when Gerald complained about rain coming through the roof Sir Frederick's reply was, "A drop of rain won't hurt you. You should have been with me in Tibet." When Sir Frederick died the following year, Gerald took over the lease with the Church Commissioners who owned the property, at a rental of £130 per annum. It was to be his home for the next ten years. According to Sir Francis Rose, the flat's interior exemplified Gerald's bad taste. "It was full of wrought-iron objects and bad seventeenth-century madonnas – the kind you find in third-rate antique shops."

From his release from Wandsworth until the end of the war Gerald's life continued to follow its usual switchback course. One moment he is forced to leave his fur coat *chez ma tante*, his euphemism for the pawnbroker's; the next, he is employed as a regular contributor to the 'Talk of the Town' gossip column in the *Evening News*. More important, in January 1943 Gerald found a wealthy patron in the person of G.B. Morgan, a Welsh company promoter, and had embarked upon a series of surreal adventures.

*

Gerald described G.B. Morgan as being "excessively dull", but no man could be entirely dull who was prepared to ruin himself financially in pursuit of a will-o'-the-wisp, which was the case with Morgan. Morgan's dream was to have himself made consul of a foreign country – it did not matter which country, so long as he became consul. When Gerald, who was introduced to Morgan in the Pandarus role, unfolded his plan of action, it met with Morgan's instant approval. "He touched a bell," Gerald recalls (people in Gerald's world never press buzzers, they always touch bells). "Miss Prince, his private secretary, came in, and he said to her, 'Bring me a packet of five hundred.' Turning to me, he said, 'I don't give cheques on these occasions'."

Gerald's plan had the beauty of simplicity. It consisted of wining and dining, at such expensive caravanserai as Claridges and the Ritz, various ambassadors from countries that were either Catholic (Gerald intended to make full use of Monsignor Barton-Brown), or in a state of transition (King Peter's Yugoslavia, and Chiang Kai-shek's Nationalist China, for example) – ambassadors who were virtually "spectral excellencies from phantom embassies", as one friend described them. In the execution of his plan Gerald had to contend with Morgan's business adviser, Dr Brynmar James Owen, D.Sc., who if anything was madder than his employer. Apart from being an inventor, Dr Owen was a swindler and a master forger who had defrauded both the Ministry of Agriculture and Oxford University (the latter took back Owen's honorary degree after it was discovered that he had diddled the university out of £75,000). He had served four prison sentences before meeting Morgan. Not even a padded cell could stop this misguided genius and, much later, after he had broken with Morgan, Dr Owen used the postal services to fleece the public of £1,000 while operating from inside a mental institution.

Possibly the better to cope with the vagaries of Dr Owen, Morgan gave Gerald official status by putting him on his staff. "He would say to me, 'Gerald, I want you to do a little staff work. I want you to order the dinner, and put the place names.'" The first of the dinners Gerald organised in the mad quest for a consulateship had Dr W.C. Chan, the Chinese *charge d'affaires* in London, as its honoured guest. "He spoke with great good humour and there was genuine wit," writes Gerald, doubling as gossip columnist in the *Evening News*.

On Ascension Day (chosen, one wonders, as a happy augury of Morgan's rise in the diplomatic world?) it was Monsignor Barton-Brown's turn to host a banquet for which Morgan picked up the tab. This time Their Excellencies the Ambassadors of Brazil and the Argentine, and Sir Edwin Lutyens, O.M., the eminent architect, were the honoured guests. Of Sir Edwin, Gerald recalls: "His skittish fingers were never idle; he was drawing designs on the table-cloth, on menu cards and even on the sacrosanct wine list of Claridge's... I still have the menu card on which he elevated our cheery host to the rank of cardinal with three or four strokes of his insistent pencil." A possible reason why Sir Edwin's skittish fingers were never idle was that he was bored. André Simon, the wine and food expert, who was a fellow guest on this occasion, gives the game away in writing to Gerald: "What, I think, made the Claridge Lunch so dull, especially when one thinks of what it must have cost, was the size of the table. It was much too big and there was no possible cohesion, still less sympathy, between the far-flung guests."

The climax to all this furious activity occurred on the

eve of Remembrance Day 1943, when Morgan entertained members of the Allied missions in London at the Dorchester, and had as his guests the Comptroller of the Royal Household, the Chairman of the London County Council, Count and Countess Oppersdorff, Lord and Lady Sempill, and Professor George Catlin. Mary Seaton found herself seated next to Count Oppersdorff, who bent her ear with talk of Silesia and the hunting of wild boar. "The Silesian boar itself," she says, "would have been a more entertaining companion." In an England of wartime rationing it was amazing how many distinguished people were prepared to endure tedium for the sake of *lobster timbale* and *faisan en cocotte*.

On the other hand Professor George Catlin, the political scientist, attended out of friendship for Gerald. Starting in 1943 Gerald became fast friends with the professor and his wife, Vera Brittain, who were his neighbours in Chelsea. A mutual interest in Catholicism and pacifism drew them together, and in July 1943 Vera Brittain was writing to Gerald to discuss the saturation bombing of Dusseldorf ("To let loose the forces of Nature on a helpless population seems to me like a challenge to the wrath of God"), while on New Year's Day 1944 Gerald attended a party at the Catlins' house in Cheyne Walk where the guests included Arthur Greenwood, the veteran socialist politician, and the cartoonist David Low.

As for G.B. Morgan, the only result of the dinners was a dent in his bank balance, which did not discourage him. In April 1946 Gerald was summoned to Lisbon by Morgan, who had gone there with his mistress Penelope. "It was the first time Gerald had ever travelled by air," relates Felix Hope-Nicholson. "He was so terrified by the prospect that as a precaution he distributed various scapulars and holy medals over his ample person." Gerald was met at the airport by Morgan, who cautioned him "Now, Gerald, don't forget Penny is registered at the hotel as Mrs Morgan." "Ah," the irrepressible Gerald replied, "a morganatic marriage."[22]

Though Gerald had failed to deliver a consulateship, Morgan continued to employ him on various futile errands. As late as November 1950 Gerald was in Paris conferring with Prince Talal of Saudi Arabia on Morgan business. The prince was interested in buying up a British bank and transferring its head office to Riyadh in order to escape British taxation. Morgan, who kept in touch with Gerald in Paris by telephone, writes to His Royal Highness: "Mr Hamilton mentioned the word 'partners' to me. There would, of course, be no partners, but it is essential that the Directors be people... of influence in the business and financial world... In the meantime, I am proceeding with the preliminary negotiations without disclosing your name or that of Saudi Arabia and will report to you in due course." Nothing came of these negotiations. Meanwhile, Gerald's bills at the Claridge in Paris were being paid by Prince Talal, who, however, allowed him no expense money. "Gerald was terribly put out," according to Mary Seaton. "Having no pin money, Gerald had to keep to his hotel room."

*

Along with the tragic loss of Snakehips Johnson, the deaths of three more of Gerald's friends, all of them in their seventies, occurred during or immediately after the war. Sir Frederick O'Connor, the Tibetan explorer, had died little more than a year after Gerald moved into Sir Frederick's house in Glebe

---

22 Morganatic marriage is marriage between persons of unequal rank – generally one royal – where the marriage is valid and the children legitimate, but the royal title is not passed on. [Ed.]

Place. As Sir Frederick had been raised a Catholic, Gerald decided to summon Monsignor Barton-Brown to the explorer's deathbed. "When I told Sir Frederick that he [the priest] was waiting in the dining room," Gerald writes, "he tossed his head and declared 'I don't believe in any God'. The Catholic nurse present… crossed herself devoutly and said, 'Glory be, he will have to be buried by the Church of England!' And this is precisely what happened."

Gerald was more deeply affected by the passing of another Catholic, this one a convert. Lord Alfred Douglas died on March 20 1945, aged seventy-five. Gerald had kept in touch with Bosie all through the years, and in February 1944 Bosie had sent him an autographed copy of the ode he had written to Churchill, in which he pictured the wartime prime minister "clothed with the Addisonian attributes of a God-directed angel". (In the early 1920s Bosie had served six months in Wormwood Scrubs for libelling Churchill in a scurrilous pamphlet entitled *The Murder of Lord Kitchener* in which among other things he accused Churchill, as First Lord of the Admiralty, of withholding news concerning the Battle of Jutland so that certain rich Jews, including Sir Ernest Cassel, could make a killing on the Stock Exchange.) Bosie, in his dotage, now directed his fire not at Churchill, but at the Labour members of the wartime coalition government, notably at Ernest Bevin, whose "filthy trick of sending Public School boys down the mines was going to collapse", or so he predicted to Gerald.

For the last four months of his life Bosie lived at Monks Farm, Lancing, near Hove, through the generosity of Sir Henry "Chips" Channon, then a Conservative Member of Parliament, who describes him as "pathetic… alone, poor, almost friendless". It was to Hove that Gerald proposed to take Mary Seaton to meet Bosie over lunch. "I was thrilled to bits," she recalls, "for I remembered how when I was twenty I had read for the first time 'Love like a lamp swung over all his days'. Afterwards I could never see a farmyard puddle, nor look down at the street lights from Parliament Hill in Hampstead, nor even at red and green traffic signals without saying to myself, 'See what a mass of gems the city wears upon her broad, live bosom, row on row... And in the mirror of the mire I know the moon has left her image unawares'."

As the great day approached a suspicion dawned in her mind. "Gerald dear, who is going to pay for the luncheon?" Miss Seaton asked. "Why, you are, of course, Mary dear," he replied. "Somehow grown men having lunch at the expense of a poor working girl appalled me. So I refused to go. Which was a pity, for Bosie died four months later, and I never had another chance of meeting him."

Another old friend whom Gerald had not lost sight of was Aleister Crowley, whom he encountered in wartime London from time to time, the Beast's presence usually being heralded by a strong smell of ether. One Easter Gerald stayed in a flat above Crowley's in Hanover Square. On his way to take Holy Communion at St. James's, Spanish Place, Gerald passed Crowley on the stairs, who greeted him with, "I hope your god will taste nice; you're such a bloody gourmet."

With the outbreak of the war, Crowley took to bombarding the War Office with suggestions for speeding up victory, the most macabre being one which he called Plan 241, whereby in the event of invasion Britons would pledge themselves to kill two Germans apiece before taking their own lives. The plan should be well-publicized by radio and leaflets, the Mage advised, so that the Germans, overwhelmed by the odds against them, would give way to despair. The Beast actually succeeded in getting a hearing at the Admiralty for one of his schemes.

In the early part of the war Gerald used to make over his sugar ration to Crowley, giving rise to the following note from the Mage on scarlet letter paper which illustrates his peculiar brand of wit:

I am looking forward to our solitary encounter at 6 on Tuesday. Can you sweeten it literally as well as metaphorically... for of late so many people, encouraged by your report of the deliciousness of Mrs Speller's chatamasha, have thronged my ancestral halls at the strygogemous hour of four, that my combinations of Carbon, Hydrogen, and Oxygen in the proportion of 12, 22 and 11 respectively are quantitively inadequate. Angelice, can you bring some shong-shong?

It was through the Beast that Gerald met the writer Maurice Richardson. Richardson had written something uncomplimentary about Crowley in a book review in the *Observer*, prompting Crowley to protest in a letter beginning, "My dear Mr Richardson, perhaps in the future before you pass animadversions on my character you will take the trouble to make my acquaintance", and ending with an invitation to lunch at Crowley's flat. At lunch Crowley, who had donned green plus-fours and a tartan bow tie for the occasion, got Richardson drunk on Cyprus brandy, and then sprang a surprise on him. Producing a fountain pen inscribed with the word "Baphomet" in gilt lettering, the Mage asked Richardson to write a note of apology for the slighting reference in his book review. But Richardson was too befuddled to write anything, so they agreed to meet again for lunch a week later. Richardson claims that he had every intention of writing some sort of an apology, but that a more knowledgeable friend warned him not to. "If you write any apology for what you said in print that's admitting liability," the friend warned. "Crowley will take it to a solicitor and he'll bung in a writ."

At the second luncheon the Beast was reinforced by Gerald Hamilton "in the role of consultant con-man", in Richardson's phrase. Richardson, who had already heard of Gerald, found that in the flesh Gerald's "bald head and naked face of quite exceptional ugliness [were] as unforgettable as Crowley's". With the brandy again flowing freely, Crowley adroitly brought the conversation round to Berlin and to *Mr Norris Changes Trains*, assuring Richardson that the real Mr Norris was even more vicious than he was painted. "What would you say, my dear Mr Richardson, if I in my role as magician were to produce him for you at this very table?" Whereupon Gerald tittered nervously and murmured, "Really, Aleister." "I did not let on that I knew," Richardson adds. "We went on drinking brandy until late in the afternoon," he continues. "Again I was asked to write a note of apology… Again I pleaded intoxication. I saw Hamilton shaking his head."

Crowley died at Hastings on December 1 1947 at the age of seventy-two. His last words, according to Frieda Harris who was with him at the time, were "I am perplexed". Gerald did not attend the cremation, but he did go along to a curry dinner organized by Lady Harris at the New Delhi Durbar Restaurant in Hampstead to mark the first anniversary of the Beast's death. "I didn't enjoy it very much, and came home at 11 o'clock," he notes in his diary.

"Postwar London depressed me beyond all measure," writes Gerald, who found himself totally out of sympathy with Attlee's Labour government. Sir Stafford Cripps, as Chancellor of the Exchequer, appeared to have banished gracious living for the foreseeable future. Instead, says Gerald, "It seemed to me to be an age of bottled salad dressing, dyed kippers, of snack-bars and jeans worn in public."

Postwar standards had invaded even the ecclesiastical world, according to Monsignor Barton-Brown, who writes, "The Holy Father is now cutting down the robes of Cardinals to bring them more in sympathy with the age." "This is terrible; I feel all the nice things are being sacrificed to the demon of democracy," Barton-Brown laments, in announcing that he intends to defy the decree for shorter robes which likewise applied to bishops and monsignors. "I am granted the privilege in a Brief and until my Brief is cancelled I shall continue to rejoice in a train." In the next breath, as if the two things were related, the monsignor complains that "crimes of violence are increasing, old ladies dare not go out in the streets at night".

*

In the immediate post-war years Gerald renewed his friendship with the Mosleys, spending a brief holiday with them on Jersey. It was then that the Mosleys, who were desperate to get out of Britain after their long internment in prison, but who had been refused passports by the Labour government, turned to Gerald for help.

"Gerald Hamilton helped me to perfect my French while at Brixton Prison," Sir Oswald Mosley explained when I talked to him. At Orsay, about twenty-five miles from Paris, 'Le Temple de la Gloire', as the Mosleys' chateau is called, is neo-Palladian, and was built in 1800 by Vignon, who designed the Madeleine church in Paris. It was the gift of his wife and mother-in-law to Jean-Victor Moreau, one of Napoleon's generals, to celebrate his victory at the Battle of Hohenlinden, and upon seeing it the general is supposed to have exclaimed, "*Voici le temple de ma gloire.*"

Sir Oswald Mosley, now in his early eighties, no longer looks, as he once did, like a taller, less athletic version of Douglas Fairbanks Senior, but his hair still retains some of its original colour and has not noticeably thinned. His eyes are still very alert and his laugh is an engaging one, his face breaking into many wrinkles and exposing many teeth. He has a pronounced limp, his left leg being one and a half inches shorter than the right as a result of an injury sustained in the First World War when, as a Royal Flying Corps pilot, he crash-landed on a training flight.

Lady Mosley retains her Dresden china shepherdess beauty, with pale blue eyes, and hair pulled back severely to show to advantage the classic profile which she shares with her Mitford sisters. She makes one feel at home immediately. The drawing room overlooks a small lake with swans on it, and is comfortable rather than elegant. It is full of chintz-covered chairs and tables piled with books.

Somehow the conversation soon after my arrival got around to scientists, with Sir Oswald delivering what sounded almost like a set piece. The two factors that have changed the world today, he said, are oil and the bomb. Oil may save Britain from bankruptcy; the atom bomb certainly has saved it from invasion by the Russians, in Mosley's opinion. "Politicians should cultivate scientists today as zealously as Lorenzo the Magnificent patronized artists in the Renaissance," he maintains. "When I was in politics Churchill made me a member of the Other Club, and it was there one evening that I sat next to Lindemann, who leaned over and said, 'Can you get me thirty thousand pounds – I need it to separate the neutron from the atom, and whoever can do that can blow up the world.' I had just come from a futile quest for government money to back Emerald Cunard's scheme for a national opera. I was not likely to fare better in going to the Ministry of Defence and saying, 'Look, I need thirty thousand pounds for a scientist who wants to blow up the world.' They would have thought me mad."

"Gerald's command of the French language was considerable," says Sir Oswald. "As France has always been *mon pays de bonheur*, I wanted to learn its language better. During the recreation hour each morning Gerald and I conversed in French as we circled the prison exercise yard. Later in the day I spent an hour with the Germans who were interned with us in learning German from scratch."

Sir Oswald was arrested on May 23 1940 at his flat in Dolphin Square, along with a general round-up of his Blackshirt followers; Lady Mosley was arrested a month later. After being held at Brixton for eighteen months Sir Oswald was reunited with his wife at Holloway prison, where the pair spent another two years in custody, Mosley being released only after he had developed phlebitis which required urgent medical care. As an autodidact, Sir Oswald's time in prison was not entirely wasted. "I read in French and German, as well as in English; learned to relate Shakespeare to Racine, Corneille to Schiller," he says. "Brixton was my college."

It was Sir Oswald's relationship with Gerald post-Brixton which interested me the most, however. When Gerald offered to get the Mosleys passports from one of the South American countries, they encouraged him. "We thought it would be a good joke on the Home Office," Sir Oswald explains. "It would make the Attlee government look silly." Gerald was given his expenses, but Mosley was vague as to how much money was involved. "He never had any great sums from us," Sir Oswald asserts. "It was never a question of X pounds." But, as was the case with Isherwood's friend Heinz, the negotiations were stretched out for some two years. In fact, Gerald's promises to the Mosleys smack of his earlier undertaking to Isherwood to get a Mexican passport for Heinz, for of course Gerald was in no position to deliver, even if he had wanted to. At one point Gerald brought in the redoubtable Monsignor Barton-Brown, getting the bibulous priest invited down to the Mosleys' house at Crowood, near Ramsbury, Wiltshire. Here Gerald gave his hosts to understand that this singular churchman had considerable clout with various Latin American legations. In the event the Mosleys, having decided to circumvent the Labour proscription by buying a yacht and setting sail for Spain, were suddenly issued passports on the eve of their departure from England in June 1949.

Before this, another episode had occurred which involved Gerald. In February 1948 Sir Oswald made a determined effort to stage a political comeback by launching the Union Movement, which had as its slogan "Europe a Nation", and which envisaged a European assembly elected by universal suffrage. But the movement for European unity was decidedly premature so far as the British electorate was concerned, besides which it contained certain features which were disturbing. Mosley's Europe, for example, included Africa, which was to be divided into black and white areas along apartheid lines, and the development of which was to be carried out by a joint-stock company of European nations. These features did not, of course, curb Gerald's enthusiasm. "Anybody who has read attentively Mosley's last book *The Alternative...* will be struck by the author's passionate belief in the Godhead," Gerald writes in a letter in the *Catholic Herald* of February

27 1948. "I have had the curiosity to consult a leaflet of the Union Movement founded by Sir Oswald Mosley," he adds, "and notice that the main object of this party is 'to resist the menace of International Communism.' It strikes me therefore that a party with such an aim in view should be able to rely at least on the tolerance and goodwill of Roman Catholics, even if it cannot count on their adherence as members." The editor apparently agreed, for in a footnote he writes, "If it ever came to Communism or Mosley, the latter would no doubt be preferable."

But Gerald's press agenting for the Union Movement did not stop with this little puff piece in the *Catholic Herald*. When I questioned Mosley about the trip to America which Gerald undertook in March 1948, partly on Sir Oswald's behalf, he was cagey. Previously, in a letter to Sir Oswald, I had pointed out that Gerald had been seeing him almost daily (I counted sixteen different occasions noted in Gerald's diary) prior to his departure for New York, and asked, "Would I be right in thinking that you were interested in obtaining American support for European Union at that time, and that Gerald may have been sent ahead to test the water?" To which Mosley had replied: "I seem to remember at some point he suggested selling my articles in America. I had there other contacts and later sold my book and appeared on television in America." When I pointed out that one of Gerald's chief contacts in New York was Merwin K. Hart, and that shortly after his return to England Gerald brought Hart to meet the Mosleys at Crowood, both Sir Oswald and Lady Diana acknowledged that Hart's name had a familiar ring, though they could remember nothing about him. "After the war Gerald telephoned frequently, offering to introduce a strange variety of people and offering a strange variety of services," Sir Oswald recalls: "He began as a joke and ended as a bore."

Operating from an eyrie on the 75th floor of the Empire State Building, Hart, who was later to head the John Birch Society in New York, still had links with Father Coughlin and Fritz Kuhn of the German-American Bund when Gerald met him. Nor was Hart the only native fascist Gerald saw during the month he spent in Manhattan. Originally Gerald had been scheduled to meet General George Van Horn Moseley, but the general was detained in Atlanta Georgia by a local election ("Our Republic is now threatened on every side," he wrote to Gerald), and hence he could not join Gerald in "New Jerusalem", meaning New York.

Instead, in his suite at the Weylin Hotel, Gerald saw a bewildering array of pro-fascist, anti-Semitic weirdos, including loud-mouthed Joseph P. Kamp, a Jew-hating publicist, who never went anywhere without his sword stick "for protection"; Frederick G. Cartwright, whose speciality was breaking up meetings of the United Nations Association; and Lambert F. Fairchild, former New York Alderman, whose dapper figure in black Homburg, bow tie and spats was a familiar one at German-American Bund rallies in the Bronx. The most colourful of all was Colonel Eugene Nelson Sanctuary, who had been indicted for sedition during the war. Pale and dressed entirely in black, the sepulchral colonel called on Gerald to convey his respects and those of Judge George W. Armstrong, the Texan millionaire with whom Gerald had been in correspondence (the judge is perhaps best known for having offered $50 million to a Mississippi military academy provided it taught the doctrine of white supremacy).

It is difficult to believe that Gerald saw all of these visitors off his own bat, or that they would have danced attendance upon him at the Weylin Hotel unless he represented interests other than his own. It is true that Gerald was concerned while in New York with securing a commercial credit for Spain in conjunction with the Wall Street brokerage house of Ladenburgh Thalmann, and that his two missions overlapped to a certain extent, Frederick Cartwright and Merwin K. Hart being ardent Franco supporters with business interests in Spain. Still, the mystery of whom Gerald represented remains. Both of the Mosleys, incidentally, feel that Gerald lacked the brains and credibility to pull off any really big business deal.

"I never heard Gerald say anything derogatory concerning the Jews," Mosley added, "possibly because he knew that I myself was not anti-Semitic." Sir Oswald is perhaps unique in this respect, because Gerald's anti-Semitism was an unfortunate hallmark of his personality, so far as most of his friends were concerned. Taxed with being anti-Semitic, Gerald usually took refuge behind some ingenious disclaimer such as this, from a letter to the *Catholic Herald* of July 9 1948: "The Arabs are, of course, a Semitic race and my well-known enthusiasm for their claims in Palestine should surely preclude anyone calling me anti-Semitic."

Lady Mosley is more critical of Gerald than her husband. While she was in Holloway the prison dentist came to her one day all excited and said, "I have just been treating a detainee at Brixton who is related to the Duke of Abercorn." "Gerald immediately sprang to mind," says Lady Diana. "After my release from Holloway I took the trouble to look up the Duke of Abercorn in *Burke's Peerage*, but there is no mention of anyone even remotely answering Gerald's description." Lady Mosley concedes that she found Gerald amusing when he visited the Mosleys at Holloway. "In prison you want someone who will cheer you up, and not make you feel down in the dumps. And Gerald did tell amusing stories. He did make us laugh. But in the end I grew weary of listening to him palm off Oscar Wilde's witticisms as his own."

Neither of the Mosleys was surprised to hear that Gerald had fed gossip items about them to the press, receipts for payment of the same being found among Gerald's papers. Sample from the 'William Hickey' diary column in the *Daily Express* for March 26 1942: "The Mosleys have their own notepaper, tastefully printed with what is, after all, a semi-permanent address – 'Holloway Prison, N7'." As late as the autumn of 1948 Gerald was still supplying the press with Mosley items, as is evident from the following note to Gerald from an editor at the *Sunday Pictorial*: "On my arrival at the office this morning I phoned Flockhart who told me (a) that Mosley had no intention of visiting the U.S. nor had he received an invitation from that quarter and (b) that it was 'completely untrue' that Mosley had a yacht. He was so positive in these denials that I do not think I can print the piece without stronger evidence on both points."

The Mosleys were surprised, however, when I told them about G.G. Smith, of the Special Branch. During the period immediately prior to Gerald's departure for New York, when he was seeing Mosley almost daily, Smith was a frequent visitor to Gerald's flat at Glebe Place, according to the entries in Gerald's diary. Almost Gerald's first appointment upon his return to London from New York on April 22 1948 is with G.G. Smith – would it be for the purpose of de-briefing? Then in August Merwin K. Hart arrives from New York and Gerald takes him to meet Mosley, as previously related. The following day, Monday August 16, this entry occurs in Gerald's diary: "Went to see O.M. Lunched alone, and then had a visit from G.G.S." In other words, Gerald had scarcely left Mosley's flat in Dolphin Square than he is seeing Smith. Sir Oswald concedes that Gerald may have been employed to spy on him ("We have had people planted on us before") but Lady Mosley is sceptical. The Special Branch was too smart to be taken in by Gerald, she maintains.

Her husband disagrees. "Special Branch on the whole is stupid. Besides, Gerald would have been capable of inventing any sort of story. He could have gone to them and said, 'Look, Mosley is planning to blow up the world.' They might not have believed him, but they would have taken it all down."

Eleven

January 1952: Tangier and the Tangeroids

Late in May 1951 an event occurred which shook Gerald considerably – the disappearance of Guy Burgess and Donald Maclean, the so-called "missing diplomats". Gerald's friendship with Guy Burgess dated back twenty years to when Christopher Isherwood had first introduced the pair. In an article in the *Spectator* Gerald admits he saw Burgess "a week or so before his final disappearance", but he told Ian Dunlop that he had seen Burgess the day before the latter went missing. "I doubt that he told this to Special Branch," Dunlop adds in telling me about the incident. "Gerald was very nervous about discussing the subject at all, but I'm convinced that he knew beforehand not only that Burgess was about to do a flit, but knew where he was headed for – Moscow."

Earlier in May, Dunlop had called at Gerald's flat, and had found Burgess there. "The only memory I have of that occasion is of Gerald reciting one of Horace's *Odes*, and of Burgess smirking, though whether he smirked because Gerald got it wrong, or because of the sentiments expressed I couldn't tell. Anyway, Burgess's attitude towards Gerald was patronising."

Dunlop had occasion to call on Gerald again, this time after news that Burgess and Maclean had absconded had leaked out. This time Gerald appears to have lost his aplomb. "He had a man with him whom he introduced as Colonel Tamlyn," Dunlop recalls. "When we were alone Gerald explained that Colonel Tamlyn was formerly the British military attaché in Egypt, and that he was now with MI6, and that the colonel had been questioning him about Guy Burgess… Obviously there had been some drama before my arrival, for Gerald appeared badly shaken, chattered away at lightning speed, hardly aware of what he was saying."

And not long after the colonel from MI6, Gerald then had a visit from his old friend G.G. Smith of the Special Branch. Obviously Gerald had reason to be in a highly nervous state if what he told Dunlop – that he had seen Burgess the day before the latter vanished – is true. If he had withheld this information, Gerald could expect Smith to take a dim view of his evasion. Gerald had kept regular contact with Smith over the years, as is evident from correspondence and entries in his diary, but the type of information Gerald fed the detective had now changed. His relations with the Mosleys having cooled, Gerald no longer supplied Smith with news concerning Sir Oswald; instead he poached on those of his homosexual friends whose positions in public life made them of interest to Special Branch. That Special Branch was in the market for such gossip may appear unlikely at first blush, but it is worth recalling that Guy Burgess himself got his start as a British intelligence agent by peddling just such chit-chat, as his biographers point out. "The kind of material Burgess had to offer – really high-grade gossip, usually culled from friends on the homosexual network – was of most interest to Section One of the Secret Intelligence Service, which dealt with political intelligence."

"I'm sure the things that Gerald told Superintendent Smith were mostly hot air," Maurice Richardson said when I talked to him. "Some of that hot air would have found its way into the columns of the *Daily Express*, for Smith used to leak stories to the Beaverbrook paper – things he wanted to be made public. I'm sure it was Smith who tipped off the *Express* about Burgess and Maclean, for it was the first paper in Fleet Street to report them missing."

In small, subtle ways Gerald made Smith aware of the class differences that separated them, according to Richardson, who had met the detective. Born the son of a Wiltshire farm labourer, Smith had served as a pantry boy, footman, and later as a valet to the Duke of Westminster before joining the Metropolitan Police. With the outbreak of the 1939–45 war Police Sergeant Smith, as he was then, was seconded to the Special Branch, where he showed an aptitude for winnowing out wartime spies. This flair was to stand him in good stead in peacetime in helping to bring to justice the "atom spies" Nunn May and Klaus Fuchs. But it was in 1961, in breaking up the so-called Portland Spy Ring, which was transmitting British naval secrets to Soviet Russia, that Smith made his name as Britain's No.1 Spycatcher. Here he pitted his wits against those of Soviet master spy Gordon Lonsdale, alias Colonel Konon Trofimovich Molody, for whom he had a sneaking admiration.

Richardson met Smith at Gerald's flat. "Gerald was always boasting to me about how well he knew Smith, so he invited me to lunch to meet the great Special Branch panjandrum. Smith was very deferential and polite. The conversation was neutral, hence banal. Afterwards Gerald twitted me, 'Why didn't you tell him about your Communist friends?' I didn't know whether Gerald was serious or not. 'What do you take me for,' I said, 'a copper's nark?' "

*

Gerald has left his impressions of Guy Burgess in an article he wrote for the *Spectator*, in the form of an open letter to Christopher Isherwood recalling old times. Isherwood had introduced the two in 1933, when Gerald had been forced by Hitler's advent to scarper from Berlin, and had rented a villa in the Uccle suburb of Brussels. Burgess even then "was showing signs of the dissipation for which he afterwards became notorious", according to Gerald. "I remember one Sunday morning he turned up, very early indeed, at the villa which I occupied at Uccle, looking, even for him, peculiarly grubby and dishevelled; he told me, so I understood, that he had just come from Mass. I remarked that I was surprised and delighted to hear it. After talking at cross purposes for some time, I realized that he was referring not to Holy Mass but to Maas, a singularly louche night haunt near the Gare du Nord in Brussels."

On another occasion, Gerald was Guy's guest at lunch at the Reform Club, where the latter's usually high spirits "seemed to take a sudden downward turn", in Gerald's words. "This club depresses me terribly sometimes; there are no page boys," Burgess is quoted as saying, to which Gerald replied, soothingly, "Come, come, dear boy, you mustn't crab your own club. Try to enjoy such solid mid-Victorian amenities as it does provide. Take another sip of this excellent Waterloo sherry."

Gerald did not encounter Burgess again until after the war, when they bumped into one another in the Christmas rush at Fortnum's and agreed to have dinner. When Burgess turned up for the dinner date he was accompanied by a friend whom Gerald, in the *Spectator* article, identifies as "Mr Q", but who in reality was Brian Howard (the character Ambrose Silk in *Put Out More Flags* is modelled on Howard). Like Burgess, Howard had found a wartime niche with the British secret services, being taken on by MI5 until his indiscretions forced that agency to get rid of him. He had to be sacked because of his habit of going up to people in bars, accusing them of being fascists, and telling them he worked for a "very secret organization."

Just how indiscreet his two companions could be Gerald was to discover when, after dinner that night, they guided him to a basement club in Soho "so manifestly louche that it reminded me... of the closing hours of the Weimar Republic". "While we were there, the place was raided," Gerald continues. "The police approached our table. Q, who was by this time very drunk indeed, on being asked... gave his name, and added, 'I live in Mayfair. No doubt you come from some dreary suburb.' Burgess, on the other hand, 'behaved with such assured nonchalance, giving his own name, address and occupation, in stentorian tones, that I could only conclude that a new – and how welcome – spirit of tolerance was prevailing in Whitehall.' " Sir Harold Acton, who knew them both, says of Burgess and Howard that "in spite of their alleged Marxism they were schizophrenic, guilty about belonging to the so-called ruling class and divided about Russia, to whose imperialism they were blind while ranting against ours".

*

"When I was in London... I telephoned your dear old number, so often dialled by stronger hands than mine, and instead of you, a WOMAN answered, very curtly, and I felt really scared, thinking perhaps you had married for the third time, which could only mean that a Third World War was imminent."

– Desmond Stewart to Gerald, August 9 1952

"So THAT is where you are! Such a shock to hear from Glebe Place that you had left and 'they did not know your address'. I thought it might be Brixton, Dartmoor, or Exeter…"

    – Basil Clavering to Gerald, February 26 1953

"Gerald, dear, WHAT ARE YOU UP TO? Why is there rioting in Tangier?"

    – Peter Gordon to Gerald, April 7 1952

Gerald fled to Tangier in January 1952, trailing behind him £3,000 in debts incurred as an undischarged bankrupt. A third of this amount Gerald owed to Captain Robert Gordon-Canning, the Etonian Mosleyite who had distinguished himself by hitting sixes over "Lenin's Tomb" (the outside lavatories) in the recreation yard at Brixton. Gerald had obtained the money from Gordon-Canning by fraud, borrowing on the strength of a legacy which he was supposed to receive, and also an insurance policy made in Gordon-Canning's favour on which only the first premium was paid. Another £500 owing was in the form of a bank loan made jointly to Gerald and to Reggie Newton, his solicitor, with a Mrs Marjorie Humphreys (of whom more later) as guarantor.

Gerald owed everyone money, from the newsboy who delivered his *Daily Telegraph* to the barber who came to his house each morning to shave him, and from Fortnum and Mason's, where in eight months he had run up a £625 bill for pressed duck and other delicacies, to John Harvey & Sons, from whom he had ordered £149 worth of wine and spirits with which to wash the said delicacies down; not forgetting his landlords, the Church Commissioners, to whom he owed nine months rent. In desperation Gerald, during his last days at Glebe Place, had pawned his signet rings and a silk dressing-gown, plus various articles which were not his. From these and other creditors, writs, judgment summonses, and "garnishee orders" had descended like autumn leaves on Gerald's head. Pulling in that head, he had made for Tangier as a haven from the coming storm.

There was a saying current in the fifties at Dean's Bar in Tangier: "If you can't make it here you can't make it anywhere." Gerald himself is enlightening on this point. "You can arrive with a trunk of solid gold bars and no questions are asked," he writes; "or if you prefer you can stay at home and, by establishing a phantom Import-Export firm in Tangier, immensely reduce your tax expenditure. For manoeuvres of this kind you require a stooge..." (a stooge which he would volunteer to be).

Tangier's population of a quarter of a million was divided into three parts: full-time smugglers, part-time smugglers, and occasional smugglers, a tribute to the fact that in Europe, despite the Marshall Plan, everything was in short supply. All three groups benefited from the fact that in Tangier there were "no controls, no taxes, no rationing, no licensing of working hours, and no trade unions", as Gerald pointed out to Ian Dunlop; "In a word, no democracy of any kind," Gerald concludes, "hence the happiness and prosperity of all concerned."

It comes as something of a shock, therefore, to learn that in this tax-free haven of smugglers and black marketeers not only did Gerald not make it as a con-man, but that he was soon as badly off as he had been in London and cadging money from everyone within reach. True, he did not arrive in Tangier with a trunkful of gold bars to salt away in one of Tangier's eighty-five banks. He was, however, capable as a stooge of setting up a dummy import-export business for some operator smarter than himself; indeed, for a time he went through the motions of trying to get himself named as

Ireland's commercial representative in Morocco. "I would not require a salary, as I would hope to recuperate expenses from business deals," he writes to the Hon. Peter Evans-Freke (later the 11th Baron Carbery), who was then a member of the Irish Exporters' Association. "It is essential to have somebody who speaks French and Spanish as I do," he adds. Gerald's offer, however, was turned down by the Irish Minister for External Affairs.

Was the competition too stiff? Was Gerald, who was sixty-one at his last birthday, slowing down? Or had he simply lost his touch? His failure to flourish in the lush soil of Tangier would seem to have been due to a combination of all these factors. To begin with, he was not in good health when he arrived; indeed, he would undergo a hernia operation within six months. Then, too, a strange torpor appears to have overtaken him from the moment of his arrival, as he admits in his letter to Ian Dunlop: "Here in this boom town I sit in the sunshine & lead a lotus-eater's life," he writes. But in his unpublished essay on Tangier he describes the city as "mentally squalid". "All these bright keen calculating brains," he writes, "create around them a kind of spiritual Dead Sea. Here, one feels, the writer would soon stop writing, the painter throw his brushes away…"

It was as an observer that Gerald sat sipping his aperitif in the cafés of the Socco Chico, where Spanish Loyalist refugees glared at former Nazi colonels while the latter in turn snubbed their Vichyite collaborators – Tangier was a Tom Tiddler's ground for fugitives of all kinds, including a "delicious sprinkling of Foreign Legion deserters", as Gerald informs Dunlop, although he also confides that he has had no sex "nor do I want any here", which was a sure sign that he was not well.

In the absence of more lively pursuits, Gerald took to sea bathing, writing to Dunlop, "I have entrusted my shapely form to the carressing waters of the sea on two occasions, much to the joy of the native population, who watched, breathless, my puffing & panting, & when finally I did emerge even as Aphrodite from the ocean, they gave vent to an odd noise which I like to interpret as an Arab cheer."

*

Mention Dean's Bar today, to those who knew it earlier, and their eyes glaze over. One half expects their lips to form the words, "Play it again, Sam." But Tangier was no Casablanca. The war was over. There wasn't any Sam, and had there been a Sam, Dean's Bar could not have housed anything bigger than a harmonium for him to play on, besides which Dean himself was no Humphrey Bogart. The trouble with Dean (real name Donald Kimfull) was that people were apt to impute to him whatever romantic notions seized them when in an alcoholic haze. Thus Michael Davidson describes Dean as possessing "the *hauteur* of a Versailles duchess, the *cortesia* of a papal chamberlain, a heart made of honey and, often, a tongue like a scorpion's sting", adding that "a silent blackball from Dean... can seem socially far more damaging than being turned down for the Royal Enclosure". Compare this with the description furnished me by another of Dean's customers: "A slim, brown, semi-literate guinea [half-caste] with enormous sad eyes which he inherited from his Egyptian parents, Dean was nothing more than a sounding-board for people who bounced their neuroses off on him."

Not to put too fine a point on it, Dean was a Man of Mystery. No one knew for certain what he did each night after he had locked up his bar, jumped into his shiny blue two-seater, and headed for the beach, where he had a house. Nor did he encourage people to enquire too closely; he had the reputation of being Tangier's loneliest bachelor. Dean had tended bar in Monte Carlo, Cairo, and Paris before becoming head barman at Tangier's El Minzah Hotel, where during the war years he had been careful to hide his pro-Allied sympathies as he served Germans and English alike. He was behind the bar when, shortly after the American landings in North Africa, the Nazi master spy Hans Auer walked in covered with dust. Auer had escaped from Casablanca after members of his own disarmament commission had been mown down by French tommy guns. He himself had talked his way through a dozen U.S. Army checkpoints on the road to Tangier, he explained to Dean, as he ordered a daiquiri and told Dean to leave the cocktail shaker on the bar.

Then, in 1947, Dean opened his own bar a stone's throw from El Minzah, and overnight it had become the smart thing upon arrival in Tangier to check in at Dean's, where the customer on the next bar stool might be Errol Flynn or Elliott Roosevelt or Guy Burgess (the latter, on a visit to Dean's in 1949, had attracted attention by singing to the tune of the Eton Boating Song a ditty about Tangier which began "Little boys are cheap today/Cheaper than yesterday"). It was here that Gerald met Francis Bacon, Robin Maugham, and Sir Cyril Hampson, a midget baronet whose ambition it had once been to become a jockey. It was here too that Gerald overheard someone ask Tallulah Bankhead's sister, "Tell me, Eugenia dear, how many husbands have you had?" and the latter's lightning reply, "Of my own, you mean, dear?"

On March 30 Gerald was making his way towards Dean's Bar from his hotel when he got caught in the riot that had broken out among Tangier's Moorish population. It had begun as an anti-French demonstration, but had quickly degenerated into an attack upon any European shop or café, with widespread looting and burning of motorcars. "I fled down a side street, banged on the first door I could find, and was at once admitted with great cordiality," Gerald records. He had in fact taken refuge in one of Tangier's better known brothels, The Black Cat, whose madame said she hoped he "would not waste valuable time in sitting in the hall".

In April, Gerald became gossip columnist for the *Moroccan Courier*, an American weekly published in Casablanca for the benefit of U.S. Army Air Force personnel. The job paid very little, but Gerald used his column to cadge free meals from restaurants which he in turn favoured with free publicity. It is obvious from his comments that Gerald did not relish assignments such as "covering" the *vin d'honneur* given for "Miss American Edition of 1952" who had won a free trip from Casablanca ("I have always noticed that at a *vin d'honneur* everything is served except wine," Gerald, who detested cocktails, writes crossly); but when the editor suggested that he report the landing of American sailors from a visiting warship, Gerald did so with alacrity, though "the crowd of shoe shine boys, souvenir sellers... and touts of all kinds that followed them about made me very angry", he writes.

Gerald could not live on the handouts he got for free publicity puffs. Owing two months' rent at the Rif Hotel, he moved to a room in the rue Rembrandt where neither the water nor the electricity had been turned on. Soon he was paying regular visits to a pawnshop in the rue Velasquez and borrowing from a money-lender named Bulchand. On top of this, his London past caught up with him with the arrival in Tangier of Mrs Marjorie Humphreys, or "La Humphreys", as he insisted upon calling her. This was the Mrs Humphreys who had guaranteed a £500 bank loan made jointly to Gerald and his solicitor Reggie Newton (the latter was to say that he never saw a penny of this loan, which was put by Gerald to his own personal use). Gerald having neglected to pay the interest on the loan, the bank now threatened to call it in, which meant that La Humphreys would be stuck with the full amount, and in turn presumably would sue both Newton and Hamilton. Whether she had followed Gerald all the way to Tangier to remind him of these unpleasant facts, or whether her presence in Tangier was pure coincidence, his one-time benefactress now took possession of Dean's Bar, which meant that it was 'Out of Bounds' to Gerald. Not only that but she proceeded to spread what Gerald called "wicked stories" about him.

In these circumstances even Gerald's cast-iron constitution deserted him. He had been bothered by a hernia for years, being forced to wear a truss, but now, suddenly, surgery became imperative. Gerald was operated on at the English Clinic on June 14th. He was on the operating table for more than three hours, his hernia proving more serious than was thought at first. It was a sobering experience. He had no intention of falling ill again so far from home, and being at the mercy of strangers. (A visit he paid to an Englishman in Tangier's Moorish prison after he had recovered from the operation also impressed him with the horrors that awaited him should he fall into the clutches of the law.) His diary for this period is punctuated by such expressions as "I am tortured by the turn of events," "I am bored with everything and have the blues," "I am sick of Tangier and the Tangerines" (the ones he disliked most he called "Tangeroids"). He preferred to return to England and to face whatever awaited him there, he decided. Better the London he knew, even though a creditor crouched behind every bush, than to continue to have his existence poisoned by Tangeroids.

*

Once more Gerald stands before an English bar of justice. Once more, he is due to be sentenced as an undischarged bankrupt who has run up debts. And once again the occasion is robbed of whatever solemnity it might have had by the comedy which preceded it. To begin with, there was a round of furious behind-the-scenes activity with Gerald trying to pull strings with his friend Detective Superintendent G.G. Smith of Scotland Yard, whom he saw on the 1, 8, and 16 of September, reporting to his solicitor Reggie Newton immediately afterwards on each occasion. Had he not given important information to Special Branch concerning Guy Burgess, among others? Would he not prove useful to them in the future? Meanwhile, could they not get him off the hook? But it was all in vain. There was nothing Smith could do to help Gerald, even if he had been so minded.

Then on the morning of his trial Gerald made the startling discovery that the judge who was to hear his case was an old Rugbeian. This was followed by an excursion to Jermyn Street to buy the requisite dark blue and green striped Rugby necktie, with his friend Maurice Richardson offering to treat him to it. "The shopman," writes Richardson, "offered us two types of tie; one in artificial silk cost only 14 shillings and looked sober and respectable; the other in real silk was almost too noticeable besides costing 24s.9d. I suggested that as he would only be wearing it once in any case the 14 shilling tie would suffice. But Gerald, with characteristic eloquence, pointed out that this kind of thing should never be done by halves."

Reggie Newton, however, was horrified when he learned of his client's plans to work the Old School Tie game: a gaffe such as this could result in the judge locking Gerald up and throwing away the key. So when Gerald appeared in the dock he was wearing a sombre cravat in keeping with the interior of the London Sessions House in Newington Causeway.

Gerald was sentenced to nine months' imprisonment at Wandsworth, which because of overcrowding (1,890 prisoners in space designed to accommodate 750) he considered to be "the worst prison in England". Fortunately for him, his sojourn was again brief, being released after serving only three months of his nine-month sentence, apparently after petitioning the Queen for clemency in coronation year – at least this was the story as told by Gerald, who claimed that he got the idea from the Duke of Alba. However, he was still in Wandsworth at Christmas, when Maurice Richardson found him in his loose-fitting grey prison garb "looking like an elderly prep-school boy". "He asked me if I would send out Christmas cards for him, giving as his return address the London Clinic," Richardson recalled. "So I bought the most expensive Christmas cards I could find, forged Gerald's signature to them, and sent them out to the Spanish Ambassador, the Papal Nuncio, the Duke of This and the Countess of That – all with 'The London Clinic' in the upper left-hand corner."

*

In going through Gerald's papers one is struck by the number of letters from jailbirds serving sentences. One comes upon long runs of letters written on narrow, feint-ruled, ivory-coloured stationery, and one knows immediately that the correspondent is an inmate of Parkhurst, or Winston Green, or The Scrubs. The number of Gerald's friends who were locked up at one time or another is perhaps less remarkable than the fact that he never lost track of them. Having spent so much time inside himself, Gerald's interest in prisons, prisoners, and all that pertained to them was an abiding one. He was a member of long-standing of the Howard League for Penal Reform; he took an active interest in the National Campaign for the Abolition of Capital Punishment chaired by Victor Gollancz; and finally, against all his priniciples, Gerald voted Labour in 1964, only because they promised to abolish the death penalty.

Some of the letters on the telltale notepaper are from young tearaways Gerald has picked up in Soho pubs frequented by rent boys. Usually they are inside for car theft, breaking and entry, or for other mindless offences, and the personalities revealed are pathetic rather than vicious. They appear to be emotionally unstable, and totally incapable of looking after themselves in a competitive world. One young offender addresses his recipient as "Uncle Gerald", perhaps to fool the prison censor. Another adds at the bottom of his letter, "P.S. Don't put anything in the letter to make it sound affectionate Gerald will you."

Others of his prison correspondents are altogether exceptional types. They range from Eric Parr, whose promising career as a writer of Runyonesque tales was cut short by lung cancer in 1967, to Richard Field, alias Richard Fabian, alias Richard Harvey, whose IQ was 164, high enough to gain him membership in Mensa, and they include an Irish fanatic, the walls of whose cell at Parkhurst were adorned by photographs of Roger Casement and other Irish martyrs. Parr, who was the son of a sergeant in the Royal Marines, Gerald met in June 1942 while he himself was His Majesty's guest in Wandsworth. Their friendship was to last twenty years, with Gerald acting as godfather to Parr's children. "Parr was a very slick operator," Maurice Richardson, who published his first stories in *Lilliput*, told me. "During the war his specialty was impersonating government officials. He would dress smartly and carry an attaché case with "H.M. Inspector" stamped in gold on it. Then he would find out which shopkeepers were violating wartime regulations, and shake them down for whatever he could get."

Richard Field/Fabian/Harvey, of the high IQ, on the other hand, was a born mythomaniac. In one of his first letters to Gerald he writes from Wormwood Scrubs, "Last week I destroyed 2 full-length novels, 20 short stories, and a mountain of such other items which I'd written." The reason for this wholesale destruction? Field, in collaboration with another jailbird, was about to launch "G.H.A.", which stood for "Gerald Hamilton Associates", and was to comprise a public relations, business consultancy, and advertising agency, with photographic studios, recording studios, two cars, and a suite of offices for the directors. Nothing came of G.H.A. but, while he was inside Shepton Mallet, Field did edit a prison magazine whose contributors included the Duke of Bedford, Lord Montagu, Dame Margaret Rutherford, Godfrey Winn, and J.Paul Getty.

As for Sean Buckley, the fanatical Irishman, here it was a case of mutual deception. Buckley laboured under the illusion that Gerald had actually met Roger Casement, while Gerald thought Buckley was doing time for some IRA offence when in reality Buckley, who had sixteen previous convictions, had been sentenced to ten years for housebreaking and larceny. Neither party sought to disillusion the other. Thus when Gerald suggested that Buckley apply for an amnesty, the latter's indignant reply was: "Do you for one moment imagine that the Sassenach would offer anything at all acceptable to anyone who had the slightest regard for that very unfashionable commodity – *honour*?"

The most interesting of Gerald's jailbird friends was the one he met in Tangier. Frank James White, alias "Eustace Hamilton Ian Stewart-Hargreaves" (was it Oscar Wilde who said that a mask tells us more than a face?) was being held in Tangier on charges of having entered Morocco on a false passport. It was a holding charge, however, for White, who had twelve convictions to his name, was wanted in England, where he had jumped bail, for more serious crimes. Piqued by that insatiable curiosity of his, Gerald made a special pilgrimage to the Moorish prison in the Kasbah to see White.

"I had hardly got back to my flat and had a bath when my Spanish maid told me there was an *hombre* at the door asking to see me," Gerald writes. "I... found myself face to face with one of the guards from the prison, whom I had seen an hour or two before. With an air of mystery he brought an important note, he said. Hargreaves [sic] had written asking me to be so kind as to give the bearer 500 pesetas as he was going to help him with certain plans he had, which he did not care to set down on paper. I felt this rather cheeky but parted with 100 pesetas and wished him well."

Born in May 1905, over a sweetshop in Hammersmith, White was the son of a parlourmaid and a costermonger father of whom by his own admission he was ashamed. At seventeen he acquired a coster's barrow and began hawking plants in Barnes, across the river from Hammersmith. "He wore his best suit," White writes of himself. "His shoes were polished and he had on a clean shirt... he offered his plants respectfully, but not whiningly, in a voice which surprised the women who responded to his knock." No doubt the neat appearance and carefully modulated voice appealed to suburban housewives, for "many of them purchased plants which they really did not want".

In between serving prison sentences for fraud, White found time to marry a girl whom he identifies as "Bobby", to father three children, and to acquire Birtsnorton, a half-timbered house with a moat in Worcestershire, which was originally the gift of Henry VI to Sir John Nanfan, a friend of Cardinal Wolsey. In that Moorish prison in the Kasbah where Gerald first encountered him, White's thoughts no doubt were with his wife and family and that moated manor house, which contrasted so sharply with the cell, measuring 15ft by 19ft, which he shared with nine other men, each with a separate heap of filthy sacking for a bed. Their only nourishment, he writes to Gerald, is "a stinking mass of bean made lurid with pimentoes served by an Arab out of a rusty bucket, a ladleful at midday and a second ladleful at night… The few men who eat it squat on the cement floor and lap it up from tin plates like dogs".

White made no attempt to escape with the hundred pesetas Gerald had given the guard. Instead, he was handed over at Gibraltar to British police, who brought him back to England where, in March 1953, he stood trial at Gloucester Assizes. He was found guilty on sixteen charges of fraud and fraudulent conversion and sentenced to eight years detention by a judge who complimented him on the "eloquence, skill, and determination" with which he had defended himself. At Parkhurst, on the Isle of Wight, where he was Prisoner No.793, White wrote to Gerald from time to time, his last letter being dated July 23 1958, or less than a month before he died at the age of fifty-two from a heart attack. His epitaph might have been the one he was fond of quoting to Gerald: "Only those of us who have touched the depths can ever hope to reach the stars." On his death certificate his profession is listed as "company director", which would have pleased him.

Twelve

June 1955: Churchill Unveiled

"It was hard not to admire Winston Churchill," Gerald writes drily in *The Way It Was With Me*, "but somehow or other I never really suceeded in doing so." In reality, Churchill was one of his pet aversions, along with women in trousers, the British royal family, and the Lord's Day Observance Society (Gerald was fond of quoting Victor Hugo to the effect that boredom was born in London on a rainy Sunday). As a pacifist, Gerald yiewed Churchill as a "warmonger" who was "temperamentally unbalanced". In particular Gerald blamed Churchill for the Yalta Conference, which he saw as a conspiracy to hand Poland "on a silver platter to the Russian criminals".

Gerald subscribed to the conspiracy theory of history. Just as individuals are governed by unseen forces, so are world events, at least according to Gerald, who blamed the disasters of history on the machinations of Jews, Jesuits, Masons, and communists, sometimes acting separately, sometimes in concert. The supreme exponent of the conspiracy theory of history was of course Adolf Hitler, who linked Wall Street and communism as part of a world-wide Jewish plot masterminded by President Roosevelt (whose real name as everyone knew was "Rosenfeld"). This kind of thinking found a ready audience among those in Germany who were victims of inflation and civil war, and who, according to a German observer, "had a secret sense that they were… being deceived by a hidden force which brought about this chaos deliberately".

In particular, Gerald was inclined to see a conspirator under every royal bed. Thus the "suicide" of Rudolf of Hapsburg at Mayerling, the assassinations of Archduke Ferdinand at Sarajevo and of King Alexander of Yugoslavia at Marseilles, the mountain "accident" of the King of the Belgians; these were all the work of unnamed Machiavels, as was the drowning of Lord Kitchener, who went down with HMS Hampshire en route to visit the Tsar in Russia. When Lord Monckton died in his bed in January 1965, Gerald hinted that he had been "accidented" because he knew too much about the abdication of Edward VIII, which in itself was the result of a conspiracy "that rang the knell of England's greatness". Gerald's political tergiversations in the 1950s and 1960s, his espousal of causes first on the left, then on the right, were in a sense due to this mad hunt for conspirators.

Besides Yalta, Gerald had other reasons for disliking Sir Winston Churchill. As wartime prime minister, was Churchill not responsible for Gerald being interned under Clause 18B of the Defence of the Realm Act? Did he not thereby deprive Gerald of his liberty, and hold him up to public disgrace? This undoubtedly was Gerald's reasoning when unexpectedly in 1955 an opportunity presented itself for Gerald to avenge himself.

*

Gog and Magog, newly gilded, looked down with oriental eyes on the gorgeous pageantry as it wound its way down the centre aisle of the Guildhall: the beadles with their wands of office, followed by the aldermen and sheriffs in scarlet robes, and finally by the members of the Court of the Common Council in mazarine blue gowns tipped with fur. The date: Tuesday June 21 1955. The occasion: the unveiling of a bronze statue of Sir Winston Churchill which the Corporation of the City of London had commissioned from sculptor Oscar Nemon. The City fathers had gathered to pay tribute to "the greatest statesman of modern times", as the Lord Mayor, resplendent in his state robe of black and gold, called him.

Promptly at 12.30 the Greatest Statesman himself, in silk top-hat and frock coat, arrived at the striped canopy in front of the Guildhall to pass between a guard of honour of pikemen from the Honourable Artillery Company in red tunics, gleaming silver helmets and breastplates. Guildhall officials from the Lord Mayor down were apprehensive of Churchill's reaction when the larger-than-life bronze was unveiled. Would that statesmanlike countenance cloud over? They were mindful of his intense dislike of the Graham Sutherland portrait of him which the House of Commons had commissioned for his eightieth birthday, and which he could hardly wait to hide in the attic, once he got it home (eventually Lady Churchill had had it destroyed). All that Sir Winston could find to say about the offending Sutherland canvas was that it was "a good example of modern art". What would he say upon this occasion? The City fathers need not have feared. Churchill was most fulsome in his praise. "I greatly admire the art of Mr Oscar Nemon," he declared. "I also admire, if I may say so, this particular example because it seems to be a very good likeness."

It was not until the following morning that the Corporation of the City of London appeared with egg on its face. For on that Wednesday morning the *Daily Express* published on its front page a photograph of Gerald Hamilton in a pose identical to that of the Nemon statue under the heading "WINSTON INTERNED HIM BUT NOW..." Gerald, it transpired, had modelled for four-fifths of the Churchill statue. Only the head, it seemed, belonged to the Greatest Statesman. There to prove it was Gerald striking a Churchillian pose for the camera, his belly pendulous, his arms extended along chair rests, his feet planted wide apart. He even wore a bow tie such as Sir Winston favoured. What had happened was that Churchill had been too busy to give the sculptor more than a half-dozen sittings, which were devoted to getting the facial expression right. "It so happens I have exactly the same measurements as Sir Winston," Gerald explained to the *Daily Express* reporter. "And, look, I've even got his stoop." In the brouhaha that followed the *Express* disclosure, Sir Winston's voice sounded almost plaintive as he inquired "Couldn't they pick anyone else?"

Meanwhile, some wag dubbed the Guildhall bronze The Churchill Chimaera, referring to the monster in ancient Greek mythology which was said to combine a lion's head with a goat's body and a dragon's tail.

*

The Suez crisis of November 1956 filled Gerald with "horror and shame", as it did many of his compatriots, the difference being that, unlike more rational minds, he saw it as a masonic plot. "Eden had apparently connived with Guy Mollet, the French Prime Minister, for a secret alliance which included Zionist elements in Palestine," he writes. "Mollet was of course the prime instigator... because he wished to please the Grand Orient and other French masonic lodges."

All of which did not prevent Gerald from trying to turn "this dangerous and disastrous piece of diplomacy", as he described it, to his profit. With the inauguration of post-Suez petrol rationing he thought he saw his opportunity. Tony Gibbs,

Gerald's publisher, drove a Rolls-Royce which did about nine miles to the gallon, so naturally Gibbs jumped at Gerald's offer of extra petrol coupons. Gerald then produced a great wad of coupons and was suitably recompensed by the grateful Gibbs. The following day the *Daily Telegraph* front-paged a story about a petrol coupon forgery being uncovered, and printed the numbers of the forged coupons. Anthony Blond, another publisher, rang Gibbs and said: "I'll bet you any amount you care to name that the coupons Gerald sold you are on that list." They were, of course, but Gibbs was more amused than angry.

*

In June 1957, Gerald was invited to lecture to the inmates of Bristol prison by their chaplain, the Reverend Richard Blake Brown, an eccentric, American-born clergyman, who had a bee in his bonnet about mad King Ludwig II of Bavaria. Blake Brown carried his Ludwig cult to the point where his Christmas cards bore swans on their covers, and his notepaper was embossed with the legend: "L.W., Drowned June 13 1886". Gerald's Bristol lecture was preceded by a certain amount of haggling with the Home Office, which refused to pay him a fee, but agreed to advance him £10 against expenses, which of course included travelling first-class.

In the prison chapel, flanked by the prison governor and by Blake Brown himself, Gerald looked down upon what must have been a familiar sight: row upon row of grey-clad prisoners. "I hear you fellows recently were subjected to a lecture on the habits of fishes, which did not go down very well," Gerald began, striking just the right note of bonhomie. "As I am not very clever about such things," he went on, "I intend to talk about myself, which is a subject I really know something about." From then on he held the convicts spellbound. During the question period "one or two prisoners got up to say that they were entirely innocent of any offence and their condemnation was a put-up job," Gerald records. "I had to be very tactful in these cases," he adds.

Gerald's lecture was a resounding success, according to Blake Brown, who, in a letter headed "The Imperial Nymphenburg Palace, Bristol", writes, "My apartment here is a Ludwig Temple, and now that I've purchased a marvellous beautiful Radiogram, I can DROWN myself in Wagner's music, and even now as I perfervidly typewrite this, the GLORIOUS Quintet from MEISTERSINGER blares forth into the post-poached egg (1.20 pm) atmosphere... all too delicious..."

Gerald continued to correspond with Blake Brown up to the latter's death in 1968. In his letters the clergyman sometimes addresses Gerald as "My Lord Bishop of Witney", and signs himself "Cardinal Crumpet", or "Richard de Wittelsbach" ("Kissing the perfervid Purple, my Lord, I hasten to subscribe myself, Richard de Wittelsbach").

*

Around this time Hamilton also knew the novelist and philosopher Colin Wilson, who then lived in London but now lives in Cornwall. Gerald, in fact, was a major cause of him moving there, in 1957. Wilson and his girlfriend Joy, now his wife, were having Gerald to supper one evening in Wilson's flat, at 24 Chepstow Villas, Notting Hill, when Joy's father burst into the room, brandishing a horsewhip and shouting that Wilson was a homosexual with a string of mistresses ("I'm not sure how he worked that out," says Wilson).

The problem was a diary that Wilson had left at the house of Joy's parents in St.Albans, when he went to visit her in hospital (she was having her tonsils out). This contained notes on the Jack the Ripper murders, among other things, for Wilson's novel *Ritual in the Dark*, in which one of the central characters is homosexual. Wilson offered to show Joy's father the diary, but he was having none of it and tried to hit Wilson with the horsewhip, at which point Wilson tried to push him away and he fell over. Joy's mother then started belabouring Wilson round the head with an umbrella shouting, "How dare you hit an old man!" while Joy's brother and sister, who had also appeared on the scene, tried to drag Joy out of the room. Wilson's neighbours in the building had now arrived to see what the noise was about, and Wilson rang the police, who finally arrived and told Joy's parents that they would have to go.

Gerald, meanwhile, had slipped away, but soon afterwards the *Daily Mirror* appeared on the doorstep complete with photographers; within minutes, more journalists and photographers were arriving in such numbers that Colin and Joy had to slip out the back of the building and stay with friends for the night. It didn't occur to Wilson that there was any connection between Gerald and the press invasion until a few weeks later, when Dan Farson met Gerald in a pub. "How much did they pay you for ringing up about the horsewhip incident?" said Farson. Hamilton began to complain and said "Do you know, they only..." when, as Wilson tells it, he "suddenly looked embarrassed and said with that wide-eyed look of his, 'Me? I assure you I had nothing to do with it.'"

Wilson nevertheless forgave him, and recalled him taking Wilson and his fiancée to Esmeralda's Barn, a fashionable nightspot of the time run by the Kray twins. Hamilton complained bitterly throughout dinner about the group who were producing soft music in the background, claiming that their noise ruined the conversation. "I always found him a most amusing old crook," says Wilson.

*

As is evident from his friendship with Colin Wilson, Gerald was not long in perceiving that, just as in the Berlin of the late twenties it was smart to be a Red (or at least a fellow traveller) so in post-Suez England the trendy thing was to be angry. If angry young men were all the rage, why not angry old ones?

Anger perhaps explains Gerald's presence on Good Friday 1958, on the plinth of Nelson's Column in Trafalgar Square under the banner of the Campaign for Nuclear Disarmament. Again, it may have been dictated by the presence among the four thousand CND marchers of such trend-setters as Miss Suna Portman, Viscount Portman's niece, and darling of the Chelsea ravers, who was escorted on this occasion by Christopher Booker, soon to become the Top People's favourite satirist. Or again, it may have been simply that Gerald sensed a conspiracy – on the part of Freemasons? communists? Jews? – directed towards the perpetuation of nuclear warfare. Whatever the reason, Gerald shared the plinth with Canon Collins and Michael Foot, both of whom in other circumstances he would have abominated. Introduced as, "Gerald Hamilton, the well-known author", he addressed a few words to the marchers before they set out for the atomic research station at Aldermaston. "Let me offer you a new slogan," he cried to the upturned faces. "Let your slogan be,

'From Fear to Sanity!' " he shouted to tumultous applause.[23]

It remains to be added that by 1961 Gerald had begun to entertain serious doubts concerning the annual CND pilgrimage, writing to Maurice Richardson, "Nobody could be a more sincere pacifist than am I, but I do not foresee anything but disaster if Britain alone decided to ban the bomb." But meanwhile Gerald had undergone another chameleon change and become a paid propagandist for South Africa's apartheid government.

*

On August 24 1958, Gerald appeared wearing a black tie in token of mourning for Johannes Gerhardus Strydom, South Africa's ferociously racialist premier. It was probably then that the idea occurred to him of doing a paid white-wash job for the South African government in the form of a travel book. In May 1959, he writes to Eric Louw, the South African Minister of External Affairs, "I think the time has come for some active propaganda to be made in England to let my fellow countrymen appreciate the real truth, instead of listening only to the abominable and seditious drivel of Father Huddleston and Michael Scott." Gerald then goes on to suggest that he visit South Africa with a view to writing "a truthful description of what I find to be the real state of affairs", a suggestion which struck a responsive chord; and early in September Gerald met Piet Meiring, director of South Africa's Information Service, to discuss the projected visit. The upshot was that the South

---

23 This story, with Gerald's Zelig-like manifestation on the CND podium, is taken from John Symonds's *Conversation with Gerald*, but things are – characteristically – more complicated. Gerald's presence is not remembered by Pat Arrowsmith, who organised the event and emphatically denies he was there [conversation 3. iv. 12]. Nor is he mentioned at the event by Maurice Richardson, in his *New Statesman* diary column, despite the fact that Richardson generally found Gerald 'good value'. [Ed.]

African government agreed to pay Sidgwick and Jackson, the publishers, £1,400 for 2,000 copies of Gerald's book, to be distributed free to incoming migrants.

Gerald, who arrived in Cape Town in October, was accorded red-carpet treatment as a guest of the Verwoerd government. "I spent nine months in South Africa and visited every town of importance," Gerald claimed of the trip later; in reality, he spent less than three months, and then ventured very little outside Cape Town, Johannesburg and Durban, the main centres of population. He was shown a hospital, visited a model prison for non-whites, interviewed Chief Luthuli, and found time for a brief excursion to Mozambique, whose postage stamps featuring tropical butterflies he admired. His recollections of this tour he entitled *Jacaranda*, but a more apt title might be "Gullible's Travels".

Having noted on page 17 that the term "native" is misleading "because the Bantu are in fact no more natives of South Africa than the whites", forgetful Gerald then uses "native" repeatedly in the remaining 174 pages of the book. Among other habitats where Gerald studied the "natives" at close hand was Leeukop Prison just outside Johannesburg, where two thousand of them were locked up. "As I and the two friends who accompanied me drove in through the gates of Leeukop we seemed to be entering the drive leading to some important country seat," he writes. "Large gardens with flowerbeds making a riot of colour lay on each side of the drive, and when we at last reached the central building we were greeted… by a very charming, merry but efficient police captain who was in charge." Inside the prison itself, Gerald found that "the walls were painted pastel shades of grey and green". If the prisoners slept on sisal mats on the floor it was because "the average Bantu regards a bed with both suspicion and dislike".

It was on a rainy Sunday that Gerald set out in a battered Morris 8 to visit Albert Luthuli, the deposed Zulu chieftain. Although Luthuli received Gerald courteously, the latter found him "a very bitter man" who dismissed as "window dressing" the model hospital and model prison that Gerald had cited as improvements in the lot of the Bantu. "If ever the day comes when the Whites really turn to loving the Natives," Luthuli is quoted as saying, "they will find that by that time we have all turned to hating the Whites." The chieftain, who was later to be awarded the Nobel Peace Prize, took Gerald in pouring rain to the centre of the village where a monument had been erected over the grave of the fallen Zulu king Chaka. Luthuli then had his picture taken with Gerald, appearing to berate him from one end of the sofa while Gerald, at the other end, stares straight ahead.

To make Gerald's conducted tour even more ludicrous, he kept bumping into Field Marshal Lord Montgomery, likewise on a visit to South Africa. "Who would have dreamed that these two would be found one day tucked up together, as it were, between the ideological sheets?" writes Maurice Richardson, then the London diarist of the *New Statesman*. Monty, who was rabidly homophobic, may have got wind of the offending paragraph, for when Richardson sought an interview with the field marshal at a later date he was turned down in no uncertain terms.

What were Gerald's real views as to the condition of the Bantu? In a letter to John Symonds from Cape Town he writes, "I admit apartheid is pretty grim. All offices are obliged to have two lifts, one for whites only. In the parks a black man may not sit on the same bench as a white, and has to get up and go if a white sits down. Separate counters at the Post Offices."

In *The Way It Was With Me* Gerald writes, "I was in South

Africa at the time of the Sharpeville incident when many Africans were fired upon and killed," but his memory is at fault. He had been back in England a good two months when this massacre occurred. Unfortunately for him, *Jacaranda*, with its rosy picture of Bantu life, had not yet appeared, with the result that Gerald was overtaken by events. The Sharpeville bloodbath in which sixty-seven Africans were mowed down by police armoured cars while demonstrating against Dr Verwoerd's detested pass laws made nonsense of Gerald's conclusion that "the Bantus [are] not only not oppressed at all, but all seeming very cheerful". Gerald then advances the official version of events, writing "something like sixteen thousand [Africans] advanced upon a small police station at Sharpeville, threatening to kill all the police who were there". "I do not know what a hundred and fifty policemen are supposed to do when they believe they are about to be attacked by sixteen thousand or more," he concludes.

Reviewing *Jacaranda* in *Punch*, B.A.Young was lightly dismissive, writing "the idea of Gerald Hamilton defending tyranny is not one that can be entertained *au serieux* for very long"; but in a review in *Tribune*, Myrna Blumberg pictures the author as "tripping with bland pleasure over the graves of a nation". Gerald, on the other hand, apologises for the book's mild tone in a letter to a New Orleans white supremacist named Betty Gaillot, to whom he sent a copy. "I had to modify the tone of this book, in order to get it published… so you may find it rather milk-and-watery, but I continue to remain a great admirer of the South African Republic, which seems to be the one country in Africa today which is properly governed and prosperous."

One other incident concerning his South African trip is worth relating. Gerald had heard that there were gay bars in Durban, but could find no one to act as his cicerone. A Durbanite to whom he was referred by Basil Clavering, and who had better remain anonymous, refused point-blank ("I wouldn't have liked to have him beaten-up, robbed, stabbed") whereupon Gerald, for reasons best known to himself, pressed this newly-found friend to acquire for him a *sjambok*, or whip made of hippo-hide. The Durbanite duly procured the real article, measuring about 4ft long, and tapering from 2in diameter at the handle to half an inch at the tip. Being in a hurry, the friend left the whip, wrapped loosely in brown paper, with the porter at the hotel where Gerald was staying. But when it was delivered to Gerald in the crowded hotel lobby he was suddenly overcome with confusion, and refused to have anything to do with it. The *sjambok* then followed him aboard the RMS Pendennis Castle, when he embarked for the return journey to England; this time the whip in its frayed wrapper being presented to him by the ship's captain. Gerald, apparently feeling that he could no longer disown it, accepted delivery of the article. The captain, whenever he encountered him thereafter, was apt to look at Gerald pensively.

*

Besides *Jacaranda*, Gerald was author, or part-author, of six other books, three of them being autobiographical. The expression "part-author" is used because Gerald never wrote anything if he could get someone to ghost it for him. *Desert Dreamers*, a piece of juvenilia, is the only work which he wrote unassisted, so far as I have been able to ascertain. His collaborators included Christopher Isherwood, Desmond Stewart, Alan Neame, Ivor Powell, James Pope-Hennessy, Maurice Richardson, and Peter Burton. The extent of their collaboration ranged from contributing a brief foreword, in Pope-Hennessy's case, to writing nine-tenths of the book in the case of Stewart and Neame. Gerald paid Ivor Powell £10 to write the last chapter of *Mr Norris and I*, which was supposed to be the *summa* of his beliefs. When Powell questioned him concerning his credo, Gerald said, "Write what you like – I don't believe in anything."

Gerald's earliest attempt at autobiography, *As Young As Sophocles*, published in 1937, is by far the best of the three versions of his life story, possibly because in the writing of it he had the unacknowledged assistance of Isherwood. The title is from a poem by an Eton master named William Johnson Cory, which reads in part:

> I'll borrow life, and not grow old,
> And nightingales and trees
> Shall keep me, though the veins be cold
> As young as Sophocles.

Gerald's veins were far from cold when he wrote *Sophocles*, which carried him from birth up to the close of the Berlin period, but the book is oddly unsatisfying, as its critics were quick to point out. Only Harold Nicolson, reviewing it in the *Daily Telegraph*, was fulsome in his praise, finding the book a "curious and moving" one which he had read "with the greatest interest". "How came it that this sensitive, intelligent, and in many ways fastidious person should have suffered so many misadventures and endured so much unhappiness?" Nicolson asks. On the other hand, J.S. Collis, reviewing *Sophocles* in the *Observer*, found it "very irritating," adding that "because his [Hamilton's] modesty is as great as his pride we close the book disappointed". Maurice Richardson, in a conversation I had with him, suggested that the book should be re-titled *As Old As Salome*: "Gerald, whether through modesty or pride, was a strip-teaser *par excellence*, adept at manipulating two half-truths as though they were fans."

"Tantalizing," is the way John Davenport describes *Mr Norris and I*, Gerald's second essay in autobiography, which was published in 1956. "One is introduced again and again to famous and infamous figures of the past, but they are as un-communicative as their glazed and dusty images at Madame Tussaud's," Davenport complains in the *Spectator*, damning the book as "a monument to good taste". "What did Roger Casement really say?" Davenport asks. If Roger Casement's conversation goes unreported I suggest that it is because Gerald, who had never met him, lacked the creative imagination to invent it.

Gerald might have made his fortune by writing a cook-book for, although he could not boil an egg, he could quite late in life still remember in detail a dinner given by the Duchess of Rutland in 1910, and tell you what wines accompanied each course. In a memorandum entitled 'Recollections of the finest dinners I have been privileged to eat', among his papers, Gerald describes this feast from the turtle soup to the *Bombe Canonnade* (vanilla ice cream with strips of ginger). "The greatest pleasures I have had in all my life," he told John Symonds, "have not been from sex, although this has contributed its share, but from well thought-out, perfectly cooked, and well balanced meals accompanied by suitable wines."

The Way It Was With Me (the title was suggested to Gerald by Brian Desmond Hurst, to whom the book is dedicated) is Gerald's third attempt at autobiography, published in 1969, and owes much of its readability to the research and editing of Peter Burton. The book's working title was "The Real Mr Norris", and in a précis intended for the publisher's eyes Gerald promises to tell all ("It is about time my definitive autobiography was written, as my life has been full of sparkle, sadness and joy"). Among the revelations promised are:

Details about well known perverts and flagellants known to me. Details of my two marriages, my first wife being the mistress of King George of Greece – indeed, it was for this reason I married her.

My role in the "Mr A" case, when the Rajah of Kashmir was blackmailed by Captain Arthur, his secretary, Monty Newton, and William Cooper Hobbs…

In the published book there is no mention of those well-known perverts and flagellants, nor of that marriage to King George's mistress, nor of Gerald's role in the Mr A blackmail case. Modesty triumphant, Gerald has once more run offstage with his rhinestone G-string firmly in place.

Of the remaining Hamilton oeuvre, *Emma in Blue*, written in collaboration with Desmond Stewart, recounts the rise at the turn of the eighteenth century of Emma Harte, illegitimate daughter of a Welsh servant girl, from London streets to marriage with doddering Sir William Hamilton, British Ambassador to the Court of Naples, to a lesbian relationship with Queen Caroline of the Two Sicilies, and finally to the bed of Admiral Lord Nelson. "You can state categorically that I wrote ninety-nine per cent of *Emma* – all in fact except the little autobiographical fragment by Gerald at the end," Stewart tells me. The book was well-reviewed in the *New Yorker* magazine which described it as "an acid period biography…

[which] though hardly agreeable reading, is an uncommonly interesting book", but it was roasted by English reviewers, who saw it as an attack on Lord Nelson and the British Navy. "If there is a public which detests Lord Nelson, despises Lady Hamilton and rejoices in abuse of the British Navy," writes George Malcolm Thomson in the *Evening Standard*, "then this is its book".

Gerald trotted out his usual conspiracy theory to account for the book not being reviewed widely in the United Kingdom, writing to Stewart, who was then in Beirut, "You know as well as I do how powerful the Jews and Masons are in Fleet Street." A more cogent reason for the book's neglect is that it appeared shortly after the Suez crisis, when Britons had other problems on their minds. As a bizarre tailpiece to *Emma*'s publishing history, Stewart reported on Empire Day 1957 that a copy of the book had been sent to Moscow to Ralph Parker of the Soviet State Publishing House with an eye to having the book published in translation in the Soviet Union. When Parker, in turn, handed it over to one of his readers for a report, the reader was none other than Guy Burgess.

"I could very easily show you which words of *Blood Royal* were written by Gerald – about .005%," Alan Neame writes. Yet when "Bloody Royal", as Neame calls it, was published in 1964, only Gerald's name appeared on the book's title page. Although Gerald in his foreword makes graceful acknowledgment of help received ("I wish he [Neame] would not smoke, and I cannot share his taste for Indian tea, but without his aid, his patience with my autocratic ways and his skill in research, this book might never have been written") there is no hint of the nature of this lop-sided collaboration. Lop-sided it certainly was – for when we met for lunch at his club, Neame presented me with a copy of *Blood Royal* in which those portions written by Gerald were marked in ink in the margins, and they were very small indeed. Neame had also marked in the margins such notations as "not true", "invented", and "made up".

The main theme of *Blood Royal* is the havoc wrought by Queen Victoria's daughters and grand-daughters, as haemophilia-carriers, on the royal houses of Russia, Prussia, Hesse, Teck, Battenburg, and Spain into which they married, all of said houses having produced their share of "bleeders". A secondary theme is the alleged illegitimacy of Prince Albert, the Prince Consort, who Gerald claims was the natural son of Baron von Mayer, chamberlain to the Duke and Duchess of Coburg and himself a Jew. Gerald's authority for this startling revelation was ex-Tsar Ferdinand of Bulgaria, who was supposed to have shown Gerald the relevant documents from the ducal archives when Gerald attended the so-called "Coburg wedding" in 1933.

Despite Neame's hard work, reviewers found *Blood Royal* boring. "What makes it so lifeless," writes John Moorehead in the *Western Mail*, "is the dullness of his writing… Hardly a character in the book has more dimensions than a gossip column could provide." H.D. Ziman, reviewing the book in the *Daily Telegraph*, was harsher still, describing it as "a rare combination of snobbery, ill-nature and pointless reminiscences". "Without wishing to dispute Mr Hamilton's personal acquaintance with the various deceased or deposed Monarchs by whom he claims to have been entertained," Ziman continues, "I feel considerable scepticism about his accuracy. It would be difficult to make more misstatements in a few pages about Leopold II of the Belgians…"

Blood Royal did better than any of Gerald's other books, but it lost him some royal friends. Queen Ena of Spain, then living in exile at Lausanne, considered it a "nasty book", according to Gerald, while Prince Nicholas of Romania, ex-King Carol's only brother, was annoyed to find himself mixed up in "this *pot au feu royale*", as he called it. Perhaps the prince took exception to the opening sentence of the chapter on Romania: "The Romanians take immense pride in descending from the bastards sired by Roman legionaries." Or again the prince may have objected to his mother, Queen Marie, being described as "egocentric, boundlessly vain, greedy for money and power", or to his brother, Carol, being pictured as suffering from satyriasis, and the victim of his mistress, Madame Lupescu, whose name translates as 'she-wolf'. Whatever the reason, *Blood Royal* got Gerald into hot water with his princely friend.

On a lighter note he may have been more amused by a letter from his friend Basil Clavering who, referring to the book's genealogical ramifications, writes, "I am at the chapter where the third illegitimate son of the second Duke of Seville has had a mild car accident and, due to bleeding, has broken off his engagement with the second illegitimate son of the third wife of the fourth Duke of Madrid by his second mother's uncle's grandson."

Thirteen

January 1964: Intrigue in Spain

Soon after his return from South Africa, Gerald moved to 17 Dartrey Road, Chelsea, the five-year lease of which he acquired from his friend Robert Jacobs ("I got the lease as a result of a property deal and made a present of it to Gerald," Jacobs told me. "Inasmuch as Gerald used only the ground floor, he had the rental of the flat above his, which gave him an income.") Gerald then set about to beautify "Dirty Dartrey", as he called it, by having his front door painted a bright yellow, and making arrangements with a local florist to keep his windowboxes supplied with blooms in season. The unpaid florist's bills are still among his papers.

From Gerald's viewpoint No 17 had the advantage of backing onto Robin Maugham's house in Seaton Street. Over the years Gerald's friendship with Maugham, who upon the death of his father in 1958 had been elevated to the peerage as Viscount Maugham, had deepened. Now that they were neighbours Gerald was constantly in and out of Lord Maugham's house, giving rise to a bizarre episode. In his book *Search for Nirvana* Maugham reveals how, before leaving for Timbuktu early in 1959, he made his will, including among the specific bequests "Item 23", £50 to Gerald. During Maugham's absence Gerald had the run of his house, dropping in daily to see that everything was in order. Upon his return to England, Lord Maugham, in searching for a photograph in the bottom drawer of his desk, came upon the will in its sealed envelope, opened it out of curiosity, and read: "Item 23: To Gerald

Hamilton of Dartrey Road I leave the sum of £5000." "I found a magnifying-glass," Maugham relates. "I looked closer. The forgery had been expert." It was another instance of "good old, bad old Gerald", but the episode did nothing to spoil their friendship.

A new friend of this period was tall, slim Maurice Leonard, then in his early twenties. Bored with his job as a music shop assistant, Leonard had inserted an advertisement in a London newspaper to the effect: "Ex-drama student, ex-RAF, with nursing experience, seeks interesting employment". Gerald, apparently from curiosity, answered, and although he had nothing to offer him in the way of employment, they became friends, Leonard being a frequent dinner guest at Dartrey Road. "Gerald would buy take-away food – usually a dab of paté and a cold bird of some kind – from Harrods or Fortnum's, while I supplied the wine," Leonard relates. "Not that Gerald would trust me to select the wine. No, he would phone up the wine shop on the corner and tell them exactly what wine he wanted, including the vintage, and I would pick it up on my way from work – and pay for it, of course."

Dirty Dartrey also produced a cleaning woman in the person of freckle-faced Violet, or Vi as she was better known. Vi had stipulated that she would not char for Gerald on Sunday, whereupon the latter had countered with "My dear lady, I am incapable of making my own bed Monday through Friday, what leads you to suppose that I could do a better job of it on Sunday?" Bowing to this logic, Vi gave in.

Possibly because she could not take Gerald seriously, Vi insisted upon calling him "Joey", a London colloquialism for a clown deriving from Joseph Grimaldi. Gerald in turn had his Vi stories, such as the note she left him: "Joey, your fiend was here while you was out." Which particular fiend had called in his absence, Gerald inquired, and had he left any mark of his fiendishness? On another occasion Vi informed Gabrielle Potter that Gerald could not come to the phone because "he's feeling queer and in bed with the doctor". "But my dear lady," Gerald protested, "I've been queer all my life." Vi would stand no nonsense from Gerald when it came to being paid. While her employer still lay abed she would rummage in his trousers until she found his wallet and extract her wages from it, sometimes returning the wallet empty.

*

Three weeks after his seventieth birthday, Gerald was knocked down in South Kensington by a youth riding a Lambretta. Fortunately he suffered no injuries, although he was badly shaken up. He was, however, highly indignant, maintaining that he never traversed the road except on zebra crossings, and then only after looking both ways, although this is contradicted by those who knew him. "He would dart out from the kerb, followed by a screech of brakes hastily applied, and the smell of scorched rubber, then he would dart back again, his hand on his heart as though he were expiring," says Mary Seaton. "He also had the quaint notion that members of the peerage, as pedestrians, had certain privileges. I remember trying to cross the Mall with him once, and Gerald shouting to the policeman on point duty, 'Look here, officer, stop the cars – I'm a peer of the realm.' "

Gerald had aged, and had become more and more excitable, his behaviour more and more erratic. Erratic is the only way to describe his interruption of Micheal MacLiammoir during a matinee performance of the latter's one-man Oscar Wilde show in January, 1961. The Irish actor had just finished reciting Wilde's *The Ballad of Reading Gaol* when, according to Maurice Richardson, Gerald "jumped to his feet and cried, in a voice quivering with perfectly genuine emotion: 'That's the way they murdered my friend Casement!' "

Meanwhile, flushed by his success in obtaining a free trip to South Africa, Gerald put out feelers concerning similar free-loading propaganda junkets first to the Taiwan government of Chiang Kai-shek and then, when that fell through, to the Rhodesia government of Ian Smith. "My idea," Gerald writes to Dr Y.S. Chen, director of the Free China Information Bureau, "would be for a clear, objective, and anecdotal book, describing a visit to the Island and individual impressions of the Government, on similar lines to those in my book on South Africa as I found it a year ago". "It would be very helpful if they [the government] would be prepared to underwrite a certain number of copies, to be decided on later," Gerald added. The authorities in Taipei took over four months to ponder Gerald's proposition, and when they did reply their offer was anything but magnanimous. "They suggest you pay your own fare from London to Formosa and back," Dr Chen writes, "but you will be treated as a guest of the Government while you are on the island. The manuscript of your book should be submitted to our Government for approval before it is published. If it is approved by them they will buy a minimum of 500 copies of the book at special reduced rate." Gerald next approached the U.S. Embassy in London to see if the Americans would pick up the tab for his travel to Formosa from London, or perhaps let him hitch a ride on a U.S. Air Force plane; but the most the Americans were willing to do was to supply him with free transport from Los Angeles to Taipei, so the whole Formosa deal fell through.

Undiscouraged, Gerald next turned to Ian Smith, Rhodesia's

prime minister, announcing his availability to do a book on that beleaguered country. But first, Gerald extended "my own good wishes for the success of your mission here" (Smith was in London discussing the thorny question of one-man-one-vote.) "We all hope that you will not give in on… matters of principle," Gerald adds. Again, nothing came of his offer to act as Smith's paid propagandist.

*

Finally there occurred an episode over which it might be charitable to draw a veil, had it not been described in some detail elsewhere. In May 1962, Gerald was the guest of Justerini and Brooks, the wine merchants, at one of their weekly wine-tasting luncheons in their wine vaults underneath Charing Cross Station to which usually ten people – the two directors and eight guests – were invited. On this occasion Gerald's friend Geoffrey Rigby was the host, and Gerald's fellow guests included Lord Maugham and Maurice Richardson. Maugham, who in his account of the episode disguises his hosts as "Messrs Helana and Faustini", writes that before lunch Gerald had made a pig of himself by gulping down quantities of a rare Amontillado "with a speed that amazed" and a "noise like dish-water being poured down an ill-adjusted drain".

At lunch, three helpings of lobster mousse disappeared down that same gullet. Gradually, according to Maugham, thawed by an exquisite Pommard, Gerald had lowered the tone of his stories from exiled royalties he had known to a sailor he had picked up in Toulon. With the arrival of the Napoleon Brandy, Gerald "began a series of interlocking tales whose length might well be likened to some pornographic saga", Maugham continues. It was terminated only by Mr Faustini's announcement that he was due at a board meeting.

What happened next is a matter of some dispute. When the other guests rose to go, "Gerald's bulk slumped on to the table; his huge head was cradled in his arms and he remained inert," according to Maugham, who fetched a luggage trolley from Charing Cross Station and, with the aid of a porter, heaved Gerald onto it and wheeled him to a taxi. According to Geoffrey Rigby, Gerald was all right until he was helped to the sidewalk, when he said, "I can't walk – my legs have given out," whereupon Maugham went for the trolley. "It was the first time I have ever seen Gerald drunk," Rigby recalls, "but there he was laid out on the barrow, his stomach pointed skywards, with a horde of commuters missing their five o'clock trains to outer suburbia in order to look on."

Rigby doesn't remember Gerald's table talk as being particularly indecent. "Gerald was a raconteur," he points out: "He amused by telling anecdotes. But I have never heard him tell blue anecdotes." Maurice Richardson, whom I questioned, likewise had no recollection of the pornographic saga. There was no dispute, however, concerning Gerald's inebriety. "In the presence of so much vintage wine Gerald was grabbing glasses with both hands," Richardson recalled.

Lord Maugham accompanied Gerald home to Dartrey Road in the taxi, and put him to bed. A few hours later Maugham was roused by a telephone call from Vi (whom he refers to as "Elsie"), announcing that Gerald had fallen out of bed and "broken his hooter". The ambulance had already arrived by the time Maugham reached No 17, but he was in time to witness a little girl, one of the horde of neighbourhood children who had gathered to watch as Gerald was lifted into the back of the ambulance, rush up to the stretcher and cry, "Give my love to Jesus!"

At Fulham Hospital Gerald had his stomach pumped, and that same night, having a horror of hospitals, he discharged himself, going by taxi in pyjamas and dressing-gown (Vi had taken his clothes away to be cleaned) first to Vi's house to get his key, then, not finding her at home, to a pub which she was known to frequent. The pub regulars looked up startled when Gerald made his entree in hospital regalia, looking like an Ali Baba who had fallen among forty thieves.

*

Meanwhile, Gerald had found a patron in the person of 'Robert Jacobs', a property developer in his early twenties. "Robert Jacobs," writes John Symonds, "looked like a schoolboy; he had a slightly self-conscious air, or, rather, a mixture of self-consciousness and expectancy – of something pleasant about to happen at any moment." Symonds adds "He was, I felt, the sort of person to whom pleasant things were happening constantly."

Mention was made earlier of how this young Maecenas had made over to Gerald the lease of No 17, which Jacobs had acquired as a result of a property deal. Not only that, but Jacobs had made cash gifts to Gerald over a considerable period of time, as is evident from the diary extracts which Symonds quotes:

28 September, 1958. He [Gerald] told me that Robert Jacobs had called on him at ten past eight that morning, thrust two fivers into his hand, and darted back into the taxi. "It's a strange world," commented Gerald. "Still, I have lived all my life in strange worlds."

29 January 1960. He was in a cheerful mood, for in spite of his debts… things looked bright. His patron, Robert Jacobs, had given him that morning £100. "He's rolling in money," said Gerald…

16 July 1961. Gerald was in a good mood. A cheque poultice had been applied to his sores… Robert Jacobs had called that morning and given him a cheque for the rent.

He showed me the cheque for £111.10s. "Childish handwriting," he commented.

It was in connection with Jacobs that he brought out his *bon mot* "I am supported entirely by involuntary contributions."

I shall continue to call him Robert Jacobs, though he now goes under a different name ("The trouble with changing your name is that they always throw it in your face when you appear in court," he complains). By the time I met Jacobs over lunch at Fino's Wine Bar in Shaftesbury Avenue he had lost whatever look of schoolboy expectancy he may have possessed. Now in his forties, he is short and swarthy with thinning black hair, and bears a superficial resemblance to Hussein of Jordan – a younger Hussein with a bushy black moustache. Far from having pleasant things happening to him constantly, as Symonds had predicted, Jacobs has spent a good part of his life in prison on fraud charges. When we met he had been out for less than three months.

I was interested in those "involuntary contributions" towards Gerald's upkeep which Jacobs had made some twenty years earlier. Was it blackmail? I knew that Gerald had busied himself, or pretended to busy himself, in procuring a title of nobility for Jacobs from San Marino ("Surely you can understand that such a delicate matter cannot be dealt with except by personal interview," Gerald cautioned Jacobs, when he became impatient for results). Still, entries in Gerald's diaries, which he used also as book-keeping ledgers, show that over a four-year period Jacobs had given Gerald more than a thousand pounds, much of the cash being contributed after June 1958, when Jacobs went bankrupt. Jacobs denies that there was anything sinister about these gifts. "I gave Gerald money because I liked him, because I found him amusing to have around. Besides, a few hundred quid would have meant nothing to me in those days. It would have been peanuts."

Jacobs looked upon Gerald as a father figure, it seemed. This was true of the upper-class dropouts who befriended Gerald in the sixties (had not Gerald himself been a dropout of sorts in his day?) It was precisely because he was disreputable that Gerald filled this role so satisfactorily, in contrast to their own fathers, who did not understand them. "Gerald was a steadying influence," Jacobs remarks. "He kept me from going completely haywire." The upper-class dropouts expressed their rebellion in various ways, some by joining the Foreign Legion, others by eloping with an heiress. Robert Jacobs, whose background was not upper-class, did it by acquiring stately homes – first Diddington Hall, a 17th century manor house in Huntingdonshire, then Brancepeth Castle near Durham, which had Saxon foundations and a moat around it. Unhappily, these castles in the air, which their *quondam* owner saw as rungs on a Jacob's ladder leading to social acceptance, came crashing to earth with the swiftness and regularity of the building societies and motor insurance companies which he floated. Undeterred, Jacobs talked of big deals in the offing when we met ("I have two office buildings under renovation in the City, and another four property deals pending," he said. "By this time next year

I shall be a millionaire.")

Jacobs harbours only one grudge against Gerald, and that is Gerald's carelessness in forfeiting the lease on No 17 Dartrey Road, which still had over three years to run. How did it happen? It transpires that those fivers and tenners which Jacobs had thrust into Gerald's willing hand some twenty years earlier, darting in and out of taxis in order to do so, were intended to cover the rent on No 17, but that they were appropriated by Gerald for his own personal use. Further, it transpires that Gerald told the owner, a Greek by the name of Soutzos, that he had been paying the rent regularly to Jacobs, and that it was Jacobs who had misappropriated it. "Why Gerald should play me such a dirty trick I do not understand," Jacobs complains. "What he hoped to gain by it is beyond my comprehension." And as he gropes for an explanation a quizzical expression crosses Jacobs's face. It is the puzzled look of a boy who has just caught his father out in a lie, and I begin to understand Symonds's reference to him as having the air of a schoolboy.

*

Gerald's abrupt departure for Madrid, in January 1964, is lamented by two shepherdesses, Tonina and Clarissa, in a Chelsea eclogue which Desmond Stewart wrote especially for the occasion.

> Clarissa: Dion has gone! Dion is snatched away!
> Dion, with whom we frolicked yesterday!
> And proud Iberia now controls the boy
> Who yestere'en was my enchanting joy.
>
> Tonina: Not thine alone, Clarissa, this sad loss.

Dion would always generously toss
His favours to far more than only you!
…
Clarissa: Mocker! See, I rend
This gilded damask. See, my velvet's torn,
And ripped in twain my handkerchief of lawn.
And so I shall forego food, clothes and sleep,
Till he returns I shall do nought but weep.

Gerald's departure was far from being mourned by those other denizens of Dirty Dartrey, Vi the char and her scavenger friends. The morning Gerald made his hasty exit for Madrid, owing £624 in back rent, these vultures descended upon No 17 and proceeded to strip his flat of its contents, disputing them noisily and loading them on to barrow and pram. One harpy claimed that "Joey" had promised her the curtains; another that he had said she could have the Hoover, while a third laid claim to his best saucepan. These harridans would have shared the carpet among themselves had they been able to prise it up. By the time they returned the following morning with the proper tools for the job the owner, Mr Soutzos, had put a new lock on the door.

Gerald had talked of settling in Madrid permanently, partly in order to be near his royal friends who lived in exile there, Prince Nicholas of Romania and the Grand Duke Wladimir, whom he recognised as the Tsar of All the Russias. But chiefly Gerald relished living in Spain because of Generalissimo Franco, whom he admired intensely. "When people ask me why Spain is today so happy & prosperous," he writes to John Symonds, "I say it is because Franco's first action on assuming power was to abolish the Cortes and forbid elections." In the back of Gerald's mind he may have seen himself becoming a paid propagandist for the Franco regime, writing articles and making broadcasts.

It was to set the machinery in motion towards this end that Gerald flew to Madrid towards the end of May 1963; but his hopes of obtaining an audience with Franco were dashed by the death of Pope John XXIII which plunged Spain into mourning, or so he wrote to Gabrielle Potter. Even so, Gerald had gone about seeking an audience the wrong way, as he admitted to Symonds, by trying to get himself recommended by the American Embassy and not the British one, which his papal contact Count Villaverde explained would have been more appropriate. However, since the British Embassy was unlikely to recommend anyone with Gerald's track record this avenue would appear to have been closed to him, and before he could explore others his hand had been forced by a notice to quit No 17.

Gerald's design for living in Madrid was simplicity itself. His rent would cost him nothing, since Mike Steen, a friend of Tennessee Williams who was in Madrid working with Nicholas Ray on a film, had offered to share his flat at Marceliano Santamaria with him. As for his living expenses, Gerald planned to bask in the sun on the £5/13/6d per week old age pension which he had been drawing from the government since reaching the age of sixty-five. He thought these 900 pesetas a week would be ample, little reckoning that ordering one meal at the Tabema Collejon, or buying his friend Prince Nicholas of Romania a champagne cocktail at the Castellana-Hilton, would gobble up the entire week's worth. Gerald was brought face-to-face with reality when having got himself invited to a party given by film producer Sam Bronson he found himself seated next to Claudia Cardinale. "We got on famously," Gerald writes to Symonds. "At the end she said

I could take her out one evening next week, what about Thursday!! Imagine me trying to take out the most expensive star in Madrid. I shall get out of it somehow."

Far from being able to wine and dine Claudia Cardinale, by the end of his second week in Madrid Gerald had not a bean to his name. Before leaving London Gerald had given his pension book to a young man whom he scarcely knew, and had signed a number of vouchers in advance so that the young man could draw the pension from the post office. Instead of forwarding the pension money to Gerald in Madrid, the young man then proceeded to get drunk on the proceeds at the Golden Lion in Soho. "I am just going mad, that is all I can say," Gerald writes to Symonds. "I feel absolutely suicidal… quite seriously I will not be alive next week unless I receive my money. I am truly almost starving."

The prospect of Gerald starving sent not only Symonds but Geoffrey Rigby rushing to help, and a few days later a cheque from the latter arrived, with comic consequences. "I went to the Bank," Gerald writes, "but the cheque was made out to 'Bearer' instead of my name. They said would I get 'Senor Bearer' to endorse it over to me & they would cash it for me. I tried to explain that Bearer meant *Portador* but they wouldn't swallow that… They are sending the cheque to London for clearance." Apparently Rigby had forgotten to transfer funds to his current account to cover the cheque, for back it came marked "Please re-present". "I hardly dare set foot in the Bank again after such loss of face." Gerald regained his composure when two days later he received a cheque for £150 enclosed in a letter signed jointly by Rigby and Mike Steen, and the visits to the Castellana-Hilton for the daily shave and facial were resumed once more – "so good for the skin and the morale, dear boy".

*

Gerald's letters contain tantalizing hints of a royalist revival in Madrid. "I now see the Grand Duke Wladimir almost daily," he writes to Symonds. "We have a wonderful plan (enemies might call it a plot) – nothing to do with Russia but about something else." To other friends he was more explicit. The royalist revival, which had the backing of Franco, would extend from Portugal right to the borders of Russia, Gerald told Robin Maugham. This was why Franco, who was himself awaiting only the opportune moment to retire in favour of Juan Carlos, gave asylum to so many crowned heads. With the ex-monarchs restored to their thrones gracious living would return to the Continent once more.

What part in this intrigue did that great exponent of gracious living, Gerald Hamilton, play? Coyly, Gerald left it to his friends to decide. But he did tell Robin Maugham that he travelled to Spain on a "special permit", whatever that may mean; and that on one visit his plane had been met by a Franco cabinet minister. That was in 1965, when Gerald stayed in an apartment at the Residencia Marquina opposite the Spanish War Office, a propinquity which Maugham, who could hear sentries clicking their heels in the street outside, found faintly sinister. Maugham observed "black-suited men" with "bulging despatch cases" leave this apartment, after which Gerald himself would depart on some "furtive assignation". On one occasion, after a man in black had arrived, Gerald had locked himself in with the stranger, whose despatch case when he emerged five minutes later seemed "less bulky". Finally, Maugham plucked up courage to ask Gerald who his visitor was, to be told that he was the private secretary of one of the "royals".

In the end Gerald could not bring himself to settle down permanently in Madrid. For one thing, despite Maugham's innuendo about bulging despatch cases, he could find no means of earning money to supplement that meagre pension of his, which fell so far short of his needs (and to make things worse, he had laid himself open to criminal proceedings by carelessly bandying about his pension book – of the three friends whom Gerald at one time or another entrusted to collect his pension, two absconded with the money). And he could not continue to cadge on Mike Steen indefinitely – Gerald had to vacate Steen's flat when Tennessee Williams arrived to stay at Easter. In April 1964 Gerald returned to London, a city that was now beginning to swing.

Fourteen

January 1966: Wickedest Man in The World

"In this century every decade has had its city... Today, it is London, a city steeped in tradition, seized by change, liberated by affluence... In a decade dominated by youth, London has burst into bloom. It swings; it is the scene" – thus *Time* magazine, in its issue of April 15 1966, begins an ecstatic tribute to 'Swinging London' in an article entitled "You Can Walk Across It On The Grass" (grass in this instance referring to London's extensive parks, not to the plant that its liberated youth were smoking). Gerald thought so highly of this article that he cut it out and kept it. It is now at the Harry Ransom Humanities Research Centre, Texas, in a Hamilton box containing among other items theatre programmes, racing cards, Old Rugbeian Society newsletters, a Gibraltar lottery ticket, a circular advertising a virility-builder known as Testerone, and an Amplivox hearing aid guarantee.

"This spring, as never before in modern times, London is switched on," the article continues. "Ancient elegance and new opulence are all tangled up in a dazzling blur of op and pop. The city is alive with birds (girls) and Beatles, buzzing with minicars and telly stars, pulsing with half a dozen separate veins of excitement." The ancient elegance that was Gerald Hamilton had no need of *Time* to remind him that London was switched on. He had only to throw open the window of his bedsit above a Chinese restaurant in Chelsea, and to look down. In the mid-sixties the King's Road "pulsed with excitement", as *Time* put it, as it had not done in the three hundred years since

Charles II and his retinue had used this highway to go from his palace in Whitehall to Hampton Court.

Did Gerald move to a furnished room at 318A King's Road, above a Chinese restaurant called The Good Earth, merely so that he could boast "It is better to be above The Good Earth than below it?" That is what some of his friends concluded after hearing his *bon mot* for the hundredth time.

The room itself was nothing to boast about, however, being furnished with only the barest necessities. "Squalid", "dingy", and "mean" are some of the adjectives applied to it by friends, who also objected to climbing the stairs. (Ivor Powell, who trudged upstairs only to find Gerald out, pinned a note to his door which reads "St. Augustine tells us that the way to a tabernacle should be steep – but to find the Shrine empty! Perhaps you are being carried in procession round the town?") Squalid it may have been, but Gerald was probably happier at 318A than he had been at any time since the war.

"The Guards now change at Buckingham Palace to a Lennon and McCartney tune, and Prince Charles is firmly in the long-hair set," *Time* assured its readers. It is doubtful whether any member of Her Majesty's Brigade of Guards now knocked on Gerald's door, as had happened so often in the past. Should a member have ventured to do so, the first thing he would have noticed upon entering was a sign reading "Visitors Are Requested Not To Smoke". That sign would have served as the visitor's introduction to the process known as "geraldization" from the verb "to geraldize", meaning to impose one's will, to force others to conform to one's lifestyle, to steamroller, and to flatten all opposition.

Should the guardsman have had the misfortune to arrive on the hour, he would have found himself unceremoniously shushed after being ushered in, for life above The Good

Earth came to a halt at hourly intervals while Gerald listened to the news on his transistor radio. It mattered not that the news varied little from hour to hour – there was always the possibility of a tidal wave in the New Hebrides, an earthquake in Outer Mongolia, or a rebellion in Peru.

In this respect, nothing that was human was alien to Gerald; he refused even to take telephone calls while the BBC news bulletins were being broadcast. As Gerald had become hard of hearing the radio was usually turned on full blast. However, if the television belonging to the neighbour below him were turned one decibel beyond what Gerald considered to be the acceptable limit he would geraldize that poor neighbour by hammering on the floor with a broom.

*

Gerald arose at 6 a.m. (Sir Cyril Hampson said "He does this so that he can pack more wickedness into his day") and had no breakfast other than a large cup of black coffee laced with brandy, arguing that miners in the Pas de Calais started their day thus "and look how *costaud* they are".

Having completed the *Daily Telegraph* crossword while still in his pyjamas and dressing-gown, Gerald would telephone Thora Brabazon-Ellis to see if she had finished it first. In fact, Gerald expected his friends to be as wide awake as he was before noon, with utter disregard for their nocturnal habits. "This is firstly to apologise for waking you up at 10 a.m. this morning," Gerald writes to James Reeve, the portrait painter. "I had been up for 5 hours, written 2 chapters before ringing you. I foolishly thought 10 o'clock was not too early to ring a friend." The sting he saved for the tail of the letter: "The reason I rang you was because I saw the Archduke Otto of Hapsburg yesterday for a brief moment and was invited to attend a reception for him today and to bring a friend. I thought at once of you, hoping you might be asked to do a portrait of him or his wife." "I am just off now to the 'do'," he concludes. There, that will teach the young whipper-snapper to lie abed while his good friend Gerald sits by the telephone waiting for him to return his call.

Distance was no safeguard against the subtle tyranny of geraldisation. Gerald kept a letter-book in which he entered the dates letters were posted to friends, together with the dates on which their replies were received, and woe to those who failed to acknowledge his letters promptly, or to answer the questions propounded therein. "Your letter dated (a trifle vaguely!) Sunday night & postmarked 11th arrived this a.m.," he writes to Ian Dunlop from Tangier. "Had you put another 1d on it & an air-mail tab I would no doubt have got it at least ten days earlier." To this same correspondent, guilty of vague dating, cheap posting and slow despatch: "Thank you so much for your letter dated March 26, but posted on April 5, indeed a long while *poche restante*."

*

"In Harold Wilson, Downing Street sports a Yorkshire accent, a working-class attitude and a tolerance towards the young that includes Pop Singer 'Screaming' Lord Sutch, who ran against him on the Teen-Age Party picket in the last election," the *Time* article on which Gerald set such store continues in its inventory of 'Swinging London'.

On October 15 1954, Gerald voted Labour for the first – and the last – time in his life, solely because the Labour Party had promised to abolish the death penalty. ("A subtler reason behind my action," he writes to David Stoker, "is the belief that when the public see what harm Labour will do, they will never install another Labour Government.")

In the general election of March 31 1966, when Labour was returned with a 97-seat majority, Gerald refused to vote at all, because "I consider the Conservatives as bad as the Socialists," as he writes to Gabrielle Potter. Gerald was incensed because the Tories were now led by a former grammar-school boy, Ted Heath, whom he accused of "lowering the standard by saying to people, when asked for his autograph... 'Just call me Ted'," he tells Mrs Potter. As an example of "this horrid democracy" that had permeated the Tory party, Gerald cites the case of "a friend of mine, a Mr Boydell, [who] stood as a candidate... he is an old Etonian, but when asked by a heckler, where he was educated, he actually replied: 'At a school near Slough.' "[24] Writing to David Stoker after the 1966 election, Gerald laments the passing of that happier time in his youth "when Lord Salisbury was Prime Minister... women did not have the vote, and Members of Parliament were noble people, who received no salary for their generous efforts on behalf of this country."

*

With the arrival at mid-morning of one or other of the ladies who took his dictation (Edith Simpson until her death in 1965, Gillian Mansel afterwards) Gerald began the main business of the day. Gerald regarded himself as the practitioner of a lost art, that of the letter-writer, and he took his letter-writing seriously. The recipients of his epistolary efforts ranged from

---

24 Gerald has his facts muddled: no Boydell stood for Parliament in 1966, but a P.T.S. Boydell stood as Conservative candidate for Carlisle in October 1964, and was defeated. The "school near Slough" anecdote has been told of many an old Etonian, but erroneously in this case: Boydell did not attend Eton. [Tom Cullen]

the Duke of Windsor to Two-Gun Cohen, from the Comte de Paris to Sir Robert Ho Tung, KBE, reputedly Hong Kong's wealthiest merchant, and included the Harvard Medical School, to whom Gerald offered himself as a suitable case for its study of eccentricity. Many of those he addressed were names he had culled from the morning's news and with whom his links were tenuous.

The line between *pro bono publico* and the begging-letter writer is a thin one, and in many respects Gerald answers the description of the latter, Genus Decayed Gentleman, as furnished by Henry Mayhew, a shrewd chronicler of London seaminess in the mid-nineteenth century. "His mouth is heavy," writes Mayhew, "his underlip thick, sensual, and lowering, and his general expression of pious resignation contradicted by restless, bloodshot eyes that flash from side to side, quick to perceive the approach of a compassionate looking clergyman, a female devotee, or a keen-scented member of the Society for the Suppression of Mendicity."

Mayhew goes on to say that such a begging-letter writer must have a keen knowledge of the nobility and the landed gentry "gleaned from the files of old county newspapers", and also be "a great authority on wines – by right of a famous sample his father 'laid down' in eighteen eleven, 'the comet year, you know'." "It is not uncommon to find among these degraded mendicants one who has really been a gentleman, as far as birth and education go, but whose excesses and extravagances have reduced him to mendicity." In common with these excessive and extravagant gentlemen, Gerald looked upon letters as bread cast upon waters, hoping it would return in the form of well-buttered toast.

To Prince Alfonso Pio, December 4 1961: "You may

wonder why I am fortunate enough to know so many Royal friends of yours…"

To Muhammad Ali, June 21 1967: "I was introduced to you by Maurice Richardson… at a restaurant in Soho called Isow's…"

To HRH Princess Beatrice of Bourbon, May 5 1967: "It might interest you to know that I was a close friend of Queen Sophia… The name of Hamilton is not unconnected with the Court of Ferdinand I…"

To Lew Thorburn, Horizon Pictures, suggesting that he be retained as technical adviser to the film *Nicholas and Alexandra*, April 1 1969: "I venture to point out that I was in Petersburg all 1912 and apart from being received at Court several times, I met Rasputin on two occasions…"

Not all of Gerald's letters were for purposes of ingratiation. He also used his correspondence as a means of venting his prejudices, however contradictory they may be. On the one hand, Gerald takes the Aberdeen Trades Council to task for opposing apartheid ("You are a foolish bunch of meddlers… Why do you not go and live in Soviet Russia?"). On the other, he takes the trouble to write to Paul Orville Crump, a Chicago negro convicted of murder and awaiting the electric chair, hoping "the pleas for clemency on your behalf will be successful".

To the United States Ambassador, November 19 1957: "Mr Gerald Hamilton thanks H.E. the American

Ambassador for his extreme kindness in inviting him to the party at the Embassy on Thanksgiving Day... but feels he must decline the honour, lest he be called upon to shake hands with the Soviet Ambassador."

To the United Nations Association, declining an invitation to a banquet in the Draper's Hall, April 13 1963: "Instead of bringing peace to the world... it [the United Nations] has only succeeded in bringing strife and discord... my own files contain details of the corruption, looting, raping and massacres committed by United Nations soldiers in the Congo."

The files to which he refers, deposited presumably in one of two battered suitcases which Gerald kept under his bed, figure again in "correspondence with *Time* magazine concerning the murder of four thousand Polish officers in Katyn Forest" ("... the most complete file on this massacre is in my possession in my London home... if it interests you or the House Committee investigating the matter").

A favourite target for abuse was the British Broadcasting Corporation, with which Gerald conducted a love-hate relationship over the years. As early as 1946 he had accused the BBC of reluctance to mention news unfavourable to Jews and Freemasons, an accusation which its director-general Sir William Haley, replying through his secretary, had vigorously denied. Unabashed, Gerald tackled Haley's successor Sir Hugh Greene for allowing "a well-known Communist" to appear on a television programme about South Africa. "The public was hoodwinked and bamboozled by the introduction of this lady as a Liberal," Gerald writes. "No doubt your Corporation would consider Stalin and Lenin also Liberals."

Yet the Beeb's alleged liberalism did not prevent Gerald from accepting a fee as technical consultant when the Third Programme did an adaptation of *Mr Norris Changes Trains*. ("It is a pity that I am not an actor," he opined, indicating his willingness to play the title role.) Encouraged by this assignment Gerald was soon putting himself forward as a possible subject for interviews on such programmes as *Tonight* and *Tall Story Club*. "Your friends, who appear to be many and assiduous, keep on asking me to have you for FACE TO FACE," writes John Freeman, whose guests on that programme had included Augustus John and Evelyn Waugh. "I am beginning to be impressed with the possibility," he adds. Nothing came of it, however.

Gerald also made a sustained effort over the years to have his name included in *Who's Who* ("I really feel I am sufficiently well-known already, but if you care to send me a form to fill up... I shall be pleased to do this.") His papers include five form letters covering the period 1959 through 1964 from A&C Black Ltd., publishers of *Who's Who*. In each case the publishers regret that the forthcoming edition has already gone to press. The letters are not even signed, but initialled, which must have been galling for Gerald's ego.

Finally, among the memoranda Gerald dictated to those patient ladies is a complaint to the police concerning the noise made by juke-boxes in Wardour Mews, where Gerald upon his return from Spain in 1965 rented a room next to a brothel. "I am a tenant of the well-known painter Arturo Ewart," the statement dated July 9 1965 begins, "and I am not an unknown author, having written a great number of books... I suffer severely owing to the loud noise from juke-boxes at a club in the Mews called "The After Five Club". The noise commences in the early evening and continues all night... What is even worse is the noise made by the young people visiting this club, who shout and scream at each other in the Mews, and even brawled on one occasion just outside my bedroom window. As I am 77 years old and not in the best of health, suffering from a heart condition, I would like to spend my few remaining months or years in comparative quietude…"

I asked Ewart how Gerald got along with the girls who plied their trade in the mews. "He got on with them very well," he told me. "Gerald always lifted his hat to them as he passed them in the doorway, and they liked him. They thought he was a real gentleman, so distinguished looking."

*

"Today, Britain is in the midst of a bloodless revolution," the *Time* article concludes. "This time, those who are giving way are the old Tory-Liberal Establishment that ruled the Empire from the clubs along Pall Mall and St James's, the still powerful financial City of London, the church and Oxbridge. In their stead is rising a new and surprising leadership community: economists, professors, actors, photographers, singers, admen, TV executives and writers – a swinging meritocracy. What they have in common is that they are mostly under 40."

Our septuagenarian hold-out against the new meritocracy had got himself in the doghouse so far as the British public was concerned when in March 1965, on a visit to Madrid, he was interviewed on Spanish television, and expressed the opinion that Gibraltar should be returned to Spain immediately. Apart from anything else, the Gibraltarians were a motley lot of Jews and Arabs, while the Britons who still clung to the Rock were for the most part smugglers. The British colony's counter-blast was not long in coming. Under the headline SPANISH

TV UTILIZES A CONVICTED CRIMINAL, *Vox*, the bi-lingual weekly, branded Gerald as being "anti-anything which is decent, moral and legal", and printed his criminal record including his conviction for "gross indecency".

But the outcry against Gerald on this occasion was as nothing compared to the obloquy visited upon him – this time, by his friends – when in January 1966 the newspaper *The People* began serializing the articles entitled 'Gerald Hamilton Confesses' written by Robin Maugham.

As early as May 1965 Gerald had laid down as conditions for his participating in the writing of the series:

> 1. I would not wish to participate in any publicity that makes the slightest anti-Franco comment, as I hope to be able to visit Spain for the rest of my life, and, anyhow, I am pro-Franco.
> 2. […] I would not be a party to any articles containing comments of ridicule on the Royals I know living in Madrid, for obvious reasons…

In July Gerald waived his right to bring a libel action against Maugham and the paper, the agreement which the paper thrust upon him reading in part:

> I hereby authorise Robin Maugham to write a series of articles about me and my life… I realise that I shall be exposed as a Fascist sympathiser who has been on Madrid radio to claim that Gibraltar should be given back to Spain.
>
> My intrigues with the deposed Royalties, including the Grand Duke Wladimir, his wife the Princess Bagration,

his Mother, Grand Duchess Cyril, and King Simeon of Bulgaria, King Leika of Albania, Geraldine the widow of King Zog, Prince Nicholas of Romania, the Carlist Pretender, Don Juan Carlos, and the Count of Barcelona, etc. will be exposed.

I may even be labelled as "Franco's Secret Agent". I realise that I may become known as the Spanish Lord Haw-Haw.

[…]

In no event will I resort to litigation against any paper that may publish these articles. In fact I agree to a complete exposure of myself and of my activities. I also agree to sign each of the articles in typescript by way of approbation before they appear and thereby clear them for publication.

In *The Way It Was With Me* Gerald writes that in return for thus signing away his birthright he expected to receive half the sum paid by *The People* for the series, but this was not to be. "Very foolishly, but needing money… I consented to accept a much smaller fee." Gerald in fact was paid a total of £1,150 for thus allowing his name to be blackened.

The *People* series was preceded by a fanfare of publicity on television. "I was watching the box on Saturday evening when suddenly Gerald's photograph was flashed on the screen," Maurice Leonard recalls. "There he was, bigger than life and wearing a panama hat, as I remember. 'This is the wickedest man in the world,' a voice announced. 'You can read all about him tomorrow in *The People*!' "

The headlines accompanying the five articles give some

idea of the sensational way the series was presented:

> January 16: "Gerald Hamilton: Traitor, Con-Man and Crook. (Even His Name is A Fake)."

> January 23: "Churchill Threw Him Into Gaol. (He Was Trying to Sell Out To The Germans)."

> January 30: "He Made Half A Million By Graft And Treachery."

> February 6: "I Palled Up With the Nazis."

> February 13: "I Worked The Perfect Crime."

The first article was preceded by a front-page blurb describing Gerald as "one of the most evil men alive today", and by a preamble, written apparently by the editor, which read in part: "Gerald Hamilton is the strangest man alive – and one of the world's biggest rogues. For 75 years he has lived a life of intrigue, imposture, knavery – and high treason… But now – old and near to death – he has decided to make a full confession of his life to author Robin Maugham."

In the opening paragraph the deathbed confessional aspect is stressed by Maugham, who says he was amazed by a letter which arrived out of the blue from Gerald in Madrid, writing "I feel the need now to tell someone the true story of my life… I want the world to know how wicked I've been and perhaps, in a way, how good."

In response to this appeal Maugham, in his role as surrogate confessor, hurried to Madrid by the next plane, he claims. "I knew him [Hamilton] to be entertaining, witty, polished and urbane... I also knew he was an outrageous crook and a traitor, who had seen the inside of a dozen prisons."

As for Gerald, after seventy-five years of dissembling, he would hardly have been capable of telling "the true story of my life" even had he so desired: the articles are largely a re-hash of material he had already published, with one notable exception: in the final article of the series Gerald goes out of his way to blacken the name of Joseph Dean, of Dean's Bar in Tangier, who alone of Gerald's friends had visited him in the Tangier hospital when Gerald was recovering from his hernia operation. Dean, who had died two years earlier and could not sue for libel, is rewarded posthumously for his kindness in *The People* of February 13 1966, where he is described as "wicked". The crime in which Gerald implicates Dean is wholly fictitious, made up by Gerald on demand.

Gerald claims that Dean was a gigolo when they first met in London in 1913, and that soon afterwards they became partners in robbing a Greek millionaire. Gerald had got a tip-off that the millionaire would be travelling on the Blue Train to Monte Carlo with his wife's jewel-case in his hand-luggage, according to his story. The partners were on the train with the unsuspecting Greek as far as Marseilles, where Dean jumped off, and bought a ticket for the Paris train which was standing alongside the Blue Train, Gerald explains. "So all I had to do was hand the jewel-case out of the window to Dean, who popped it under his arm and took it back to Paris." When the theft of the jewel-case was discovered there was a terrific hue and cry, according to Gerald, who told Maugham that his share of the loot was between £40,000 and £50,000.

The robbery Gerald relates, naming Dean as his accomplice, is almost a carbon copy of one that had taken place in Paris in 1898, and which had involved a duchess and a charming jewel thief named Willie Johnson, better known as "Harry the Valet". The duchess, returning from the Riviera, had been robbed of her famous collection of jewels while her train was still standing in the Gare du Nord. The jewel case had been placed in charge of her personal maid, who had travelled in a different compartment, and who had quit the train at the station for a few minutes, when the robbery presumably took place. Harry pleaded guilty at the Old Bailey, and was sentenced to seven years.

The reason for Gerald's cock-and-bull story is not hard to find. The Great Train Robbery had taken place in England shortly before the Maugham series began to appear and the papers were full of this audacious exploit – so much so that "the then Editor (of *The People*) telephoned Robin Maugham, who was in Madrid with me at the time, saying they must have some reference to a train robbery", Gerald writes. "When Maugham answered that as far as he knew I had never had anything to do with a train robbery, the Editor said, 'Oh, let him think back and he might remember some such occasion.' "

*

Gerald took refuge in the Canary Islands soon after the series began, and appears to have been totally unprepared for the horrified reaction of his friends. "Of course I knew that there was a seamy side to your life, but had no idea it could be as dreadful as this," Gabrielle Potter, one of Gerald's oldest friends, writes. In his reply, Gerald pointed out "This is the age of the anti-hero," rather lamely trying to compare himself to Jean Genet, pederast and ex-thief, who "is now the leader of the Sartre set in Paris." But in a letter to Sir Frederick Bowman,

KCE,[25] whom he had known when both were 18B internees at Brixton, Gerald described the series as "a conspiracy between Robin, myself and the Editor of *The People* to lure sixpences from the British public". "Three-quarters of the lurid drivel is absolutely fictitious, especially the train robbery, which did not happen."

In his tribulations Gerald was somewhat consoled by the reaction of his landlord, the Chinese proprietor of The Good Earth who, when the articles appeared, assured him "I was so relieved to find that the articles were not about you, but about a total stranger – someone quite frightening." "There's Chinese politeness for you," Gerald later told a friend.

Arturo Ewart told me that shortly after the first article appeared, his dentist, who also happened to be Gerald's, commented, "They'll get him, all right – they'll get him." Ewart asked, "What do you mean?" "Dr McNab – the National Assistance Board," the dentist replied. "They'll read about him amassing half a million pounds in his lifetime, and then they'll discover he's drawing supplementary benefits. They'll get him all right – mark my words."

As the dentist had predicted, "Dr McNab" was not long in getting on to Gerald's trail, forcing the latter to reply,

---

25 "Sir" Frederick Bowman (1893-1969), Liverpool actor and eccentric, was a pacifist, animal rights activist and sometime Muslim convert who finally found an agreeable berth in obscure and esoteric San Luigi Catholic Orders such as the Order of the Crown of Thorns and the Order of the Lion and the Black Cross. A member of the Marquess of Tavistock's pro-fascist British People's Party, Bowman was interned in Brixton, where he founded the Frederick Bowman Freedom League and attempted to escape while disguised as a clergyman. Released in 1943, he was knighted by Count Potocki de Montalk, only to be stripped of his knighthood the following year after a disagreement. His obituary in *Les Chroniques de Chevaliers* remembered "a life of kind and useful service to humanity and animals. Devoted to the Orders and the ideals of true chivalry; staunchly celibate, he left no next of kin, but many friends in Liverpool and far beyond. The Grand Prieur will remember him with especial affection as a loyal comrade." I have been unable to decide what KCE means. [Ed.]

through his solicitor. "The articles contained a lot of highly coloured material as to Mr Hamilton's wealth… I can only describe that as journalistic licence," the solicitor writes. "You know Mr Hamilton's means as well as anyone." He then goes on to mention a fortnight's holiday at Las Palmas, which "Mr Hamilton is not sure he told you about… he gets distinctly nervous when faced with government officers." As to the holiday in the Canary Islands, "he lived very modestly in a bedsitting room (not a luxury hotel) and every penny of expenses was paid for by his friends."

In reality Gerald, with the £1,150 from the series in his pocket, had put up at the high class Hotel Atlantico intending to spend the whole of the winter there. Unfortunately, shortly after his arrival he slipped on the hotel's marble staircase, fell on his back, and spent two expensive days in hospital. There were no bones broken, but one slightly dislocated, and he was forced to return to London.

It was Arturo Ewart who introduced him to Mrs Starr, an osteopath in Seymour Street, Marylebone, whom Ewart describes as being "about ninety-five years old, but very nimble". "After poking him for a few minutes Mrs Starr said, 'Oh, I know what's wrong – you've got a slipped disc. We'll soon fix that. Off with your vest.' At this point poor Gerald's eyes began to roll like those of a calf being led to the knacker's yard." (Here Ewart gave a comic imitation of Gerald rolling his eyes and murmuring, "Oh, dear, Oh, my!") "Mrs Starr got his arm round her shoulder somehow, and pressed her hand into his back, and I heard it – heard the click as the bone snapped back into place. When we got outside Gerald said, 'I thought she was going to throttle me.'"

"Dr McNab" was not the only one accorded the privilege of supporting Gerald in his "anecdotage", as he liked to call it.

He had become expert in milking various funds. From 1960 to 1968 Gerald received four grants from the Royal Literary Fund, founded in 1787 after public opinion had been shocked by the death in a debtors' prison of Floyer Sydenham, a scholar noted for his classic translation of Plato. The Prince Regent had granted the Fund its royal charter; Albert, the Prince Consort, was another early patron; and in its day the Fund had given aid to writers as diverse as Samuel Taylor Coleridge and "Baron Corvo"; James Hogg and Joseph Conrad; D.H. Lawrence and James Joyce.

Gerald got under the wire even though successful applicants must not only be published writers, but pass a test of literary merit. "Several of us on the committee knew all about Gerald's past," John Lehmann, the Fund's president, told me. "And you gave him a grant in spite of his past?" I asked. "We gave him more because of it," Lehmann replied.

Gerald took no chances, however, but lined up such old friends as Professor George Catlin, Professor Peter Campbell, and Robin Maugham to support his applications. In addition, at the time of his death, Gerald was about to receive a grant of £250 from the Arts Council.

*

After Gerald had finished his morning's dictating he would dress carefully before going out. More often than not it would be to keep a luncheon date in the West End. "One of the remarkable sights of London in the sixties was to see Gerald standing on the corner of the King's Road, waving down a taxi, with that ebony walking-stick of his poised in mid-air," remarks Geoffrey Rigby, who had witnessed the phenomenon many times. "Then you would hear him tell the driver to take him to the Savoy, knowing as you did that he had barely the cab fare let alone the price of lunch in his pocket, but lived in expectation that at the other end someone somehow would take care of both…"

In August 1968, this routine was varied pleasantly, Gerald being collected on the street corner by James Reeve, who was painting his portrait, and who drove Gerald to a studio in Kensington. "Gerald was thrilled to bits," Reeve recalls, "especially as his portrait entailed me giving him lunch every time he came for a sitting." "He was an excellent sitter," Reeve, who is now in his early forties, adds. "Knowing that I dislike talking to people as I paint, he saved all of his gossip for the lunch table." Reeve had in common with Gerald a loathing for Rugby school, which both had attended, although Reeve stuck it out for four years, eventually winning a scholarship to Oxford.

"Gerald didn't give a damn what his portrait looked like," Reeve continues. "He was haughty, like those royals he admired so much. If the family of Carlos the Fourth had been bothered about their looks Goya probably would never have painted them." Reeve's portrait of Gerald – on the cover of this book – is if anything flattering, which is remarkable considering that Reeve did not altogether approve of his sitter. "I suppose he was a 'friend' in the sense that the snake is to a rabbit," Reeve had written to me before we met. "It was his quite unique nastiness which fascinated me I imagine… I am sure [he] would not have hesitated to slander me if it was to his advantage."

Reeve gave a small dinner party to introduce Gerald to his cousin Elizabeth, the Countess of Longford. Gerald had been a great admirer of Lady Longford's biography of Queen Victoria, writing to compliment her on her achievement, but also to set her straight concerning Albert's parentage, insisting that the Baron Mayer was the father of the Prince Consort. Meeting Lady Longford in the flesh affected her admirer strangely, according to Reeve. "Gerald fairly grovelled before her," he says. "All evening long it was "My Lady" this, and "My Lady" that – I never saw such obsequiousness."

Reeve also gave a party on what was supposedly Gerald's eightieth, but in reality his seventy-eighth, birthday. Among the guests were Lady Antonia Fraser, Sibylla Jane Flower, James Pope-Hennessy, Mark Amory, and Bevis Hillier, with the birthday boy looking distinctly saurian amid so many gifted youths. Miss Flower gave Gerald a bottle of claret of rare vintage, and Bevis Hillier presented him with an expensive book, but was hardly out of earshot before Gerald was heard to say "Pity he inscribed it – I could have sold it as a review copy."

Gerald in turn introduced Reeve to John Sergeant Cram III, an eccentric American millionaire, whose philanthropies in Manhattan's Lower East Side, where he ran a drug rehabilitation centre, had earned him the title of "the Prince Myshkin of the Bowery". Reeve's portrait of Cram shows him sitting gingerly on a gilt chair with the marbled columns and potted palms of the Ritz in the background. Unfortunately the portrait exists today only as a photograph, Reeve having painted over it when the millionaire's cheque bounced.

Cram, who was notoriously absent-minded, had neglected to have funds transferred from New York to his London bank. What really angered Reeve, however, was when Gerald demanded a commission for having introduced Cram – that and Gerald's boast about using his influence to free some of Reeve's paintings that were being held by Spanish Customs before an exhibition which was due to open in Madrid.

"Whenever I exhibit abroad I seem to have trouble with Customs officials," Reeve told me. "But in this case Gerald had nothing to do with breaking the log-jam. He would have been the last person in the world I would have gone to for help."

*

Gerald's habit of rising early meant that he now retired at 9.30 p.m. ("I am like an animal," he would say, "I like to go to bed when it gets dark") and this in turn changed his whole lifestyle. For one thing, it limited his theatre-going to matinees. Just how far out of touch with the theatre he had become was revealed while staying in Brighton, when Gerald was invited to a cocktail party given by Cuthbert Worsley, the drama critic, at which mostly theatre people were present. Gerald found himself chatting with an elderly gentleman whose conversation was so absorbing that when it came time to leave he could scarcely tear himself away. "I've been absolutely enthralled by your talk of the theatre, which remains my first love," Gerald began, "but, dare I confess it, I have no idea to whom I have been talking all this while." "Silence fell upon all present, who looked at me with horror," Gerald recounts. "Sir Laurence himself seemed slightly surprised and said, 'My name is Olivier.'"

Being in bed by 9.30 also meant that if Gerald wanted to do any cruising it had to be done in the afternoon. As he had done all his life, Gerald continued to cruise Soho pubs frequented by homosexuals, a large part of whom were "rent", always in search of youth ("I like to surround myself with youths," he told John Symonds. "If I am with old fogeys, I feel one myself.") But as he grew older Gerald's definition of youth became more elastic:

Gerald: I met the most divine boy at Ward's Irish House
last night.
Peter Burton: Really?
Gerald: Yes, he was heavenly.
Peter: And how old was this boy?
Gerald: Oh, only about forty.

Burton, who was then editing the gay magazine *Jeremy*, lived
almost opposite Gerald at 217 King's Road, and used to look
in on him daily to see if Gerald was in good health and his
needs catered for. One evening in November 1969 he returned
home to find a note from Gerald slipped under his door saying
something had happened, and that he would be grateful for a
visit as soon as possible.

"Gerald was less than his usual avuncular self when I
arrived," Peter recalls, "but the usual glass of red wine (from
his latest Wine Society consignment) was served before
Gerald explained what was worrying him." After lunching
with a friend Gerald, it seems, had gone round to the Golden
Lion, where he had picked someone up and brought him home.
After they had sex the man pulled a gun on him and demanded
that Gerald hand over all his money, threatening to shoot him
otherwise. "Gerald never had much by way of cash," Peter
explains, "and so he handed over only a few pounds. The man
said this wasn't enough money, that Gerald had better get
some more, and that he would be in touch."

Gerald had been most reluctant to involve the police, but
he did, and the blackmailer was arrested after Gerald, this time
acting as a police decoy, had agreed to meet the man again.
Nor was this the only incident of its kind. In June 1962, Gerald
picked up someone in the White Bear at Piccadilly Circus,

who robbed him of his cuff-links, later traced to a pawnbroker in the Edgware Road. Earlier still, Gerald had been forced to call the police twice to deal with a rough customer, as the following diary extracts indicate:

> June 15 1958: Beautiful summer day. I lunched at the Grill and Cheese, where unhappily, I met a certain Tom whom I brought home with me.
> June 16 1958: Turbulent night. Tom rang the bell incessantly at 2.30 a.m. I had to call the police.
> June 17 1958: The monstrous Tom came back and I had to call the police.
> June 23 1958: Troubled day. Tom called again.

Gerald in his seventies was still quite highly sexed, according to Burton. "Once when I left the room for a moment Gerald touched up my friend Ian," Peter tells me. "The temptation must have proved too strong. Anyway they were both embarrassed." On another occasion Gerald asked Peter and Ian to show him something of London's gay life, so they took him to The Boltons, a Kensington pub. "Mindful that Gerald had to be tucked up in bed by nine-thirty, we arrived at seven-thirty, and of course the place was empty," Peter recalls. "Gerald kept waiting for the action to happen, and when it didn't he became full of scorn." The London scene wasn't a patch on what he had known: "Now," said Gerald, "if you had been with me in Berlin in the early thirties…"

Fifteen

June 1970: Exit Gerald

Gerald's ability to hold friends, once he had made them, is little short of astounding. "I am not everybody's cup of tea," he told John Symonds, "But I am certain people's liqueur." Of all Gerald's friends Christopher Isherwood was certainly the most faithful (most long-suffering, some might say). Neither Gerald's dishonesty nor his political views, which many found repellent, put Christopher off. "I disapprove of your politics, but it would take a bigger man than Franco, or Mosley, to come between us," Isherwood wrote to Gerald. Shortly after Gerald suffered a mild stroke in 1967, Maurice Richardson wired Isherwood in Santa Monica that Gerald was in need of help. Without hesitating Isherwood sent a sizeable cheque, and he added that although Richardson had suggested he had an obligation of some kind to provide assistance, what he felt instead was simply the wish to help an old friend.

Perhaps Isherwood's feelings towards Gerald at the end of the latter's life are best summed up in a dream he had. "I had an almost clairvoyant dream," he writes to Gerald,

> in which I sat with you in that park in Amsterdam near the Emmastraat, watching the ducks on the lake. Nothing special happened, but it was unforgettably vivid, with the weeping willow and the sunlight on the water and the quacking of the ducks, and you, elegant as usual in grey, with a soft grey hat and your walking stick with the gold band; and there was a friendly relaxed atmosphere of mid-morning leisure.

Unexpectedly, in July 1967, Gerald was reunited with that other friend of his Berlin days, Wystan Auden, whom he had not seen in years. The reunion occurred through the good offices of David Stoker, a young poet whom Gerald had met on the Isle of Man. On July 12th Stoker came up to London for the Poetry International Fiesta held at the Queen Elizabeth Hall, at which Auden, Allen Ginsberg, and Pablo Neruda read their poetry. "The tickets were all sold out," Stoker explained to me, "but I managed to squeeze myself in backstage where, during the interval, I met Auden, who was in the wings chain-smoking Du Maurier cigarettes. Auden was also trying to fend off a Hungarian woman admirer who represented the Martin Buber Society, and who insisted upon drawing parallels between Buber's writings and Auden's poetry. I was having dinner with Gerald at his flat that evening…"

One reason Gerald was so successful in holding on to his friends was that he was generous in sharing them. He liked nothing better than to bring together two people whom he esteemed. Mike Steen met Robin Maugham and Hermione Baddeley through Gerald, and Mike in turn introduced him to Tennessee Williams. It then remained only for Gerald to square the circle by bringing Williams and Maugham together, which he did at a luncheon party at the Ritz which Maugham hosted. "Our host always had a particular table in the restaurant facing across Green Park," Gerald explains. He then goes on to recall the convivial mood of the occasion compounded of "sunshine, the good wine and food, the humourous talk and badinage, more often than not directed against me." "When our host said, 'Gerald, of course, prefers Claridges or the Connaught,' I answered at once, 'My dear, I never mind roughing it at the Ritz, when it's in such delightful company.'"

At about this time Gerald, in the company of a young Mauritian friend named Roddy, made a pilgrimage to Berneval in Normandy, where Oscar Wilde had stayed immediately after his release from Reading Gaol. The Hotel de la Plage, where Wilde had registered as "Sebastian Melmoth" in an effort to throw reporters off his trail, had been pulled down, but Gerald was able to resurrect an old woman aged ninety-four who had been a *femme de chambre* in Wilde's time, and who remembered the flow of visitors coming to see Mr Melmoth from all over Europe.

The following year Robin Maugham invited Gerald to come to Paris aboard the Golden Arrow Pullman train for a long weekend. It was to be Gerald's last trip abroad. Gerald stayed at the Hotel San Regis near the Champs Elysees, had dinner that night with Robin and friends at a restaurant called La Rose-Bleue, lunched the following day at L'Escargot du Grand Palais, and they returned to London on the Monday. "It's not the same Golden Arrow I knew," Gerald complained. But then nothing was the same.

*

Gerald's pulse was quickened by the receipt of a letter from the Duke of Windsor, writing from his home in the Bois de Boulogne, Paris. In December 1969, Gerald had sent the duke and duchess a copy of *The Way It Was With Me*. It so happened that James Pope-Hennessy was staying with the Windsors when the book arrived, and the duke asked him if he knew the author. Pope-Hennessy owned that he did, whereupon the duke wrote to Gerald – unwisely, as it turned out.

A photocopy of the duke's letter, the original of which is marked "Private and Confidential" is to be found among

Gerald's papers. In it the duke thanks Gerald for the favourable references to himself and the duchess in Chapter 12, which they had read with great interest and some nostalgia. In this chapter Gerald states baldly that King Edward VIII "was hounded into exile" by a "camarilla" headed by Prime Minister Baldwin and "that Caiaphas of Canterbury", Archbishop Lang. Gerald goes further, and asserts that had "the real King" occupied the throne, then the Second World War might never have broken out at all. "The whole attitude of the Royal Family seems to me to have been beyond contempt," he continues; "even Queen Mary... referred always to the Duke of Windsor in conversation as 'my poor son', as if he had some terrible disability."

Referring to Gerald's assertion that had he remained king, World War II might have been averted, the duke writes that he had used his influence to warn against the folly of such a holocaust. Where he had clashed with Baldwin and his cronies was that he, Edward, had never been a part of the Establishment. This made them suspicious that he would not always 'yes' to them. The duke thought that Gerald's analysis of Churchill was perfect (Gerald had described Churchill as a "warmonger" and "temperamentally unbalanced").

Gerald hastened to reply to this letter, regretting that "the late Duke of Bedford is not alive... He always maintained that you would have succeeded, had you remained on the Throne, in finding means somehow of avoiding the last war." "I was in Germany as an assistant correspondent of *The Times* when Hitler came to power," Gerald continues, "and, although he did so much good at the beginning, especially with regard to unemployment, he became in my view quite mad and I honestly believe the Germans would have got rid of him themselves..." Rudolf Hess he describes as "not only brave but also politically sensible when he foresaw the danger to the world of any form of Russian supremacy and in my humble view, we should have joined with Germany against Russia…" Gerald concludes by wondering whether, on his next visit to Paris, he might be allowed to pay an afternoon call.

Meanwhile, Gerald had not been idle in hatching out schemes to dispose of the letter to the highest bidder. Timothy d'Arch Smith, a rare book dealer whom he approached with this end in view, refused to have anything to do with the letter since it was marked "Private and Confidential". Bevis Hillier was pressured into trying to interest *The Sunday Times*, for whom he was then reviewing books, but Hillier was lukewarm to what struck him as a dubious venture. Claiming that he had been offered £500 for the duke's letter, Gerald even tried to borrow money on the strength of it, offering the letter as security. The £500 offer apparently came from Charles Potter in Guernsey, who attached as conditions to it that no copies of the letter be made and that Gerald retain the original. On April 24th Potter wires, "Copy having been sent to America deal off STOP Our deal depended on original and copies never leaving your hands… My offer now for original and envelope is limited to £75." Gerald, having proved once more that he was his own worst enemy, settled for the £75.

*

At Easter 1970 Gerald was saddened by the news of Vera Brittain's death after a long illness. "I have so many happy recollections of the days when I lived in Glebe Place and Vera once or twice came to my table with Cyril Joad," he writes to her husband, Professor Catlin. Gerald himself had not been feeling well. On March 23 he notes in his diary, "Lost blood and stayed home all day… Mrs Mansel and Mrs Daltry helped me a good deal." (Lily Daltry was the daily who now did for Gerald at 318A.) "I haven't eaten anything, and I feel feeble," he adds. He spent the greater part of the following day at Fulham Hospital undergoing various tests, but reports to James Reeve, "It was nothing serious – just a blood vessel which broke, but I hate the sight of blood and was very frightened at the time." Four days later he had sex with Don, who "left me completely worn out", he notes in a diary entry beginning "Unforgettable day…" Don, a thirty-two-year-old married man, was Gerald's sexual partner during the last year of his life, the routine being that they had sex after Don came to lunch on Saturdays.

Gerald continued to see Roddy, who was known to Gerald's friends as "Mauritius", but theirs was mainly a platonic relationship (Roddy is the only one of Gerald's friends to whom he applies adjectives such as "gay", "charming", and "debonair" in his diary – usually when he mentions someone there are no qualifying adjectives). Among his papers is a poem dated June 11 1966 in which he compares Roddy's eyes with the empyrean ("I always thought the sky was blue/But now I know, 'twas merely grey.") Roddy is the only person to whom Gerald makes a bequest in his will. In a codicil, dated December 23 1969, Gerald left his friend £100.

On May 16 Gerald went to Robin Maugham's birthday party given jointly by Hermione Baddeley and her daughter Joan, Lady Assheton-Smith, at the latter's flat in Westminster Gardens. Gerald's thank-you note to Lady Assheton-Smith recalls the Narrator's leave-taking at the Princess de Guermantes' reception with which Proust closes his great novel (did Gerald, too, sense that this would be the last evening party he would ever attend?)

In any case, in writing to his hostess Gerald remarks her "extreme kindness and courtesy in coming downstairs twice when I was leaving… to make certain that there was a taxi to whisk me away. I really was touched by this gesture on your part because you had so many important people upstairs to look after… I would have liked to have stayed much longer if I had not been so old."

Gerald's diary for the last fortnight of his life contains constant references to his health ("I feel ill"; "I am not at all in a good state"). He complains of rheumatism, but is well enough to go to the Hilton for a manicure, to Harrods for carrot juice, and to sit on a bench near the public library in Manresa Road, watching the Chelsea scene pass by. On Wednesday, June 3 he keeps a luncheon date with two publishers whom he was hoping to interest in a book he proposed to write on "Kings in Exile". "I couldn't eat a thing," he notes, adding, "Back home I went to bed quickly." His last diary entry is dated Sunday, June 7: "Spent the entire day at home in bed. Lily was kind enough to come in afternoon. I am suffering from fibrositis. Fine day of […]." Gerald never finished the sentence.

The story is taken up by John Symonds. "Early on Monday morning, the 8th June, I received a telephone call from Mrs Eileen Sweetland, one of Gerald's oldest friends," Symonds writes. He then reports the following conversation:

"He's lost the use of his legs, won't eat –"
"That's bad," I interjected.
"– and he's raving about a little black boy and some jewels."

The Emir's jewels? wonders Symonds. The following day, Gerald died in hospital, but with the mention of "the little black boy" and the "Emir's jewels" the transmogrification of Gerald had reached a new level.

*

On the face of it, Gerald unconscious and raving about a blackamoor and the theft of a pearl necklace in Milan nearly half a century earlier (for the "Emir's jewels" can only refer to that) is no more absurd than the other stories that have circulated concerning Gerald's death, no two of Gerald's friends being agreed as to manner of his departure from this world. Not surprisingly, in death as in life Gerald was to assume mythic proportions.

One apocryphal story has it that Gerald died twice, the first death being staged for the benefit of his creditors. "To put his creditors off his scent, Gerald got Robin Maugham to write his obituary notice, which duly appeared in the *Observer*," Felix Hope-Nicholson assured me, adding "A week later a mutual friend saw what appeared to be Gerald's ghost circling Sloane Square in a taxi-cab and keeled over in a faint."

A Sloane Square taxicab figures in another version, this time of Gerald's actual death. "Gerald had a heart attack that Sunday," Geoffrey Rigby told me, "but then the phone rang next day with an invitation to lunch at the Hilton. Gerald simply couldn't resist the thought of that sumptuous meal awaiting him, so he got out of bed and dressed. He died in a taxi as it made its way across Sloane Square."

The version told by Brian Desmond Hurst appears to be the most reliable – up to a point. Hurst had gone that Monday forenoon with Gerald to Harrods where the latter partook of his usual glass of carrot juice – "Harrods is the only place where one can be sure the juice is not diluted," Gerald informed his friend. It was there, at the juice counter, that Gerald had his heart attack. "I took him by taxi to the home of a woman friend – I think it was in Fulham," Hurst told me. (Actually it was the home of Mrs Thora Brabazon-Ellis in Thistle Grove,

SW10.) "Gerald opened his eyes long enough to say, 'I must say goodbye now' – those were his last words – then sank into a coma. Later he was taken to the hospital and died that night."

But Gerald did not die that night. Gillian Mansel, who went to St Stephen's Hospital, Chelsea, the following morning, Tuesday, June 9, to see Gerald, takes up the story. "I took some letters I had typed from his dictation for Gerald to sign," Mrs Mansel told me. "The letters didn't need his signature really, but I thought it would cheer him up and reassure him that he was going to live if he had something to do."

In the event Mrs Mansel did not see Gerald. "I was met by a nurse, who asked me if I were any relation to Gerald. I said, No, only a friend. She then said that Gerald had had another heart attack and was very, very ill. Not only that, but he was delirious and shrieking the ward down, disturbing all the other patients with anguished cries of remorse for his past life."

> As I recall, I could hear those shrieks, coming at me distantly from the labyrinth of corridors – perhaps it was my imagination. I suddenly had a picture of Gerald terrified at the prospect of death, of being cut off unshriven, like the ghost of Hamlet's father, "even in the blossom of my sin". It was horrible. I couldn't bear to see him in these circumstances, so I turned and fled.

"I have always regretted that I didn't send for a priest," Mrs Mansel added. "I knew that Gerald was a lapsed Catholic – very lapsed, I would say. I doubt that a priest could have arrived in time, for Gerald was dying right there and then. Still, the priest might have made it, and Gerald might have derived some comfort from the sacrament of extreme unction, who knows."

Had Mrs Mansel but known it, the late Canon Alfonso de Zulueta was not far away in Chelsea, and would have come running at such an opportunity to save an erring soul. Canon Zulueta, known to his friends as "Zulu", was a friend from Gerald's Glebe Place days, and shared his predilection for royalty. He was once hearing confessions in a very smart part of Paris when he thought he recognised a voice. "Do I have the honour of hearing the confession of the Duc de Guise?" he asked. "Alas, my father," came the reply, "I am only the Comte de Paris."

Zulu counted Gerald as one of his failures, I gathered, when I talked to him at the rectory of the beautiful church of the Most Holy Redeemer and St Thomas More in Chelsea. A tall, spare, white-haired man in his late seventies, Canon Zulueta told me how periodically he would have a go at bringing Gerald back to the practice of his faith, but was always put off. "I'll get in touch with you, Father Alfonso," Gerald would say, "But he never did." "Gerald always struck me as a mystery man, some sort of secret agent," he concluded. "I think he rather enjoyed giving me that impression."

*

The transmogrification process did not stop with Gerald's death. His death certificate got his birthplace wrong, giving it as the Irish Republic. Gerald's obituary notice did not appear in *The Times* until nine days after his death, because of a newspaper strike. Owing to the strike not many of Gerald's friends learned of his death in time to attend his funeral at the Putney Vale Crematorium (Gerald had expressed a preference for cremation, having been assured the Catholic Authority had lifted its objections.)

Those who did attend disagree as to the details of the funeral. Robin Maugham has given the fullest account of the ceremony. Admitting that his memories are "slightly clouded by a form of retrogressive amnesia", Maugham's impression of the funeral cortege was that it consisted of black Daimlers, from which alighted elderly gentlemen in mourning clothes. Geoffrey Rigby says the Daimlers were two Bentleys, one of which belonged to Maugham himself, the other to Lady Beryl Rose, wife of Sir Francis Rose. The others present at the crematorium were John Symonds, Peter Burton, literary agent Olwyn Hughes, the sister of Ted, Brian Desmond Hurst, Keith Gossop, Mary Seaton, Cecil Woolf, Gillian Mansel, and Lily Daltry. Mrs. Daltry was the only one of Gerald's creditors to be paid. She was given a cheque for £5 owed in back wages, but never banked it.

The mix-ups had only just started. "I wandered round to the side of the crematorium," continues Maugham, "where the coffins were laid out with the wreaths tastefully disposed upon them... I passed by a large-sized coffin which might have belonged to an overweight giant from a circus and was numbered 1701. Next to it was a small coffin which might have been appropriate to a child or a dwarf or a pygmy. On it was written the number, 1702, and the name Gerald Hamilton." Peter Burton agrees that "considering Gerald's bulk, and he was rather a fat man, the coffin seemed pathetically small". He quotes Maugham as saying, "My dear, we've got the wrong funeral. That is a child's coffin and they certainly cannot have got Gerald into it."

Maugham claims that the officiating clergyman, by way of a text, read a blood-curdling Old Testament account of the Israelites warring against their enemies ("We will smite the Philistines. We will cut off their foreskins and hang them from our girdles") which was singularly inapposite in view of Gerald's anti-Semitism. Burton, too, remembers the reading as being inappropriate, and followed by "an entirely unsuitable hymn". Then, says Burton, "the coffin slid away" and the mourners retired to the nearest pub for "champagne, cheese sandwiches, and Gerald Hamilton stories".

Coda: Jury Still Out

"Hamilton was a true eccentric: an extravagant sensualist, a man with political views which would have seemed repellent in anyone who made less of a vaudeville of his own life."
– Gerald's obituary in *The Times*

"Here, Heaven knows, is no monster."
– Christopher Isherwood, Prologue to *Mr Norris and I*

"I should keep away from him if I were you. He's like Aleister Crowley, a dangerous man."
– Julian Maclaren Ross to John Symonds

"Gerald was a darling, sweet, loveable man. Of course he was a wicked old rogue and a con man, but there was nothing evil about him."
– Maurice Leonard

"…though he was consciously and consistently wicked, he was one of the happiest men I have ever met."
– Robin Maugham

"His immense capacity for enjoyment and his ability to communicate this to his companions… it is this above all that causes me to remember 'P.F.G.'."
– Professor Peter Campbell

"Gerald is getting too expensive for me. When one dines with him it is no longer a question of caviar or foie gras, but of caviar and foie gras. And he will order the most expensive brandy on the wine list."

– Peter Watson

"I was always irritated by his lies and fantasies and that bloody awful royal snobbery. I never, in fact, found him amusing or entertaining – but that was the moralist in me."

– Colin Spencer

"I don't know why we put up with Gerald, he was so awful. But he was amusing; he made us laugh. He used to tell the same stories over and over, but somehow one didn't mind – they were always funny."

– Felix Hope-Nicholson

"He lacked a tragic sense of life… Gerald had what I would call a Noel Coward sense of life: gay, witty, humorous, light… But on a deeper level, he was lacking, sometimes sadly so."

– Professor William Gray

"What a life! He's BEEN everywhere and GOT nowhere!"
– Bristol Prison inmate after reading *Mr Norris and I*

"A committee of psychiatrists, physiologists, professors of morals and ethics, priests and schoolmasters, might confer endlessly about his character and never agree."

– Maurice Richardson, 'Epilogue' to Hamilton's *Mr Norris and I*.

Personal Recollections of Tom Cullen
by Reed Searle

Tom Cullen was born in Oklahoma City in 1913. He became a British resident after the Second World War, and died in London in 2001. He lived most of his later years in a council flat in Belsize Park. He developed glaucoma and became completely blind in the late 1990s.

I met Tom in the early 1980s and spent many, many pleasant hours being and talking with him until his death. What follows is gleaned from some of those conversations. Tom was reluctant to talk about himself and his background. I didn't have to pry information from him, but I did approach these issues carefully.

After the War, Tom was discharged from the U.S. army in France and decided to remain there. He used his G.I. Bill to study at the Sorbonne, then moved to London. The major reason he did not return to the U.S. was related to his political activities during the Thirties.

Tom was a left-wing thinker and an active homosexual, as well as a writer of true crime books. There was considerable prejudice against communists and homosexuals (particularly when combined) during most of his life. He kept his sexual and political preferences reasonably discreet, although they were arguably the most important influences on his life.

He had been an active member of the U.S. communist party during the Thirties and into the Forties. He lived and worked in Los Angeles, where left-wing orientation was widespread during the Thirties. He was active in the EPIC (End Poverty in California) movement, led by Upton Sinclair. He became the chair of a national communist party committee responsible, as I recall, for the mobilization of young people. When the U.S.S.R. and Germany entered into the non-aggression pact, Tom faithfully followed the party line. He told me that since he believed in the aims and goals of the party, he believed he should follow their directives. I believe the event that caused him to become disenchanted with the party was the Hungarian "freedom fighter" uprising in 1956.

Soon after he became resident in England, on a visitor's visa and a U.S. passport, Tom learned that the U.S. authorities had a subpoena waiting for him should he return to the U.S. The government wanted him to testify before the Un-American Activities Committee. When the U.S. Embassy in London asked him to come along and bring his passport, saying that there was a technical matter to be worked out, he did so, handed over his passport and was given a document valid only for return to the United States (prescient of the passport valid only for return to the U.S. that was more recently issued to Edward Snowden).

He knew that criminal prosecution under the Smith Act (which made it a crime to be a member of a group which sought to overthrow the U.S. government) was probably waiting if he returned to the U.S. But he was now without legal permission to be in the U.K. So he went to the Home Office and explained the situation. As he told me, the Home Office representative listened carefully, then told him that the Brits just did not feel comfortable about their American Cousins (I use the words as Tom related the story to me) interfering with people in the U.K. They gave Tom a U.K. visitor's passport and asked him, please, not to become too involved in British politics.

301

This endeared the United Kingdom to him, and led to his decision to become a U.K. citizen some years later. He did not take the step lightly, in part because the Thatcher era intervened and Tom contemplated returning to France.

After receiving his U.K. citizenship, he took his U.S. passport to the U.S. Embassy and left it there. Some weeks later he received a letter from the Embassy asking him why he or any U.S. citizen would ever want to renounce U.S. citizenship. The letter offered him the opportunity to visit the U.S. Embassy and to reconsider his decision. He declined the opportunity.

Some years later, Tom asked for and received a copy of his F.B.I. file, as permitted by the Freedom of Information Act. It comprised two volumes, each six inches thick. About half of every page was blacked out, no doubt in an effort to protect the names of informers. I was able to read what was left. Much of the file was hearsay and, according to Tom, generally inaccurate. I begged Tom to let me have the file or at least to copy it because it had clear historic interest as a reminder of the times and the communist scare, but he insisted on destroying it.

By the Seventies, the communist scare had abated, Smith Act prosecution was precluded, and Tom was able to visit the U.S. without fear of prosecution. The F.B.I. had not lost interest in him – agents followed him wherever he travelled in America. One long series of entries in his file related to a trip he took to various cities in the U.S. By happenstance, Tom's itinerary took him to several cities where, at the same time, the then U.S. President was visiting. As Tom told it and as I gleaned from the file, everywhere he went on that trip, he was followed by armed agents, ready to shoot him if he got close to the President. (Tom chuckled about this incident: the F.B.I.

informant had mistaken Tom for someone else.)

Tom was an active homosexual most of his life. He became married to a confirmed lesbian, a writer and a close friend. He may never have lived with her. The relationship was simply one of convenience.[26] He kept his sexual activities separate from the rest of his life until his very last years. His gay friends were separate from, for example, his rambling or political activities. But he frequented many of the homosexual pubs and meeting places of London. At one time he compiled a list and description of them. The list and descriptions would have provided an interesting history of the times, but unfortunately it has been lost.

Tom "came out" following a lunch with some friends at Kenwood House on Hampstead Heath. During the lunch, a friend appeared and mentioned that a gang were assaulting some homosexuals on the Heath. Tom was incensed, and said that this was too much. The next day he helped organize and then led a gay rights march in Central London. At that time Tom's books were in circulation, *The Times* picked up his presence, and his sexual preferences were publicized.

Writing books was his retirement occupation. He had been a correspondent for several U.S. media and received pension money, together with some income from book royalties. As he said, he had always wanted to be a journalist instead of just being a reporter. He mostly wrote true crime. His books were translated into several languages and enjoyed a respectable circulation, but they never made him wealthy. Tom was used as an expert in the controversy over the so-called "Jack the Ripper Diaries". Tom reported that they were a fraud and a

26 Cullen married Winifred Louise Hunt, a Los Angeles schoolteacher, in 1942, and she spent a good deal of time with him in Germany and Paris circa 1947-49, so they may have had a closer relationship than Cullen suggested when he came to look back in later life. She died as Winifred Louise Cullen in 1958, in Los Angeles. [Ed.]

forgery. After his death, there was some interest in a TV series or a film about one of his books, as I recall it was "Crippen: The Mild Murderer", but the project was abandoned.

Weekly rambles in and around the Home Counties with the City Lit Rambling Club were his major outdoor activity; until he became substantially unable to walk or to see he was an avid walker. It was on these rambles that I met him. We became best friends – two expats, each somewhat disenchanted with the U.S.

In the last seven or eight years of his life, in addition to losing his sight, his walking ability deceased. But friendship continued and deepened. When I was in London, I saw him most days, escorted him to whatever appointments he had – generally medical – took him the the theatre and to concerts, and spent many wonderful hours talking with him. Notwithstanding his physical problems, he was always aware of and interested in current world affairs and had considerable knowledge of and perspective on history.

This was Tom's last book. When Tom and I talked of it, Tom showed me the manuscript and several filing boxes containing notes of his research on Gerald Hamilton. He had substantially finished the book but he was stopped at the last moment. We had talked about it and about Hamilton many times. While cleaning and emptying Tom's flat after his death, I found the manuscript. I brought it with me when I returned to the U.S. It is indeed gratifying that the book is now being published.

*

References

Epigraph

"It's marvellous…": E.M. Forster to Isherwood, May 11 1935, cited *Christopher and His Kind* (Eyre Methuen, 1977) p.155

Introduction:
The Importance of Being Gerald

"Uncle Gerald, your charm is a mystery": 'Ode to the New Year', quoted in Charles Osborne, *W.H. Auden: the Life of a Poet* (Eyre Methuen, 1979) p. 181

"sacred cause": Hamilton, *The Way It Was With Me* (Leslie Frewin, 1969) p.41

"…tea-stirring times": Peter Parker, *Isherwood: A Life* (Picador, 2005) p.275 cf Christopher Isherwood, *Mr. Norris Changes Trains* (Hogarth Press, 1935) pp.33; 106.

"robot, Gerald-as-I-choose-to-see-him": Isherwood, 'Prologue: Gerald and Mr. Norris' in Hamilton, *Mr. Norris and I* (Allan Wingate, 1956) p.9

"football crowds, drinkers of bad beer, and fornicators in general": John Symonds, *Conversations with Gerald* (Duckworth, 1974) p.53.

"…a privilege to have assisted at its obsequies": ibid. p.14

"the last of the dangerous men": Maclaren-Ross cited in *Conversations with Gerald*, p.viii.

"Goodness gracious me! Young men today seem to want to live forever!": ibid.

"one of the most evil men alive today": *The People*, 16 January 1966

"I'm sorry you died friendless, ugly, broke": John Lehmann, 'The Rules of Comedy', *New and Selected Poems* (Enitharmon, 1985) p.66

"An old-queen voice…": William S Burroughs, *The Place of Dead Roads* (John Calder, 1984) p.193

References

"I do have a few bits of equipment myself…" Kyril Bonfiglioli, *Don't Point That Thing at Me* (Weidenfeld and Nicolson, 1972) p.12

"…contrived to rhyme 'plastic rainwear' with 'Mr Norris changes train-wear'": Barry Humphries, *More Please: An Autobiography* (Viking, 1992) p.192

Ronald Searle cartoon: 'Sister Hamilton', *Mr. Norris and I* facing p.149.

The People exposé: first instalment 16th January 1966

"…wittiest man in Europe, well, really…": Daniel Farson, *Soho in the Fifties* (Michael Joseph, 1987) p.119

"enchantingly 'period'": Isherwood, *Christopher and his Kind* (Eyre Methuen, 1977) p.62

"…very easily capable of misinterpretation." Isherwood, *Mr. Norris Changes Trains*, p.154

Bullied at his first school: see Hamilton, *As Young As Sophocles* (Martin Secker and Warburg, 1937) pp.15-16

"like a greedy animal which you can't leave alone in the kitchen": Isherwood, *Christopher and His Kind* p.63

"quite literally a familiar": interview with Alan Wilde, 13 January 1964, cited in Alan Wilde, *Christopher Isherwood* (New York, Twayne, 1971) p.62

"quite marvellously himself"… "so polished and gross and charming and hideous"… "… as terrific as the picture of Dorian Gray": Isherwood, *Liberation: Diaries Volume Three 1970–1983* ed. Katherine Bucknell (Chatto, 2012) p.19

"both of them ultimately downers": ibid. p.646

"I had an almost clairvoyant dream…": Isherwood to Hamilton, letter of 3 October 1942, formerly in the possession of Alan Clodd

"This morning, lying in bed, half-awake…": Isherwood, *Diaries Volume One 1939–1960* ed. Katherine Bucknell (Methuen, 1996) p.91

"But I do remember all the fun we had together…": Isherwood, *Liberation: Diaries Volume Three* p.87

The Man Who Was Norris

Tom Cullen's manuscript is a little under-referenced in its surviving form – although the manuscript was saved, two concertina files of correspondence and notes were lost. Cullen has not dated conversations or put page references on published sources. The main or default published source for the first half of the book is *As Young As Sophocles*, and quotations from it exceed those he

References

has noted. I have left his references to Crowley material in the "Warburg", a resonant word for a couple of generations of scholars and researchers, although it is now more properly known as The Yorke Collection, Warburg Institute, University of London (this is the same Gerald Yorke who figures in the present text as Brother Volo Intelligere), and it has since been catalogued in more detail. The main unpublished source, particularly in the second half of the book, is the Gerald Hamilton Archive at the Harry Ransom Center, University of Texas at Austin, which I have abbreviated as HRC.

Norris refers to Christopher Isherwood, *Mr Norris Changes Trains* (Hogarth Press, 1935); *Sophocles* to Gerald Hamilton, *As Young As Sophocles* (Secker and Warburg, 1937); *Conversations* to John Symonds, *Conversations with Gerald* (Duckworth, 1974); *Christopher* to *Christopher and His Kind* (Methuen, 1977).

Prologue

"…onlie begetter": Hamilton in *Conversations*

"I must have been staring very rudely…": *Norris*

"…his Hero-Father": Christopher Isherwood, *Kathleen and Frank* (Methuen, 1971)

"…Gerald's fellow-criminal": *Christopher*

"…like an absurd but nostalgic artwork…": ibid.

"…orgy of ice-cream": *Sophocles*

"…as demanding and unrewarding as witchcraft": *Christopher*

"…seem to want to live forever": Maclaren Ross in *Conversations*

"…encouraged him to live his own life more boldly": *Christopher*

"…zestful hedonism was often an encouragement to others": Maurice Richardson, 'Epilogue' to Gerald Hamilton, *Mr Norris and I* (Allan Wingate, 1956)

Chapter One

"If indeed to be premature is to be perfect…": *Sophocles*

"…'Father is here'": *Sophocles*

"…faintly ducal": Hamilton, *Mr Norris and I*

References

"Iron has entered...": the author is indebted for information concerning the Souter family to Lt.Col. the Lord Dunalley, and to his brother the Hon. Terence Prittie, who are distantly related to the Souters.

"the mutiny left in its wake vibrations of uncertainty...": Patricia Barr, *The Memsahibs* (Secker and Warburg, 1976)

"...a second little Lord Fauntleroy...": *Sophocles*

"...organized bullying...": *Sophocles*

"...condemn as 'unnatural vice'...": *Sophocles*

"...putting me into an office": *Sophocles*

"...fifteen Mexican dollars": *Sophocles*

"...sever the ties that bound me...": *Sophocles*

"...terrible story of a god crucified": *Sophocles*

"...Church of which my father was so militant a supporter": *Sophocles*

Chapter Two

"...each with a revolver in his hand": *Sophocles*

"As I knelt and kissed the ring of St Peter...": Hamilton, *The Way It Was With Me* (Leslie Frewin, 1969)

"...regret today that I wasn't wiser with the money...": Hamilton in BBC interview, October 27 1963.

"...as I had ample money for the moment...": *Sophocles*

"...unreasonable as it was imperative": *Sophocles*

Tsar, Tsarina, Tsarevitch: *Sophocles*

"...cornflower-blue uniforms": *Sophocles*

"...and despised particularly the Bloomsbury intelligentsia": Hamilton reviewing a biography of Douglas by William Freeman, *World Review*, March 1949.

"...details of his sexual life with Wilde": *Conversations*

"...invited the lady to lunch with him at the Cafe Royal": *Sophocles*

"I shall try not to be so funny again": Hamilton in BBC interview, October 27 1963

References

"...told me that he was really the Baron von Koenig, the notorious millionaire crook": *Sophocles*

Chapter Three

Wingfield to Aladon PRO/FO 371/246/16817

"...the habit of getting up and leaving the court...": *Sophocles*

"Harcamone... a kind of Dalai Lama...": Jean Genet, *The Miracle of the Rose* (Anthony Blond, 1965)

"...not because I was at the time associated in any way with Casement...": Hamilton, *Labour Monthly*, August 1966

"I knew positively that a rising in Ireland had been planned...": *Sophocles*

"...thoroughly enjoyed myself that morning": *The Way It Was With Me*

"...from the modest five shillings or three-and-six to a sovereign": Xavier Mayne [pseud. Edward I Stevenson] *The Intersexes* (privately printed, 1908)

"...I should change him into a toad": Lance Sieveking, *The Eye of the Beholder* (Hulton Press, 1957)

"...rather presumptuous to style yourself as the Great Beast 666...": Sir Francis Rose to author

Chapter Four

"...hard work he did for the Fight The Famine Council and the Save the Children Fund...": *Christopher*

"...regarded children as a peculiarly sacred trust...": *Sophocles*

"...if a receiving order is made against me...": letter attached to petition in bankruptcy filed against Gerald, July 10 1918.

"a small sum from a Sinn Fein agent...": PRO/FO 371/3816/F951

"...any information as to the genuine character of Hamilton's mission?": PRO/FO 382/2389

"...it was felt that Mr Hamilton was an unsuitable person to work through": ibid.

"It really might have been a monk's cell...": Francesca M Wilson, *Rebel Daughter of a Country House* (Allen and Unwin, 1967)

50,000 pesetas: *SCF International Union Bulletin* no.7, March 20, 1920

References

"Beware of anyone called Hamilton – he is probably a fraud and a rogue'": Eglantyne Buxton to author, March 1978

"…a more active part in assisting my martyred country": *Sophocles*

"…plot to assassinate both Kitchener and Sir Edward Grey: Basil Thomson, *Queer People* (Hodder and Stoughton, 1922)

"…must regretfully believe that I was the real Representative": *Sophocles*

"…about my frequenting members of the military mission": ibid.

"…photographs of Roger Casement, who was his closest friend": PRO/FO 371/4783

"…with some such name as 'Liberators of India'": PRO/FO 371/6844/N5259

"…why should he not buy a title?": *The Way It Was With Me*

"…other occasions when Your Grace deigned to help me with similar requests": Hamilton Papers HRC

Chapter Five

"War cripples and profiteers, filmstars and prostitutes…": Klaus Mann, *The Turning Point* (New York, Fischer, 1942)

"I had never before met anyone of such magnetic charm…": *Sophocles*

"…a sort of incubus which I had wilfully accepted… ": ibid.

"…sometimes nothing had been seen or heard of him for several days.": ibid.

"…rusty cage (for gilded in your case does not apply)…": Tinker Dare to Gerald, August 28 1959 [HRC]

"…no matter what they were discussing…": *Conversations*

"…determined never to forgive him this last mad freak of his": *Sophocles*

"…thoroughness of his work of extermination": ibid.

"… think I am about to meet God": Hamilton review of a biography of Kreuger by Allen Churchill, *Spectator*, August 2 1957

"…cork lifts inside the heels of his shoes": Gerald to actor Julian Somers (who acted Harris in a play about Wilde)

"He would toss over £10,000 to me…" 'Gerald Hamilton Confesses', *The People*, January 23 1966

References

"…the insignificant and the careless, the tools and the fools…": *Sophocles*

"the famous pearl necklace which brought so many tears…": ibid.

"…a cheque to settle my account with Gatti": ibid.

"…the 'Deus ex Machina' in the whole bloody business": de Tilleghem to Hamilton, March 11 1948 [HRC]

"…feel that I was taking part in some horrible nightmare": *Sophocles*

"…mosquitoes and gnats that buzzed in the foetid air": ibid.

"…in the opinion of H.M. Consul-General in Marseilles no purpose would be served in taking up the matters with the authorities": Foreign Ofice to author, December 11 1978

"…if the weaker partner showed reluctance": *Sophocles*

"…My inspiration and my deity": 'Idolatry' [HRC]

"…a world… in which appalling things could happen to you as a matter of course…": *Christopher*

Volume One of a two-volume work: *Sophocles*

Chapter Six

"…full of cabals, and of cabals within cabals…": William Shirer, *The Rise and Fall of the Third Reich* (Secker and Warburg 1960)

"…betterment of the conditions of those less fortunate than myself": *Sophocles*

"…I found myself suddenly launched into this most respectable and responsible post": ibid.

"…seen Socialist Cabinet Ministers, hard-boiled bankers, and Austrian dukes, behave like schoolboys in his presence": Arthur Koestler, *The Invisible Writing* (Collins, 1954)

"…unclean instrument…": *Christopher*

"…found himself up against hard-nosed professionals…": ibid.

"…said that she didn't blame me for what I was doing…": *Conversations*

"…with the official wearing his sash of office": 'Gerald Hamilton Confesses', *The People*, January 16 1966

References

"…He had come to help them… He was their friend": *Norris*

"…would insist upon passing the girl he was sleeping with off as his wife…": Claud Cockburn, *I, Claud* (Penguin, 1967)

"Under these conditions…" Royle: *Times* archive

"…a kind of travelling circus, and may move elsewhere at any moment": ibid.

"…a dark striped suit, light hat, and was wearing his monocle": ibid.

"…for sheer stupidity and obstructiveness…" *Norris*

Chapter Seven

"…cure for our personal problems": Stephen Spender, *World Within World* (Hamish Hamilton, 1951)

"…Berlin meant Boys": *Christopher*

"…most shameless rituals of the Tantras…": Christopher Isherwood, *Down There on a Visit* (New York, Simon and Schuster, 1962)

"…dirty plaster frontages embossed with scrollwork and heraldic devices": Christopher Isherwood, *Goodbye to Berlin* (Hogarth Press, 1939)

"…laughing with Hamilton over his classic struggles with the bailiff": *Christopher*

"…partly because they knew it excited their clients": ibid.

"Now, Miss Jean, you behave properly, or I'll fetch Mr Crowley to you": Warburg Collection

"…that he wasn't interested in anything, even in damnation": Christopher Isherwood, 'A Visit to Anselm Oakes', *Exhumations* (New York, Simon and Schuster, 1966)

"The maniac must have rung up all the old cats in Berlin the moment I left him…": Warburg

"…he knew I was a disbeliever": *Conversations*

sought to recruit Crowley to spy on the Theosophical Society: Gerald Yorke to author

"…long memoranda about the consumption of goat's blood": Bruce Page et al, *Philby: The Spy Who Betrayed a Generation* (Andre Deutsch, 1968)

312

References

"…something in the nature of spiritual debauch": Warburg

"…the ruffians broke and fled": Warburg

"…all his complex – homosexuality and pacifism": Warburg

"…serenely unconscious of anything untoward happening": *Conversations*

"Only a sizeable gift of money succeeded… ": Jonathan Fryer, *Isherwood* (New English Library, 1977)

"…capable of pawning his best pal's overcoat during a cold snap": Warburg

"…Genug!": Warburg

"…Encourage that idea": Warburg

"…Be *bloody* careful!": Warburg

"… province had belonged to Hungary before the Versailles Treaty… ": *Sophocles*

"…most soothing": ibid.

"…grease which submerged everything": Alexander Harrison, *Eye-Witness in Czechoslovakia* (Harrap, 1939)

"…the problem of alleviating the distress there": PRO/FO 371/15900

"…probably played a double game…": Renn to author, letter of July 21 1978

Chapter Eight

"…an egg which has as many hairs on it": *Conversations*

"…some curious ingredient in a curry": Claud Cockburn, *I, Claud* (Penguin Books, 1967) [p.188]

"…agent of a French armament manufacturer": ibid.

"as a conjurer produces rabbits out of his hat": Koestler op.cit.

"…manipulators of the Comintern's propaganda apparatus in western Europe.": Andrew Boyle, *The Climate of Treason* (Hutchinson, 1979)

"…like an aspirin on my rentier-guilt": John Lehmann, *The Whispering Gallery* (Longmans, Green and Co., 1955)

"…hundreds, if not thousands, of rifles are brought…": Hamilton, 'Arms and the Chinaman', *New Statesman* May 12 1934

References

"…all the local radical and communist elements": PRO/FO 371/17143

"…a barbarity and cold-blooded cruelty that the so-called 'Reds' have not yet shown": Hamilton in PRO/FO 371/21368/W4440

"…emergency which demanded all Gerald's art as a host…": *Christopher*

"Uncle Gerald, your charm is a mystery / I shall not attempt to define…" : 'Ode to the New Year', quoted in Charles Osborne, *W.H. Auden: the Life of a Poet* (Eyre Methuen, 1979)

"…one weakness and that was my love of food and drink": Hamilton, *The Way It Was With Me*

"…Wystan replied, 'Neither can I'.": *Christopher*

"…two dozen Chateau Yquem '21.": Hamilton in Driberg papers, Christ Church Library, Oxford.

"What the authorities were supposed to do…": Isherwood to author, letter of October 6 1976

"…I greatly admire his lack of self-pity and general calm": Isherwood to Hamilton, May 20 1952, HRC

"…terrified of being found out and punished for it, in this and the next world": *Christopher*

"…Christopher would believe him but would feel subtly disappointed": ibid.

Chapter Nine

"honoured, excited, amused" … "Delighted": *Christopher*

"…what are buggers for?": cited P.N. Furbank, *E.M. Forster: A Life* (Secker and Warburg, 1978)

"…several thousand quid for Gerald in that girl's belly": cited Cockburn, op.cit.

Gerald told Arturo Ewart: Ewart to author

"…willing pupil in the glories of a worthwhile cellar": Hamilton in *Ridley's Circular*, June 16 1942

"…the pink-and-plush atmosphere of a pre-war nightclub": Peter Chambers in *Evening Standard*, October 7 1952

"…again the sensation of the ground slipping from beneath my feet": Hamilton in *Ridley's Circular*, June 16 1942

References

"...though by no means seeing myself as a Saviour, I did see myself as a man with an idea": Hamilton, 'My Peace Bid' [HRC]

The little drama of Hamilton's Peace Bid has been put together from Hamilton's autobiographical writings, notably *Mr Norris and I* and *The Way It Was With Me*; a four-page synopsis entitled 'My Peace Bid', in James Graham Murray's writing, but apparently dictated by Hamilton, in the Harry Ransom Humanities Research Center; and *The Sword and the Umbrella* by James Graham Murray. [Ed.]

"...integrity of the British Empire should be respected": Hamilton, *Mr Norris and I*

"...a course of action which might have changed the History of the World": Hamilton, 'My Peace Bid'

"a meeting was arranged between the three of us": James Graham Murray, *The Sword and the Umbrella* (Douglas, Isle of Man, The Times Press, 1964)

"...hoped for an opportunity for Peace discussions with me": Hamilton, 'My Peace Bid'

"...begun quite favourably": *The Way It Was With Me*

"...offered to finance him to the extent of £1,000 once he arrived in Eire en route for the Vatican": Graham Murray op.cit.

"...six nuns, prayer books and rosaries in hand, would not be interfered with": *The Way It Was With Me*

"I was gratified by this statesman's agreement with much of what I said": ibid.

"...not a matter which can be effected by simply going to Rome and asking for it...": Mgr. Barton-Brown to Hamilton, October 10 1954 [HRC]

"...never met him, but always admired him": 'Gerald Hamilton Confesses' Feb 6 1966

"deluging all sorts of people with a series of pamphlets...": John, Duke of Bedford, *A Silver-Plated Spoon* (Cassell, 1959)

"if handled with sympathetic imagination": Lloyd George papers, House of Lords Record Office

"to encourage the peace movement in England": German Foreign Policy document quoted in Graham Murray, op.cit.

"...only one man to whom, by reason of his reputation and record...": Lloyd George Papers

"...a piece of disguised spivvery": Graham Murray to Hamilton, undated,

References

circa December 1963 [HRC]

"…Jiggery-Pokery": ditto, January 25 1964 [HRC]

"…Pro-Nazi, pro-Vichy, pro-Verwoerd, pro everything that I regard with horror": ditto, February 4 1964 [HRC]

"Call him Sir Oswald, you bastard!": *The Way It Was With Me*

"…but I do know that you're a damned nuisance": Graham Murray op.cit

"Ere, 'Amilton," he said, "You're for outside": Maurice Richardson, 'Epilogue' to *Mr. Norris and I*

Chapter Ten

The Mosley interview in this chapter took place in August 1978.

"…when a dangerous air raid is in progress": Hamilton, 'Three Months' Imprisonment, or Holy Ground' [HRC]

"…more conscious than ever… that he too is an outcast of society": ibid.

"…the illusion that I was sitting with my friends once again at the Abri Bar at the Ritz.": ibid.

"One of those with me here today considers me to be no better than a murderer". [e.g. *Conversations* p.199]

"…You should have been with me in Tibet": *Mr Norris and I*

"…full of wrought-iron objects and bad seventeenth-century madonnas…": Sir Francis Rose to author

"…Bring me a packet of five hundred": *Conversations*

"Gerald, I want you to do a little staff work…": ibid.

"His skittish fingers were never idle…": Hamilton, obit for Lutyens, *Ridley's Circular*, January 1944

"…still less sympathy, between the far-flung guests": André Simon to Hamilton, July 13 1943 [HRC]

"Silesian boar itself": Mary Seaton in conversation with author

"To let loose the forces of Nature on a helpless population…": Vera Brittain to Hamilton July 7 1943 [HRC]

"…holy medals over his ample person": Felix Hope-Nicholson to author

References

"…a morganatic marriage": *Conversations*

"…without disclosing your name or that of Saudi Arabia and will report to you in due course" [HRC]

"…he will have to be buried by the Church of England!": Hamilton letter to *New Statesman*, March 10 1967

"filthy trick of sending Public School boys down the mines…": Alfred Douglas to Hamilton, February 8 1944 [HRC]

"pathetic… alone, poor, almost friendless": Henry Channon, *Chips: The Diaries of Sir Henry Channon* (Weidenfeld and Nicolson, 1967)

"…and I never had another chance of meeting him": Mary Seaton in conversation with author

"I hope your god will taste nice; you're such a bloody gourmet": *The Way It Was With Me*

"…Angelice, can you bring some shong-shong?": Warburg

"…I saw Hamilton shaking his head": Maurice Richardson, 'Luncheon with Beast 666', *Punch* September 7 1955; review of Somerset Maugham, *The Magician*, *TLS* May 26 1978

"…old ladies dare not go out in the streets at night": Mgr. Barton-Brown to Hamilton, December 3 1952 [HRC]

"…he suggested selling my articles in America…": Mosley letter to author, June 29 1978

"…without stronger evidence on both points": Fred Mullally to Hamilton, September 1 1948 [HRC]

Chapter Eleven

"…Burgess's attitude towards Gerald was patronising": Ian Dunlop to author

"…Gerald appeared badly shaken…": ibid.

"…Section One of the Secret Intelligence Service, which dealt with political intelligence": Bruce Page et al, *Philby* (Andre Deutsch, 1969)

"…first paper in Fleet Street to report them missing": Maurice Richardson to author

"…a copper's nark ?": ibid.

"…louche night haunt near the Gare du Nord in Brussels": Hamilton,

References

Spectator November 4 1955

"...Take another sip of this excellent Waterloo sherry": ibid.

...telling them he worked for a "very secret organization": Bruce Page op.cit.

"...a new – and how welcome – spirit of tolerance was prevailing in Whitehall": Hamilton, *Spectator*, November 4 1955

"...to whose imperialism they were blind while ranting against ours": Harold Acton, *More Memoirs of an Aesthete* (Methuen, 1970)

"...For manoeuvres of this kind you require a stooge...": Hamilton, 'Tangier: Outpost of Anarchy' [HRC]

"...hence the happiness and prosperity of all concerned": Hamilton to Ian Dunlop February 13 1952 [HRC]

"It is essential to have somebody who speaks French and Spanish...": Hamilton to Peter Evans-Freke, March 23 1952 [HRC]

"nor do I want any here": Hamilton to Ian Dunlop February 23 1952 [HRC]

"...sprinkling of Foreign Legion deserters": ditto February 13 1952 [HRC]

"...an odd noise which I like to interpret as an Arab cheer": ditto February 23 1952 [HRC]

"...far more damaging than being turned down for the Royal Enclosure": Hamilton, 'Tangier: Outpost of Anarchy' [HRC]

"...waste valuable time in sitting in the hall": *Mr Norris and I*

"...this kind of thing should never be done by halves": Richardson, 'Epilogue' to Hamilton, *Mr Norris and I*

"...all with "The London Clinic" in the upper left-hand corner": Richardson to author

"...parted with 100 pesetas and wished him well": Hamilton review of *Man on the Run* by E.H.I. Stewart-Hargreaves [pseud. Frank James White], *Spectator*, September 28 1957

"...purchased plants which they really did not want": Frank James White, *The Hargreaves Story* (Bodley Head, 1953)

Chapter Twelve

"...hard not to admire Winston Churchill...": *The Way It Was With Me*

"on a silver platter to the Russian criminals": ibid.

References

"…a hidden force which brought about this chaos deliberately": Stefan Zweig, *The World of Yesterday* (Cassell, 1945)

"…rang the knell of England's greatness": Hamilton letter to *South African Observer*, January 15 1965

"…the Grand Orient and other French masonic lodges": *The Way It Was With Me*

…Gibbs was more amused than angry: Anthony Blond to author

"…had to be very tactful in these cases": *The Way It Was With Me*

"My apartment here is a Ludwig Temple…": Blake Brown to Hamilton, July 6 1957 HRC

"…not foresee anything but disaster if Britain alone decided to ban the bomb": Hamilton to Maurice Richardson, April 6 1951

"…seditious drivel of Father Huddleston and Michael Scott": Hamilton to Eric Louw, May 5 1959, HRC

"…spent nine months in South Africa and visited every town of importance": *The Way It Was With Me*

"…with flowerbeds making a riot of colour…": Hamilton, *Jacaranda* (Sidgwick and Jackson, 1961)

"…not only not oppressed at all, but all seeming very cheerful": *Jacaranda*

"I do not know what a hundred and fifty policemen are supposed to do…": *The Way It Was With Me*

"…so you may find it rather milk-and-watery…": Hamilton to Betty Galliot, May 18 1962 [HRC]

"Write what you like – I don't believe in anything": Ivor Powell to author

"The greatest pleasures I have had in all my life…": *Conversations*

"…perverts and flagellants known to me…": Hamilton precis, 'The Real Mr Norris', circa 1968 [HRC]

"…about .005%": Alan Neame to author, June 9 1977

"this *pot au feu royale*": Nicholas of Romania to Hamilton, November 27 1964 [HRC]

References

Chapter Thirteen

"…the rental of the flat above his…": Robert Jacobs to author

"…The forgery had been expert": Robin Maugham, *The Search for Nirvana* (W.H. Allen, 1975)

"…stop the cars – I'm a peer of the realm": Mary Seaton to author

"That's the way they murdered my friend Casement"": Maurice Richardson in *The Sunday Times*, January 29 1961

"…very helpful if they would be prepared to underwrite a certain number of copies…": Hamilton to Dr Chen, May 13 1961 [HRC]

"…500 copies of the book at special reduced rate": Dr Chen to Hamilton, August 30 1961 [HRC]

"…hope that you will not give in on… matters of principle": Hamilton to Ian Smith, circa September 1964 [HRC]

"…some pornographic saga": Robin Maugham, *The Search for Nirvana*

"…the sort of person to whom pleasant things were happening constantly": *Conversations*

"…was to abolish the *Cortes* and forbid elections": Hamilton to John Symonds, September 26 1965 [HRC]

"…I shall get out of it somehow": Hamilton to Symonds, January 7 1964 [HRC]

"…truly almost starving": ditto, January 16 1964 [HRC]

"…hardly dare set foot in the Bank again…": ditto, January 23 1964 [HRC]

"…a wonderful plan (enemies might call it a plot)…": ditto February 10 1964 [HRC]

…private secretary of one of the "royals": Maugham, 'Gerald Hamilton Confesses'

Chapter Fourteen

"…but whose excesses and extravagances have reduced him to mendicity": Henry Mayhew, *London Labour and the London Poor*, vol.IV (London, Griffin, Bohn and Co., 1862)

"…met Rasputin on two occasions…" [HRC]

"…a foolish bunch of meddlers…": Hamilton to Aberdeen Trades Council,

References

March 20 1964 [HRC]

"the pleas for clemency on your behalf": Hamilton to Paul Crump, July 21 1962 [HRC]

"…committed by United Nations soldiers in the Congo" [HRC]

"…if it interests you or the House Committee investigating the matter": Hamilton to *Time* magazine, dated February 19 1952 [HRC]

"No doubt your Corporation would consider Stalin and Lenin also Liberals": Hamilton letter to Sir Hugh Greene, Jun 29 1966 [HRC]

"…pity that I am not an actor": Hamilton to BBC, letter circa May 1957 [HRC]

"…beginning to be impressed with the possibility": John Freeman to Hamilton, July 2 1960 [HRC]

"…I am sufficiently well-known already…": Hamilton to *Who's Who*, September 8 1962 [HRC]

"…I am 77 years old and not in the best of health…" [HRC]

"a real gentleman, so distinguished looking": Ewart to author

"…would not wish to participate in any publicity that makes the slightest anti-Franco comment…": Hamilton to Robin Maugham, May 13 1965 [HRC]

"…I hereby authorise Robin Maugham to write a series of articles about me…": agreement dated July 30 1965 [HRC]

"…read all about him tomorrow in *The People*!": Maurice Leonard to author

"…share of the loot was between £40,000 and £50,000": Maugham, 'Gerald Hamilton Confesses', *The People*, February 13 1966

"…let him think back and he might remember some such occasion": *The Way It Was With Me*

"…but had no idea it could be as dreadful as this": Gabrielle Potter to Hamilton, January 18 1966

"…now the leader of the Sartre set in Paris": Hamilton to Gabrielle Potter, February 28 1966

"…especially the train robbery, which did not happen": Hamilton to Sir Frederick Bowman, February 18 1966

"…Chinese politeness for you": John Symonds to author

"…discover he's drawing supplementary benefits…": Arturo Ewart to author

References

"...every penny of expenses was paid for by his friends": Aidan Evans to National Assistance Board, June 15 1966 [HRC]

"We gave him more because of it": John Lehmann to author

"...you would hear him tell the driver to take him to the Savoy...": Geoffrey Rigby to author

"Gerald was thrilled to bits...": James Reeve to author

"Gerald didn't give a damn what his portrait looked like": ibid.

"...a 'friend' in the sense that the snake is to a rabbit...": James Reeve to author, July 13 1978

"...that the Baron Mayer was the father of the Prince Consort": Hamilton to the Countess of Longford, April 11 1968 [HRC]

"...I never saw such obsequiousness": James Reeve to author

"Pity he inscribed it...": Bevis Hillier to author

"...the last person in the world I would have gone to...": James Reeve to author

"My name is Olivier": unused notes by Hamilton for book on Tennessee Williams by Mike Steen [HRC]

"...If I am with old fogeys...": *Conversations*

"Oh, only about forty": Peter Burton to author

...reluctant to involve the police, but did...: ibid.

Chapter Fifteen

"...But I am certain people's liqueur": *Conversations*

"...it would take a bigger man than Franco, or Mosley, to come between us": Isherwood to Hamilton, March 7 1946, formerly in the possession of Alan Clodd

the wish to help an old friend: Isherwood to Hamilton, March 7 1946 [Clodd]

"I had an almost clairvoyant dream...": Isherwood to Hamilton, October 3 1942 [Clodd]

"...I was having dinner with Gerald at his flat that evening": David Stoker to author

"...I never mind roughing it at the Ritz...": unused notes by Hamilton for

References

book on Tennessee Williams by Mike Steen [HRC]

Visitors coming to see Mr Melmoth: Hamilton, 'Wilde at Berneval', *London Magazine*, June 1967

"...attitude of the Royal Family seems to me to have been beyond contempt...": *The Way It Was With Me*

Correspondence with Duke of Windsor, January 14 and 19 1970 [HRC]

"...so many happy recollections...": Hamilton to Professor Catlin, March 31 1970 [HRC]

"...I hate the sight of blood and was very frightened at the time": Hamilton to James Reeve, April 3 1970 [HRC]

"I always thought the sky was blue...": Hamilton, 'To R.A., June 11 1966' [HRC]

"...if I had not been so old": Gerald to Lady Assheton-Smith, May 18 1970 [HRC] "– and he's raving about a little black boy and some jewels": *Conversations*

"...Gerald's ghost circling Sloane Square in a taxi-cab...": Felix Hope-Nicholson to author

"...died in a taxi as it made its way across Sloane Square": Geoffrey Rigby to author

"...taken to the hospital and died that night": Brian Desmond Hurst to author

"...a mystery man, some sort of secret agent...": Canon Alfonso de Zulueta to author

...fullest account of the ceremony...: Robin Maugham, *The Search for Nirvana* (W.H. Allen, 1975)

"...a child's coffin and they certainly cannot have got Gerald into it": Peter Burton, 'Meetings with Mr. Norris', *Gay News* no.110, 1977

Sure there wasn't any mistake: Burton to author, December 11 1978

"...and Gerald Hamilton stories": Burton, 'Meetings with Mr. Norris'

Bibliography

Acton, Harold, *More Memoirs of an Aesthete* (Methuen, 1970)

Barr, Patricia, *The Memsahibs* (Secker and Warburg, 1976)

Bedford, John, Duke of, *A Silver Plated Spoon* (Cassell, 1959)

Boyle, Andrew, *The Climate of Treason* (Hutchinson, 1979)

Burton, Peter, 'Meetings with Mr Norris', *Gay News* no.110 (1977)

Channon, Sir Henry, *Chips: The Diaries of Sir Henry Channon* (Weidenfeld and Nicolson, 1967)

Cockburn, Claud, *I Claud* (Penguin, 1967)

Davidson, Michael, *The World, The Flesh and Myself* (David, Bruce and Watson, 1973)

Forster, E.M. *Two Cheers for Democracy* (Edward Arnold, 1951)

Fryer, Jonathan, *Isherwood* (New English Library, 1977)

Furbank, P.N., *E.M.Forster: A Life* (Secker and Warburg, 1978)

Gray, Charles [pseudonym of Charles Potter], 'Gerald Hamilton' [unpublished essay]

Hamilton, Gerald, *Desert Dreamers: A Romance of Friendship* (At the Sign of the Tiger Lily, 1914)

Hamilton, Gerald, *As Young as Sophocles* (Martin Secker & Warburg Ltd, 1937)

Hamilton, Gerald, *Mr Norris and I* (Allan Wingate, 1956)

Hamilton, Gerald, with Desmond Stewart, *Emma in Blue* (Allan Wingate, 1957)

Hamilton, Gerald, *Jacaranda* (Sidgwick and Jackson, 1961)

Hamilton, Gerald, *Blood Royal* (Isle of Man, Times Press and Anthony Gibbs & Phillips, 1964)

Hamilton, Gerald, 'Wilde at Berneval' *London Magazine* (June 1967)

Hamilton, Gerald, *The Way It Was With Me* (Leslie Frewin, 1969)

Harris, Frank, *Oscar Wilde* (Constable, 1938)

Henderson, Alexander, *Eye-Witness in Czechoslovakia* (Harrap, 1939)

Hyde, H Montgomery, *The Other Love* (Heinemann, 1970)

Isherwood, *Mr Norris Changes Trains* (Hogarth Press, 1935)

Isherwood, Christopher, *Goodbye to Berlin* (Hogarth Press, 1939)

Bibliography

Isherwood, Christopher, *Down There on a Visit* (Methuen, 1962)

Isherwood, Christopher, *Kathleen and Frank* (Methuen, 1971)

Isherwood, Christopher, *Christopher and his Kind* (Eyre Methuen, 1977)

Koestler, Arthur, *The Invisible Writing* (Hamish Hamilton, 1954)

Lehmann, John, *The Whispering Gallery* (Longmans, Green, 1955)

Macardle, Dorothy, *The Irish Republic* (Gollancz, 1937)

Magnus, Philip, *King Edward the Seventh* (John Murray, 1964)

Mann, Klaus, *The Turning Point* (Oswald Wolff, 1984)

Maugham, Robin, 'Gerald Hamilton Confesses', *The People* (January 16 to February 13 1966)

Maugham, Robin, *Escape from the Shadows* (Hodder and Stoughton, 1972)

Maugham, Robin, *Search for Nirvana* (W.H. Allen, 1975)

Mayhew, Henry, *London Labour and the London Poor*, Vol.IV (London, Griffin, Bohn and Co., 1862)

Mayne, Xavier [pseud. Edward I Stevenson] *The Intersexes* (privately printed, 1908)

Murray, James Graham, *The Sword and the Umbrella* (Douglas, Isle of Man, Times Press, 1964)

Page, Bruce et al, *Philby: The Spy Who Betrayed a Generation* (Deutsch, 1968)

Reid, Benjamin L, *The Lives of Roger Casement* (Yale, 1976)

Richardson, Maurice, 'Mr.Hamilton Regrets…', Epilogue to Hamilton, *Mr Norris and I*

Richardson, Maurice, 'Luncheon with Beast 666', *Punch* September 7 1955 [now collected in *Fits and Starts* (Michael Joseph, 1979)]

Richardson, Maurice, review of Somerset Maugham's *The Magician*, *Times Literary Supplement,* May 26 1978

Shirer, William, *The Rise and Fall of the Third Reich* (Secker and Warburg, 1960)

Singleton-Gates, Peter, *The Black Diaries* (Paris, Girodias, 1959)

Spender, Stephen, *World Within World* (Hamish Hamilton, 1951)

Symonds, John, *Conversations with Gerald* (Duckworth, 1974)

Thomson, Basil, *Queer People* (Hodder and Stoughton, 1922)

White, Frank James, *The Hargreaves Story* (Bodley Head, 1953)

Wilson, Francesca M, *Rebel Daughter of a Country House: The Life of Eglantyne Jebb* (Allen and Unwin, 1967)

Zweig, Stefan, *The World of Yesterday* (Cassell, 1943)

Acknowledgments 1980

Tom Cullen particularly wished to thank Christopher Isherwood for answering his questions and reading his manuscript, and the late Peter Burton, who gave him the idea of writing this book in the first place. Sadly none of them lived to see it published.

In researching Hamilton, Cullen drew on Hamilton's papers at the Harry Ransom Humanities Research Center at the University of Texas. Although it only covers Hamilton's life from 1940, the Hamilton collection there comprises some 11,000 items in forty-one boxes. Cullen particularly wished to thank the Center's then director Warren Roberts, and librarians Ellen S Dunlap, Lois Garcia, and Erica Wilson.

Although there was later some disagreement, in the wake of Robin Maugham's objections to the book, at the time he finished this manuscript Tom Cullen very much wanted to thank John Symonds, Hamilton's literary executor, for research help and for permission to consult the Hamilton archive at the Harry Ransom Center.

Cullen also conducted his research among materials in the Gerald Yorke Collection at the Warburg Institute; the Public Record Office at Kew; the Records Office of the House of Lords; the library of Christ Church College, Oxford; and the archive of the *Times* newspaper. He wished to thank all the relevant librarians and archivists, and particularly named Dr JFA Mason at Christ Church and Gordon Phillips at *The Times*.

One of the things that makes Cullen's account of Hamilton valuable is the number of people he was able to speak to, thirty-odd years ago, who had known the man in person and were willing to be interviewed and quoted. This includes many of the people on the following list. Begging the forgiveness of anyone he had inadvertently left out, he specifically wished to thank for their help with this book AP Arnold, Hermione Baddeley, Eric and Irene Barton, Anthony Blond, Ilinka Bossy, Mrs Thalia Buckley, David Buxton, Miss Eglantyne Buxton, Professor Peter W Campbell, Lady Catlin and Sir George Catlin, Alan Clodd, Barry Davis, Commander Charles H Drage, Ian Dunlop, the Lord Dunalley, Aidan Evans, Arturo Ewart, Sibylla

Acknowledgements

Jane Flower, Jonathan Fryer, Charles Goeller, Professor William S Gray, Geoffrey Handley-Taylor, Jack Hewit, Bevis Hillier, Felix Hope-Nicholson, Brian Desmond Hurst, David Hutter, 'Robert Jacobs', Mrs Connie Jebb, John Lehmann, Maurice Leonard, Mrs Jenny Macrory, Mrs Gillian Mansel, Miss Audrey Moser, Sir Oswald and Lady Mosley, Alan Neame, Ivor Powell, the Hon. Terence Prittie, David Fara Proudlove, James Reeve, Maurice Richardson, Geoffrey Rigby, Sir Francis Rose, Mary Seaton, Timothy d'Arch Smith, Colin Spencer, Ann Spraike, Desmond Stewart, Mike Steen, David Stoker, Hugh Trevor-Roper, Willy Trebich, Colin Wilson, and Canon Alfonso de Zulueta.

Acknowledgments 2014

I would particularly like to thank Reed Searle and Tom Symonds for making this publication possible, and James Reeve for permission to use the painting on the cover, with equally sincere gratitude to Mark Bostridge, Bill Breeze, the late Peter Burton, Geoffrey Elborn, Bevis Hillier, Torsten Højer, Sheena Joughin, Maurice Leonard, Edward Platt, Kate Pool, Rosanne Rucho, Tim d'Arch Smith, Laura Susijn, David Sutton, Gabriel Symonds, Mark Watson, and Rick Watson of the Harry Ransom Center.

Gerald Hamilton's copyright belongs to the estate of John Symonds, and Aleister Crowley's copyright belongs to Ordo Templi Orientis: material from WH Auden, Vera Brittain, and Christopher Isherwood is copyright of their various estates. I have been unable to trace a number of estates including those of Richard Blake Brown, Basil Clavering, and Desmond Stewart, among others.

Index

Index

Index

Index

Index

Index

Index

335

Index

Index

Index